SCHOOL DEVELOPMENT SERIES

General Editors: David Hopkins and David Reynolds

MERGING TRADITIONS

OTHER TITLES IN THE SCHOOL DEVELOPMENT SERIES

MERGING TRADITIONS
The Future of Research on School Effectiveness and School Improvement

Edited by

John Gray,
David Reynolds,
Carol Fitz-Gibbon
and David Jesson

CASSELL

Cassell
Wellington House
125 Strand
London WC2R 0BB

127 West 24th Street
New York
NY 10011

First published 1996

British Library Cataloguing-in-Publication Data
A catalogue record for this book is available from the British Library

Library of Congress Cataloging-in-Publication Data
Merging traditions : the future of research on school effectiveness
   and school improvement / edited by John Gray . . . [et al.].
      p. cm. — (School development series)
      'The chapters presented in this book were first given at a seminar
   series funded by the Economic and Social Research Council' — Pref.
      Includes bibliographical references and index.
      ISBN 0–304–33653–X. — ISBN 0–304–33647–5 (pbk.)
      1. School improvement programs—Research—Great Britain.
   2. Educational evaluation—Research—Great Britain. I. Gray, John
   (John Michael), 1948–   . II. Series.
   LB2822.84.G7M47   1996
   371.2'007—dc20   96–6375
                                                          CIP

ISBN 0–304–33653–X (hardback)
      0–304–33647–5 (paperback)

Typeset by Action Typesetting Limited, Gloucester
Printed and bound in Great Britain by
Redwood Books, Trowbridge, Wiltshire

Contents

Contents

Conclusions: Facing up to the Challenge of Securing Improvement

List of Contributors

Sally Brown, Department of Education, University of Stirling
Tony Bush, School of Education, University of Leicester
Jill Duffield, Department of Education, University of Stirling
Carol Fitz-Gibbon, School of Education, University of Durham
John Gray, Homerton College, Cambridge
David Hopkins, School of Education, University of Nottingham
David Jesson, Division of Education, University of Sheffield
Peter Mortimore, Institute of Education, London University
David Reynolds, Department of Education, University of Newcastle upon Tyne
Sheila Riddell, Department of Education, University of Stirling
Pam Sammons, Institute of Education, London University
Louise Stoll, Institute of Education, London University
Sally Thomas, Institute of Education, London University
Peter Tymms, School of Education, University of Durham

Preface and Introduction

In recent years two simple questions have come to dominate the policy-making agenda. How does one tell a 'good' school from a 'bad' one? And how does one set about improving them? In this volume leading British researchers in school effectiveness and school improvement explore recent research evidence from their respective perspectives and seek to identify ways of integrating the two 'traditions'. The result is a distinctive mix of approaches and perspectives harnessed to the cause of improving both the quality of research and the quality of the practice of judging and improving schools.

Until recently, the two traditions have largely gone their separate ways. Much (but not all) school effectiveness research has been premised on the search for generalizations across samples of schools; quantitative evidence has been the common currency in this search. School improvement research, on the other hand, has usually started with the problems presented by the school. Given the position a school has reached, how can it be helped and encouraged to move forward? Qualitative evidence, relying on the generation of case studies to furnish insights, has been the norm. Only a small number of studies have attempted to cross traditions.

The chapters presented in this book were first given at a seminar series funded by the Economic and Social Research Council. In agreeing to make contributions, the authors to a greater or lesser extent accepted the challenge of interrogating the key questions about what their research had to say about effectiveness and improvement from their respective positions. Given their starting points some found it easier, others more difficult. What drove those who came from the school effectiveness side was the sense that whilst they could delineate the characteristics of so-called 'effective' schools, their tradition had rather little to say about how the schools had achieved their status. How a school *maintains* its effectiveness may differ from the ways in which it *becomes* effective. Amongst those on the school improvement side there were matching concerns. How far had change and improvement come about? And what 'hard' evidence, if any, could be marshalled to demonstrate that it had?

PART ONE

The four contributors to Part One of the book seek to provide up-to-date accounts of the research evidence in their respective fields of school effectiveness and school improvement and to identify their implications for school change and development.

In an extensive review of the research evidence on school effectiveness Pam Sammons, Peter Mortimore and Sally Thomas explore how far different studies

have indicated a high degree of consistency concerning schools' effects on different educational outcomes and areas of school pupils' experiences, as well as their
effects over time and across different phases of schooling. They are also interested
in how far these effects apply for different social and ethnic groups. In broad
terms, they conclude that schools are more consistent over time than they are
across different educational outcomes, whilst the verdict on differential effectiveness for different groups of pupils is still to come in. However, the most significant
feature of their analysis is the extent to which it shows how complex the research
findings have become. Such complexity, they argue, is something that needs to be
embraced rather than shied away from. There are likely to be few remedies for
school improvement, at least based on research on school effectiveness, that cross
countries, contexts and circumstances.

Is it premature to talk of 'theories' of school improvement? In his contribution to the book David Hopkins suggests, on the basis of research with which he
has been involved, that there are a variety of conditions which need to be fulfilled
if improvement efforts are to be successful. These include the schools' commitments to: enquiry and reflection; collaborative planning; staff development; staff
and student involvement; coordination and leadership throughout the school. The
messages from the North American studies he considers are somewhat more
diverse but also hold out the prospect of more generic frameworks. Crucially,
schools need to become more aware of the options for change that are available
and more skilled at analysing which particular ones will meet their specific
concerns. In this contribution some of the assumptions underlying the different
improvement options begin to be spelt out.

Louise Stoll also addresses the challenges of harnessing and converting the
school effectiveness and school improvement paradigms into on-the-ground
change strategies. She argues that there are sufficient pointers in the research
evidence to justify interventions and then proceeds to analyse some of the characteristics of 'action projects' (most of which she has played some part in
implementing) which have arisen out of what she terms the 'blended research
literature'. Subsequently she considers some of the unresolved issues which, she
maintains, can impede improvement efforts. Prominent amongst these constraints
are questions about the relevance of the research evidence to the changed circumstances of schools in the 1990s and the extent to which the characteristics
identified in 'effective-schools' research lend themselves to the practicalities of
implementation.

The need to help schools to integrate the 'broad, reproducible, simple
patterns' that come from working across large quantities of data with the 'need
to recognize the immense complexity at the level of action at which schools must
operate' is the conundrum which Carol Fitz-Gibbon considers. Drawing on the
relatively new field of 'complexity theory' she argues that 'local control' and 'self-
organization' are crucial handles on the self-improvement process. The key
challenge for managers, she argues, is to ensure a better flow of high-quality
information to decision-makers at all levels of the system and also, crucially, to
classroom teachers. Drawing on her own experience of a major monitoring-with-
feedback project, she suggests that to formulate effective strategies teachers need
to know both what the broad patterns are across schools and some of the reasons

why their own position may be different. The challenge is to offer simplicity whilst respecting complexity. To meet it, information systems (and the assumptions underlying their construction) will need to be reconfigured.

PART TWO

Part Two brings together a number of recent studies conducted within the two research traditions.

The contribution by Sally Brown, Sheila Riddell and Jill Duffield is based on four case studies of schools facing different challenges during a period of rapid educational change. Two of the schools served areas of social advantage; two served areas of social disadvantage. Within each pairing of social context one of the two schools was chosen because it seemed to be 'less effective'. A number of important findings emerge from the study of which two, in particular, stand out. First, many of the patterns reported in previous research on school effectiveness appear to have been more strongly correlated with the schools' social compositions than with their effectiveness. If these conclusions hold in other settings, then they offer some additional purchase on why many school improvement efforts may have stumbled – they have failed to disentangle causes from correlations. Second, the authors are struck by the paucity of commonalities 'between, on the one hand, the more effective and, on the other hand, the less effective pairs of schools'. In brief, there were few pointers to success – schools will probably have to sort out their own particular routes to improvement.

Peter Tymms returns to the theme of 'complexity' in his chapter. Using simulated data, and comparing it with the results of actual teachers and students at A level, he suggests that 'even if it were possible to arrange for exactly the same class to have exactly the same teacher for two years in the same classroom living through the same two years, the outcomes would not be the same'. Consequently, he is sceptical of attempts to find 'blueprints for success' at school, LEA or country level. Given so much 'complexity', the 'ability to respond to feedback and to absorb new data must surely be an attribute of successful behaviour in chaotic situations'. The 'effective teacher' is likely to be the one who can 'read' a class better than others and who is capable of monitoring and diagnosing the occasions when action is required.

The need for schools to take hold of their own futures is captured in Tony Bush's piece on the moves in Britain and elsewhere towards greater autonomy in school management, captured in the concept of the 'self-managing' school. He reviews some of the recent experiences of schools which have gone 'grant-maintained' and explores how their 'greater freedom' may (or may not) have contributed to their subsequent improvement. It is clear from his analysis that improvement is not an unambiguous correlate of greater autonomy. 'The international trend towards school autonomy,' he argues, 'has been accompanied by claims that it will foster beneficial change by allowing those most concerned with the school to determine their objectives, allocate resources in support of those aims and to monitor whether and to what extent they have been achieved.' 'This hypothesis,' he concludes, 'has been well-supported in government rhetoric and by the management literature but has (to date) received only limited empirical verification.'

David Reynolds concludes the section by reporting on work undertaken within the sites of historically ineffective schools, using his experience to interrogate existing policies followed to 'improve' such schools. He argues for the schools to be seen as distinctive, not simply processing a deficit of factors seen within more effective institutions, and outlines characteristics of the culture, organization and ethos within two schools he has been involved with. The failure of the change attempts of a conventional kind to generate enhanced outcomes is then used to draw up situation-specific improvement programmes, on the lines of David Hopkins's attempted context-specific theorizing outlined earlier in Part One; these involve directive skilling, quasi-therapeutic interventions and heavily means-orientated improvement programmes, which are argued to be necessary to meet the challenge of securing improvement in these schools.

In their conclusions to the volume, John Gray, David Jesson and David Reynolds attempt to draw out the usefulness of the knowledge bases outlined in the book for the practical improvement of schools. They note that there are many school improvement programmes in the United Kingdom and the United States but that we lack hard evidence about 'what works'. It seems that only a small proportion of schools seem to improve their outcomes markedly more than others over time. They argue that the historically separate knowledge bases of school effectiveness 'factors' that are argued to generate success, and the improvement literature on the programmes that are argued to develop schools' capacity to acquire these factors urgently need integration; their assessment that the proportion of schools currently possessing a capacity to improve may be as low as a third of the total, suggests a need for both considerable and urgent action to develop appropriate knowledge about *what* is a 'good' school, and in particular *how* to make more schools better schools.

The Conclusions themselves finish with pleas for a merger or integration of effectiveness and improvement perspectives, particularly through the study of those historically ineffective schools which turn the corner and start to improve. The current range of initiatives, programmes and sanctions being utilized with 'failing' schools would strongly suggest that educational policies need the still, silent voice and truths of research knowledge more than ever before.

John Gray
David Reynolds

Part One

The Research Inheritance

Chapter 1

Do Schools Perform Consistently Across Outcomes and Areas?

Pam Sammons, Peter Mortimore and
Sally Thomas

INTRODUCTION

The purpose of this chapter is to endeavour to answer the question framed in its title. Over the past 20 years in which research studies of the effectiveness of individual schools have been promoted, there has been an *implicit* assumption – and in rare cases 'explicit' investigations – that school effects are consistent. Without such a general assumption researchers would be hard put to justify the expense of detailed investigations into what may be seen as ephemeral effects. The assumptions and the achievements of researchers have also to be seen in a context in which there is a widespread presumption that 'schooling must have a positive effect' (Husen *et al.*, 1992) and yet, paradoxically, in which many governments across the world are expressing the view that schooling is simultaneously increasing in costs and decreasing in quality! Perhaps because of the obvious political nature of this research context, studies of school effectiveness have often proved controversial. At times, the political discussion has focused on researchers' purpose in carrying out the work; at other times, it has been concerned with the methodology adopted. In the United Kingdom, publication of *Fifteen Thousand Hours* produced an avalanche of comment; highly critical and eulogistic in almost equal parts (see Mortimore, 1991). Similar examples include the study of high-school achievement (Coleman *et al.*, 1982) and from Wales, *The Comprehensive Experiment* (Reynolds *et al.*, 1987).

In most writing on the subject of school effectiveness (Reynolds and Cuttance, 1992; Scheerens, 1992) there is a common acceptance that schooling effects can be found; that they are substantial; and that – in many cases – they are differential. Some schools promote positive effects and others, negative ones. Although studies of variations between schools exist in both simple and more sophisticated forms, the majority tend to take account of the differences in the characteristics of students entering and attending schools. Whilst the methodology for doing this has improved considerably over the past 20 years a number of studies are still considered statistically weak. The criteria for an adequate study of such differences have recently been described (Scheerens, 1992). These are:

- taps sufficient 'natural' variance in school and instructional characteristics, so that there is a fair chance that they might be shown to explain differences in achievement between schools;

- uses adequate operationalizations and measures of the process and effect variables, preferably including direct observations of process variables, and a mixture of quantitative and qualitative measures;
- adequately adjusts effect measures for intake differences between schools (e.g. in previous achievement and socio-economic status of pupils);
- has units of analysis that allow for data analyses with sufficient discriminative power;
- uses adequate techniques for data analysis – in many cases multilevel models will be appropriate to do justice to the fact that we usually look at classes within schools, pupils within classes and perhaps even schools within specific types of environments;
- uses longitudinal data.

There is thus considerable agreement on many of the initial concerns of researchers in this area. What becomes even more important, therefore, is how best to deal with the problems of different effects and of consistency. Accordingly, in this chapter, we will attempt to pose and answer a series of sub-questions relating to its title.

Do schools perform consistently on different outcomes?

- in different aspects of academic attainment;
- in different boards of the same examination;
- in different measures of attendance;
- in different measures of attitudes towards the school;
- in different measures of behaviour;
- in different aspects of self-concept;
- in different kinds of outcomes (academic and affective/social);
- betwixt and between all of these.

Do schools perform consistently over time?
Do schools perform consistently across different phases of schooling?

- infant phase;
- junior phase;
- secondary 11–16;
- post-16.

Do schools perform consistently across differing school memberships?

- in terms of different levels of prior attainment;
- in terms of gender differences;
- in terms of ethnic differences;
- in terms of age differences;

- in terms of socio-economic differences.

It is also our intention to identify some of the most serious methodological and conceptual problems that underpin the question of consistency in this area of research. We will draw on the published literature and, where appropriate, our own data in order to clarify particular points.

At this stage it is important to clarify the definition of consistency, as it is meant here. First, there is the consistency of individual school effects where *within school* comparisons are made across:

- different cognitive (e.g. academic, vocational, subject-specific) and non-cognitive (e.g. attendance, behaviour, attitudes) outcomes;
- different year groups within each school;
- different school memberships such as boys and girls or high ability and low ability at entry to the school;
- different time periods.

Secondly, there is the consistency of school effects across different groups of schools where *between school* comparisons are made across:

- different regions or countries;
- different phases of education, such as primary, secondary and higher education;
- different types of school, such as county or voluntary or according to size.

In addition to clarifying the definitions of consistency it is also important to distinguish between the different methods employed to measure school outcomes when considering the issue of consistency in school effects. The magnitude of school effects may vary too according to the nature and extent of background factors controlled for in the method of analysis and this may, in turn, have some bearing on estimates of consistency. Previous research has indicated that substantial differences between schools are shown when raw outcome measures are reported, but that these differences are much reduced when the impact of background factors is taken into account. Background factors in general may be grouped into two distinct categories: the first comprise the prior achievements of pupils on school entry and measures of schools' effects that account for this kind of factor are often referred to as 'value-added'. All other characteristics of individual students, such as their age or sex, social class or ethnic background comprise the second category of background factors and outcome measures that account for this kind of factor may be referred to as 'adjusted scores'. In both cases estimates of school outcomes that take account of the intake characteristics of students are commonly viewed as fairer and more accurate than raw measures in the sense that 'like-with-like' comparisons can be made between schools and, ideally, school effectiveness studies should make as full control as possible for intake differences in terms of prior achievement and other background factors.

DO SCHOOLS PERFORM CONSISTENTLY ON DIFFERENT OUTCOMES?

There is considerable evidence from the school effectiveness literature that schools can vary substantially in their effectiveness in promoting students' academic attainment (see discussions by Reynolds, 1992; McPherson, 1992; or Scheerens, 1992, for example) and broad agreement as to appropriate methodology for the analysis of such effects. However, rather less evidence exists concerning schools' effects on other important aspects of student development (e.g. behaviour, attendance, attitudes, self-concept). The majority of studies have focused on only one or two measures of academic attainment, most commonly basic skills (reading/mathematics) at primary and total examination scores at secondary level. Only a minority of researchers have attempted to examine consistency in schools' effects on a range of different educational outcomes including social/affective and academic outcomes (examples of studies which have paid some attention to this issue include Reynolds, 1976; Rutter *et al.*, 1979; Gray *et al.*, 1983; Mandeville and Anderson, 1986; Cuttance, 1987; Mortimore *et al.*, 1988a; Brandsma and Knuver, 1989).

Different Aspects of Academic Attainment

At the primary-school level, Mortimore *et al.*'s (1986, 1988a) work provides evidence that some schools were more effective at promoting particular aspects of academic outcome than others, although there were few schools which were very effective in one cognitive area and very ineffective in other cognitive areas. Modest positive correlations were reported between schools' effects on reading and mathematics (r=0.41) and writing and mathematics (r=0.28). However, school effects on oracy were not related to those on other language measures (reading or writing). Overall 19 schools were reported to have positive effects on all or three of the four cognitive outcomes examined and 12 positive effects on none or only one cognitive outcome out of a sample of 47 schools for which data on all outcomes were available. Subsequent reanalysis of the data set has shown that, using a more complex model the relationship between schools' effects on reading and mathematics may be somewhat closer (r=0.61), Sammons *et al.* (1993a).

Tizard *et al.*'s (1989) infant-school study also examined school differences in pupil progress in reading and mathematics but did not report on whether schools which were effective in one area were also effective in another.

A UK recent study (Thomas and Nuttall, 1993) concerning Key Stage 1 (KS1) attainment in the National Curriculum reported correlations between school effects for the four subjects, English, mathematics, science and technology. These analyses took account of a variety of pupil-level background characteristics but did not provide estimates of the value-added by the school because no measures of prior attainment were available. The correlations reported ranged between a maximum of 0.68 for English and mathematics effects to a minimum of 0.42 for English and technology.

Bosker and Scheerens (1989) provide a useful review of various aspects of stability in school effects. In connection with stability across effect criteria they note American studies by Mandeville and Anderson (1988) and Mandeville (1987) which, like the Mortimore *et al.* (1988a) study, investigated the correlation between effects on mathematics and reading. The results indicate fairly substantial stability (r near 0.70), a figure in line with that reported by Bosker's (1989) study of elementary schools in the Netherlands (r = 0.72) and higher than that reported by Mortimore *et al.* (1988a).

In the USA work by Crone *et al.* (1994) examined the consistency of achievement measures of school effectiveness across years. In particular, the issues of the validity of using narrow measures of school performance to establish school effectiveness was investigated. The study's methodology was limited due to the reliance on aggregated data and absence of adequate control for intake differences.

Schools' residuals were classified as effective if actual scores were 0.674 standard error (SE) units higher than predicted, negative if 0.674 SE units lower. Contingency tables were analysed to establish the extent of consistency in classifications for each year and test score. It was found that reading measures were more variable than either mathematics or composite achievement measures and it was concluded that 'the composite score of multiple-test types and years appears to provide a broader, more stable and consistent basis from which to construct a model to judge school effectiveness' (p. 10).

Another recent elementary study of reading and mathematics achievement by Yelton *et al.* (1994) demonstrated a fairly high level of consistency in school effects for these two outcomes within years. However, the study was based on aggregate data and therefore suffered from the same methodological weaknesses as the Crone *et al.* research. An analysis of outliers revealed that 'eight of the fifteen or sixteen outliers identified for each year were outliers in *both* reading and maths achievement' (pp. 9–10). Outliers were classified as residuals plus or minus one standard deviation larger than expected.

Few studies have examined consistency in different measures of attainment at secondary school. Cuttance (1987) reports correlations for Scottish secondary schools of 0.47 and 0.47 for English and arithmetic respectively with an overall achievement indicator. Work by Willms and Raudenbush (1989) and Smith and Tomlinson (1989) has also found some positive correlations between schools' effects in English and mathematics and overall exam score but, as with the primary-school research, the correlations are by no means perfect. Smith and Tomlinson concluded

> Differences between schools are greatest if specific subjects are
> considered rather than the sum of the results across all subjects.
> There is a considerable tendency for schools that are successful in
> one subject to be successful in another and across all subjects, but
> there are also some important contrasts between the level of success
> achieved by the same schools with different subjects (p. 276).

Fitz-Gibbon (1991) has developed an A-Level Information System (ALIS). One of ALIS's aims is to report to schools how their students' examination results compare with those of similar students in other institutions. Only departmental indicators are produced. Evidence of significant differences between departments is reported after control for relevant background factors and prior attainment. It is noted that the results 'do not lend strong credibility to the notion that schools

7

doing well with students in one aspect will be effective in all aspects' (p. 80), but no correlations were reported of departmental effects at A level on different subjects. Fitz-Gibbon's work controlled for mean O-level grade and a measure of student ability at age 17. It is arguable that this procedure may mask some significant earlier school/departmental effects which could have raised/depressed pupils' examination performance at age 16 and/or affected their decisions to stay on for A level. In addition, the small numbers of students involved in analyses at the departmental level at A level mean that very large standard errors will apply in cases with five or fewer students.

More recent work conducted on behalf of the Association of Metropolitan Authorities (AMA) has examined consistency in secondary schools' effects, in terms of the 1991 GCSE results in English and mathematics for 116 schools in nine LEAs (Thomas et al., 1993). This multilevel analysis took account of prior achievement and background factors and found a positive correlation between schools' effects on these two areas of 0.48.

Luyten (1994) conducted an interesting and wide-ranging analysis of the stability of school effects in secondary education examining performance in 17 subjects across five years. Although the Luyten research utilized individual-level examination data no intake characteristics details were available, thus little control for variations between schools was possible (although control for curriculum track was made.) This is likely to have affected the results of the study because a value-added approach was not possible. It was concluded that 'differences between subjects within schools appear to be of more importance than the general school differences' (p. 21). Luyten argues that the findings confirm the conclusions of recent studies that departments play an important role in secondary schools. In total 40 per cent of the school-level variance in student achievement was attributed to subject differences (where the school level represents 15 per cent of the total variance in student achievement).

In summary, the evidence concerning consistency in schools' performance in promoting different aspects of academic attainment or subjects is fairly limited being confined to language/reading and mathematics/arithmetic in the main. Given the differences between secondary and primary schools (the greater use of subject specialist teachers and departmental organization) it might be anticipated that the concept of overall school effectiveness would be less applicable than of departmental effectiveness and Luyten's (1994) analysis supports this view. However, many studies of the process side of school effectiveness have pointed to the importance of particular school-level factors (e.g. headteacher's leadership) at the secondary level in particular. The extent of consistency in departmental/secondary school effects on different academic outcomes is an area that requires further investigation. Our present ESRC study of Differential School Effectiveness: Departmental Variations in GCSE Attainment (Nuttall et al., 1992) which utilizes the AMA data for eight London LEAs across three years (1990–1992), provides further evidence concerning the interrelationship between school and departmental effects for a wider range of subjects (English language, English literature, French, history, mathematics and science) at GCSE (Sammons, Thomas and Mortimore, 1995).

In Different Boards of the Same Examination

In England, the General Certificate of Secondary Education (GCSE) is currently administered by four independent groups of examination boards. Previously, the General Certificate of Education (GCE) examinations had been administered by up to seven independent boards. In such circumstances, it is difficult to ensure common grading standards. The existence of possible systematic differences in the proportions of high grades awarded by the boards, was investigated by Martini *et al.* (1985).

The researchers examined the records of 40,000 London candidates. They used two methods of comparison between the two boards with the largest number of entries. The first method compared separately the results of two boards for candidates of different known abilities (as measured at age 11). The second method used performance in one subject in a particular board to compare with the results of the same pupil taking another subject *in either the same or a different board*. Both methods produced the same outcome: systematic differences in the proportion of high grades awarded by the two boards. Paradoxically, the board with the reputation for setting more straightforward questions actually produced a lower proportion of candidates with high grades than did the other board.

The possibility of a systematic bias in the examination results of pupils, therefore, has to be recognized. Investigators of school effectiveness studies might be advised to check that differences in academic outcomes based on public examinations have not been caused artificially, by the choice of a particular examination board.

In Different Measures of Attendance

Little work has been conducted on school differences in effectiveness in promoting pupil attendance at primary, in comparison with that at secondary level. Mortimore *et al.* (1988a, 1986) found that the school did have an impact upon attendance though the effect was small. Two measures of schools' effects on attendance were reported. One on attendance in Year 5 (the third year of junior schooling) and one on change in attendance over time (controlling for first year [Year 3] attendance at the pupil level). The results of these two measures of schools' effects were closely related ($r = 0.89$).

At the secondary level Rutter *et al.* (1979) and Reynolds (1976) investigated variations in attendance. They found marked differences between secondary schools. The Rutter *et al.* study examined school differences for two different measures of pupil attendance at secondary school (mean attendance for pupils of middle ability and the proportion of very poor attenders). The rank ordering of schools was very similar on these two measures (0.93).

In Different Measures of Attitudes

Mortimore *et al.* (1986, 1988a) examined schools' effects on children's attitudes towards a variety of curriculum areas, and towards school. It was not found appropriate to draw up a composite measure of attitudes because individual-level analyses demonstrated that children had very specific attitudes towards different activities, and that relationships between attitude to school and to school activities were weak. In all cases it was found that school membership was more important than background factors, sex and age in accounting for variations in the attitude data.

It was reported that the correlations between schools' effects on the different areas were generally weak, although positive and significant. In particular, effects on attitude to school and on attitude to mathematics (r = 0.38), and on attitude to reading and on attitude to writing (r = 0.33) were related.

Fitz-Gibbon (1991) reports positive but fairly weak, correlations between attitudes to subject and attitude to school at A level (r = 0.30 for attitude to geography and attitude to school for those taking geography A level, r = 0.48 for attitude to mathematics and attitude to school for those taking A-level mathematics).

In Different Measures of Behaviour

Mortimore et al.'s (1988a) work examined schools' effects on a measure of pupil behaviour. Because of difficulties involved in using individual teacher-based assessments, an overall measure (based on aggregated assessments over three separate years) was used. Evidence of substantial school differences was reported. Positive correlations were also noted between schools' effects on behaviour and on attitude to school and attitude to mathematics.

At the secondary level, Reynolds (1976), and Rutter et al. (1979), found evidence of substantial school effects on different student behaviour measures. The Rutter study investigated pupil behaviour using a combination of pupil self-report and observational measures for several different age groups of children. In addition, delinquency data were obtained from police records. The rank correlation of schools on these two measures was 0.72.

Different Measures of Self-Concept

Mortimore et al. (1988) reported the existence of significant differences in school effectiveness in promoting pupil self-concept at school. School effects on self-concept were found to be positively correlated with effects on attitude to school and attitude to mathematics also (r = 0.36 and r = 0.36 respectively).

In Different Kinds of Outcomes (Academic and Affective/Social)

The studies of secondary schools by Reynolds (1976) and Rutter et al. (1979) found fairly strong intercorrelations between schools' academic effectiveness and their social effectiveness (in terms of attendance and delinquency rates). The Rutter et al. (1979) study concluded 'On the whole, schools which have high levels of attendance and good behaviour also tend to have high levels of exam success' (p. 92). Substantial rank correlations were reported for delinquency and attendance (0.77); for delinquency and academic outcome (0.68); for delinquency and behaviour (0.72). However, later work by Gray et al. (1983) suggests that outcomes such as liking school and attendance were partially independent of schools' academic outcomes.

Fitz-Gibbon (1991) reports significant but modest positive correlations (ranging between r = 0.26 and r = 0.53) between attitude to school, on attitude to subject and on aspirations and effects on A-level subject performance for chemistry and mathematics.

For primary schools, although Mortimore *et al*. (1988a) found some significant positive associations (and no negative ones) between particular cognitive and affective outcomes (e.g. attitude to mathematics and on self-concept with effects on mathematics progress), it was concluded that the two dimensions of school effects upon cognitive and upon non-cognitive areas were independent. Nonetheless, it was also noted that a number of schools had positive effects upon outcomes in both areas (14 out of 47 schools) whereas very few recorded positive effects for cognitive outcomes but were ineffective in non-cognitive outcomes (3) and six were broadly effective in promoting non-cognitive outcomes but were unsuccessful in most cognitive areas.

Recent work in the Netherlands, Knuver and Brandsma (1993) on the relationships between schools' effects on a variety of affective measures and on language and arithmetic attainment indicated that the correlations are very small but never negative. Interestingly, this study also found that 'the strongest relationship between cognitive and affective outcomes can be found when subject-specific affective measures are under study' (p. 201). In line with Mortimore *et al*.'s (1988a) work it was concluded that the two domains are relatively independent at the school level.

Evidence on the extent of consistency of schools' effects on different kinds of educational outcomes appears to be mixed. At both secondary and primary level significant and positive, though far from perfect, correlations between schools' effects on different kinds of academic outcomes have been reported. However, few studies have examined both cognitive and academic/social outcomes. Of those that have, primary studies suggest that schools' effects on the two domains are weakly related and may be independent. At the secondary level results suggest that effects on academic and affective/social outcomes may be more closely linked, particularly for examination results and attendance and behaviour. Nonetheless, further research is needed to investigate the issue of consistency in schools' effects on different kinds of outcomes in greater depth and in a wider range of contexts before firm conclusions can be drawn.

DO SCHOOLS PERFORM CONSISTENTLY OVER TIME?

Bosker and Scheerens (1989) review evidence concerning two aspects of stability over time. They make the assumption that 'since we might expect that organizational characteristics of schools are more or less stable over time, we must know if the rank order of schools on output remains the same no matter when we measure the effect' (p. 747). In addition they comment that 'Another aspect of stability over time is the possible existence of grade-specific effects. If school effects vary across grades this would mean – especially in primary education – that these effects are in fact teacher effects' (p. 747). However, this would only be the case if prior attainment is controlled. Moreover, the extent to which schools' organizational characteristics remain stable over time is, of course, debatable. Evidence from Mortimore *et al*. (1988a) has demonstrated that many inner-city primary schools were subject to substantial change during a three-year period. In the UK in recent years the implementation of the 1988 Education Reform Act has, of course, led to many far-reaching changes.

11

The evidence on whether the effects of schools vary over time is mixed. Early British secondary studies (Reynolds, 1976; Rutter *et al.*, 1979) examined students' examination outcomes for different years and found in general consistency over time (rank correlations of 0.69 to 0.82 for the Rutter study). Work by Willms (1987) and Goldstein (1987) in the UK reveals correlations ranging between 0.80 to 0.60. In the Netherlands figures ranging between 0.75 (Roeleveld and de Jong, 1989) to 0.96 (Bosker *et al.*, 1988) have been identified.

However, Nuttall *et al.*'s (1989) research in inner London points to the existence of lack of stability in secondary schools' effects on student total examination scores over a three-year period, although no indication is given of the correlation between years in the estimates of individual schools' effects. These authors note that 'The lack of stability may also be partly to do with the unreliability and lack of comparability of the examination scores' (p. 775). They also report that statistical adjustment for prior attainment in their analysis is limited because the only measure available was a crude three-category variable (verbal reasoning band). Nuttall *et al.* conclude 'This analysis nevertheless gives rise to a note of caution about any study of school effectiveness that relies on measures of outcome in just a single year, or of just a single cohort of students. Long-time series are essential for a proper study of stability over time' (ibid.).

In her A-level work, Fitz-Gibbon (1991) also draws attention to the need to examine departmental residuals over several years. She notes that the problem of reliability of residuals for departmental effects is particularly acute with the small samples typical of A-level analyses for schools. She concludes 'Only steady trends year after year could provide a basis for strong inferences' (p. 78).

Like Nuttall *et al.* (1989), Raudenbush (1989) also draws attention to the importance of adopting a longitudinal model for estimating school effects and their stability. He notes that 'The estimated "effect" of a school includes its average effect over the period under study – its stable component – plus an effect specific to each point in time – its unstable component' (p. 733). He summarizes results from a study of school effects over two time points (1980, 1984) in Scotland. He concludes that 'school effects on overall attainment are not nearly as unstable as the estimated school effects make them appear to be. The estimated true score correlation is reported to be fairly high (r = 0.87).' However, in the original analyses Willms and Raudenbush (1989) also looked at English and arithmetic results separately in addition to overall examination results. It was found that 'school effects on overall attainment were the most stable ... school effects on examination results in specific subjects were less stable'. More recent multilevel research on stability in examination results for secondary school effects is reported by Sime and Gray (1991). In contrast to Nuttall *et al.*'s (1989) conclusions, but in line with those of Raudenbush (1989), these authors found evidence of considerable stability in schools' effects on pupils' mean examination results over a period of three years in one LEA and over two years in another (correlations ranging from 0.86 to 0.94).

More recent work conducted in the Netherlands (Luyten, 1994) has examined the stability of school effects in secondary education over a period of five years. This study attempted to investigate stability across subjects (17 in all) and across years and to examine the interaction effect of instability, across years and subjects. Unfortunately, because no measures of prior attainment were available for the analysis the results cannot be interpreted in a value-added context and it is possible that, with more adequate control for intake, the results might differ. Nonetheless, it was concluded that 'schools produce fairly stable results per subject across years' (p. 20). It was further noted that 'the interaction effect of subject by year is substantial' and 'the general year effect turns out to be very modest' (p. 21). In terms of percentage of student variation attributable to school (15 per cent of the total), 25 per cent was found to represent a main school effect, 27 per cent an interaction of subject and year and only 8 per cent a year effect. The remaining 40 per cent was attributable to a subject effect.

Less attention has been paid to the stability of school effects at the primary than the secondary level, although Mandeville (1987) reports correlations in the USA ranging from 0.34 to 0.66. However, Bosker and Scheerens (1989) point out that these figures may be 'deflated' because of the inadequacy of the statistical model used.

Although no correlations were reported, another example of USA research (the Louisiana School Effectiveness Study) examined selected schools which were consistent outliers either negative or positive terms in the state basic skills test (which focused on reading). Stringfield et al. (1992) reported in their study of 16 outliers 'most schools appear to have remained stable outliers, either positive or negative, for at least seven years' (p. 394).

Two recent studies of elementary schools in the USA have also pointed to the existence of substantial stability in school effects over time. Crone et al. (1994) investigated the issues of stability and consistency in classifications of schools as effective/ineffective at one point in time. The study examined two years of state-wide assessment at four different grade levels. Unfortunately, the study utilized aggregate school-level data in regression analyses and thus no account was taken of the multilevel structure of the data. In addition no prior-attainment measures were available and the intake data available for control was limited. This is likely to have had a substantial impact upon the estimate of schools' residuals obtained and thus the results should be treated with caution. Crone et al. reported correlations of residuals over the two years ranging between 0.49 and 0.78. It was concluded that stability was greater for composite measures of achievement and for mathematics results than for reading or language.

Research by Yelton et al. (1994) used comparative path models to investigate the stability of school effectiveness for 55 elementary schools. Unfortunately, like the Crone et al. (1994) study, the research used aggregated data in the analysis. No prior-attainment data were included and the control for intake characteristics was severely limited. Given this the results should be interpreted with care. It was found that of the 14 reading-achievement outliers (plus or minus 1 SD) identified for each year, nine were outliers in both years. For mathematics achievement 15 outliers were identified over two years with eight being outliers in both years. However, only three schools were identified as outliers in both cognitive areas and in each of the two years.

In the UK, Tizard et al.'s (1988) infant-school study of an age cohort suggests that generally school differences are greater over a single year period than over a longer period (three years). These authors argue that their findings point to the greater importance of teacher than of school effects for this age group.

13

Stability Across Grades/Age Groups

Bosker and Scheerens (1989) argue that, from a theoretical point of view, stability across grades is a more interesting question than stability over time. However they note that 'Only little is known about this topic' (p. 748). Using USA data Mandeville and Anderson (1986) report very low correlations at the elementary level (near 0.10) for mathematics and language. However, in the Netherlands, Bosker (1989) found an intra-school correlation between grades for arithmetic of 0.50, and for language 0.47.

At the secondary level Bosker et al. (1988) cite rank correlations ranging from 0.40 to 0.80 between grades but Bosker and Scheerens also note 'these figures may be somewhat inflated because of dependency in the observations' (p. 748). In the UK, Rutter et al. (1979) report rank correlations for pupil misbehaviour across grades ranging from 0.23 to 0.65. The relationships were far stronger for attendance (near 0.80).

Overall these results suggest a fair degree of stability in secondary schools' effects on academic outcomes over time (correlations are fairly strong and all positive), particularly for overall examination results and, to a lesser extent, for basic skill areas in the primary sector. There is much less evidence concerning stability for specific subjects at secondary school or concerning social/affective (non-cognitive) outcomes of education, although the Rutter et al. (1979) research demonstrated considerable stability in school differences in attendance across years (rank correlations ranging between 0.60 and 0.90). It is clear that there is a need for further research to examine the extent of stability in school/departmental effects for a wider range of outcomes and in different sectors.

The fact that measures of stability are not perfect over time should not be too surprising. It is important to recognize that change in outcomes is likely over time periods of more than one or two years due to changes in staff, in pupil intakes and in ethos. Schools may also change rapidly as a result of outside intervention (e.g. new principal, inspection or in the face of particular issues). Therefore a method of identifying and separately measuring time and school effects is required in order to evaluate schools more accurately. In addition, further work on school processes related to effectiveness is needed to investigate mechanisms for change and ways in which it may be most successfully introduced.

DO SCHOOLS PERFORM CONSISTENTLY ACROSS DIFFERENT PHASES OF SCHOOLING?

Evidence for the existence of school effects has been found across all phases of schooling and for a variety of outcomes. For example, in the UK context, Tizard et al.'s (1988) study of infant schooling demonstrated the existence of effects for reading and number work; Mortimore et al. (1988a, 1988b) produced evidence for a variety of cognitive and non-cognitive outcomes concerning the junior phase. Studies by Cuttance (1987); Reynolds et al. (1987); Rutter et al. (1979); Nuttall et al. (1989); Willms and Raudenbush (1989); and Jesson and Gray (1991) demonstrate the existence of secondary-school effects on examination results at age 16 years. For the post-16 phase work on the existence of specific school effects is limited, although Thomas et al.'s (1992; 1993) work on A-level league tables for the Guardian project indicates the existence of significant school effects. Furthermore, Fitz-Gibbon's (1991) analyses at the departmental level indicates the importance of departmental effects for A levels.

Value-added studies for higher education institutions are lacking as yet but should prove to be a fruitful area for further investigation.

Bosker and Scheerens (1989) discuss effect size as a function of the choice of dependent and independent variables. They note that specific characteristics of instructional processes show up more clearly when curriculum-specific tests rather than general scholastic aptitude tests are used as the dependent variable (as was demonstrated by Madaus *et al.* (1979)). They conclude 'Effect sizes are also relatively higher when subject matter areas are tested that depend more exclusively on schooling and instruction; so, effects in arithmetic and mathematics are usually somewhat higher than effects in a subject like (native) language, which is also learned at home' (p. 745).

Research in the Netherlands (Brandsma and Knuver, 1989) examined the effects of school and classroom characteristics on pupil progress in language and arithmetic. It concluded 'schools can influence arithmetic progress more than language progress. These results are congruent with ... similar research in England (Mortimore *et al.*, 1988a). This may be caused by the fact that arithmetic is a subject that is more uniquely learned at school, while language acquirement is more a joint operation of school and home environment' (p. 787). Thus, it appears that the school is important in accounting for variance in pupils' progress in mathematics than in language at the primary level (a point we will return to at a later stage). However, Brandsma and Knuver did not report correlations on the extent to which schools which were effective in arithmetic were also effective in language.

It is difficult to compare the *relative* size of school effects in different school effectiveness studies because these are often reported in different ways. One approach is to examine the report of average between school variance reported in different studies. Bosker and Scheerens (1989) reviewed 12 Dutch studies of which only six computed the between school variance. 'The average percentage of the total variance accounted for by the factor school is 12' (p. 745). However, these authors do not indicate whether these studies were based on primary or secondary schools or a mixture. A later review by Daly (1991) of secondary-school studies only reports figures of between 8 and 10 per cent. However, Scheerens (1992) notes that 'More insight into the *practical* significance of school effectiveness is gained when the relevant difference can also be expressed in money or time. Thus the difference of 0.67 standard deviations is compared to an entire school-year's difference between the average pupil in the most effective schools and the average pupil in the least effective schools' (p. 71).

In a recent multilevel reanalysis of the Mortimore *et al.* (1988a) *School Matters* data, Sammons *et al.* (1993a) note rather higher figures for reading and mathematics scores at primary school (between 14 and 15 per cent of the overall variation in reading and mathematics attainment for pupils in Year 5 of junior school was attributable to school). As part of further analyses conducted to examine the issue of continuity of schools' effects at secondary school for the sample followed up at age 16 years it was noted that the equivalent figures for secondary schools (i.e. the percentage of total variation in students' total examination scores attributable to school) was somewhat lower, at 11.5 per cent (Sammons *et al.*, 1993b).

It was noted that differences amongst primary schools in basic skills attainment thus appear to be rather larger than those amongst secondary schools in GCSE attainment. It was also found that, after controlling for prior attainment and background effects at secondary school, the proportion of unexplained variance in students' GCSE total examination score accounted for by the school was reduced to just under 9 per cent. This estimate is markedly lower than that obtained in the equivalent multilevel analyses of primary schools where estimates were in the region of 18 to 19 per cent for reading and mathematics respectively.

There are likely to be a number of reasons for this apparent difference in the size of the school effect. Only pupils for whom a valid examination score was available were included in the secondary analysis (i.e. no information was available about students who were not entered for GCSEs). This may reduce estimates of the effects of schools because low ability students (or those of higher ability who leave early or are absent) will be underrepresented.

It is also possible that overall GCSE examination performance is affected by departmental/subject variations within schools. 'Departmental differences may be more marked than overall differences between schools in total examination performance scores and the concept of overall school effectiveness may be less relevant to secondary than to primary schools' (Sammons *et al.*, 1993b). Clearly the issue of *counterbalancing* effects will be especially relevant to any schools which are found to be effective in some subjects but ineffective in others. For these schools, overall examination performance scores will obscure important subject differences in students' GCSE attainment.

Thomas *et al.*'s (1993) work on AMA examination data suggests that, when the school-level variation is compared, school differences may be more substantial in some subjects than in others and this is likely to reflect departmental effectiveness. Using a measure of total examination score alone may mask such differences. For example, they report differences in the intra-school correlations for mathematics ($r = 0.13$) compared with English ($r = 0.08$). The intra-school correlation for total examination score was 0.11.

Substantial subject differences are also apparent at the infant level. Thomas and Nuttall (1993) have reported that there is greater variance attributable to schools for science KS1 assessment (27 per cent) than for English (10 per cent). However, overall it was found that 20 per cent of the variation in pupils' total KS1 score is attributable to schools and this result alone would mask the differences according to subject. Unfortunately, no measures of prior attainment were available for these KS1 analyses and thus the results do not provide value-added estimates of school effectiveness (although data concerning socio-economic factors was utilized).

Sammons *et al.* (1993b) also investigated the issue of continuity in primary school effects upon pupils' later performance at secondary school. Evidence of small but continuing differences in students' overall performance at GCSE related to primary school attended was found. Estimates of the proportion of unexplained variance in total examination scores attributable to primary school attended ranged from 4.2 to 5.6 per cent (in models where attainment at entry to secondary school and background factors were controlled and accounted for around 38 per cent of total variance).

Overall there is considerable evidence that significant school effects can be identified for all phases of schooling. There is some indication that they may be larger for younger rather than older age groups. Further exploration of differences in the relative importance of school effects for different phases of schooling is required to examine this issue.

DO SCHOOLS PERFORM CONSISTENTLY ACROSS DIFFERING SCHOOL MEMBERSHIPS?

The importance of controlling for prior attainment in studies of school effectiveness so that the value-added by the school can be estimated is now widely recognized (McPherson, 1992) as standard practice (with a few notable exceptions such as Preece, 1988). Controlling for prior attainment much reduces the apparent importance of background factors. Nonetheless, there is evidence that a number of pupil-level characteristics remain of statistical and theoretical importance (see Nuttall et al., 1989; Sammons et al., 1993a). Willms (1992) argues that, of such factors, measures of socio-economic status are particularly important. Absence of control for variables such as father's social class, eligibility for free school meals and so on will tend to favour particular schools. 'Schools with more advantaged intakes appear to be performing better than they are; schools with disadvantaged intakes appear worse' (p. 45).

In considering whether schools perform consistently across differing school memberships it is important to distinguish contextual or compositional effects as they are sometimes labelled, from differential effects. Contextual effects are related to the overall composition of the student body (e.g. the percentage of high ability or of high SES students in a given year group or in the school's intake as a whole) and can be identified by between school analyses across a sample of schools. Differential school effects refer to *within* school differences in a school's effects for individual pupils according to specific characteristics (e.g. sex, SES group, ethnicity).

Contextual Effects

In addition to control for effects related to individual background characteristics (e.g. age, sex, social class, ethnicity, etc.), some studies have addressed the issue of contextual effects. Willms (1992) notes that 'the composition of a school's intake can have a substantial effect on pupils' outcome over and above the effects associated with pupils' individual ability and social class' (p. 41) (see Brookover et al., 1978; Willms, 1986 or Willms and Raudenbush, 1989 for example). However, it is important not to confuse contextual effects with differential within school effects related to social class. Willms (1986) examined social-class segregation and its relationship to pupils' examination results in Scotland. It was noted that 'some of the observed differences between schools in their adjusted outcomes were associated with school composition' (p. 239). It was concluded that pupils at all levels of ability tend to benefit from attending high SES schools.

Willms (1985) also found contextual effects related to the balance of high-ability students within a school. Students of average ability in high-ability schools scored more than a full examination grade higher than comparable students in schools where the majority of pupils were of low ability.

In contrast to the Scottish study of secondary schools, Mortimore *et al.* (1988a) found no evidence of contextual effects related to social-class composition for their sample of junior schools (a finding supported by the later reanalysis). Similarly, Bondi's (1991) analysis of reading attainment in Scottish primary schools noted 'In contrast to the results obtained for secondary schools in the same area (Willms, 1986) there is no evidence that the mean socio-economic status of a school influences variations in outcomes between schools after adjusting for the background characteristics of the child' (p. 211). Bondi argues that the contrast between primary and secondary schools suggests that peer group effects are more marked among adolescents than among young children.

Nuttall's (1990) research into inner London secondary school effects over three consecutive years noted some evidence of positive compositional effects related to the concentration of high ability students (percentage VR band 1) and negative effects related to the concentration of students eligible for free school meals.

Thomas and Nuttall (1993) looked at a variety of contextual effects in relation to Key Stage 1 attainment in the National Curriculum. The only significant finding was that of mean age of pupils in Year 2 implying that relative age is a factor that should be considered in relation to the attainment of seven-year-olds. No significant contextual effects were found for gender, English as a second language or free school meals.

Differential School Effects

The importance of differential school effects (or differential school slopes) is a topic of increasing interest in school effectiveness research especially in the UK field. Differential school effects concerns the existence of systematic differences in attainment between schools for different pupil groups (those with different levels of prior attainment or different background characteristics), once the *average* differences between these groups has been accounted for.

Prior attainment   Although the study by Rutter *et al.* (1979) did not utilize multilevel techniques it did examine schools' examination results for the most and least able children and compared the results for children of different levels of prior ability (using a three-category measure at intake – VR band). It was found that 'the pattern of results for each school was broadly similar in all three bands' (p. 86). In addition, the rank correlation of schools on a lower exam pass measure correlated highly (0.83) with that on examination score. The analysis of high examination results for top VR groups also showed 'a ranking of schools which was broadly similar (0.70) to that obtained with the overall weighted pass measure' (p. 89).

Smith and Tomlinson's (1989) study of multiracial comprehensives investigated school differences in effectiveness in promoting examination performance (total exam score, English exam score and mathematics exam score). Some evidence of differential effectiveness for pupils with different levels of prior attainment (measured by second-year reading tests) was found. In particular, differences in English exam results between schools were found to be greater for pupils with above-average, than for pupils with below-average, second-year reading scores. The authors conclude that this is 'largely because the exams are such that even the best school cannot achieve a result with a pupil having a below-average reading score' (p. 273). However, Smith and Tomlinson found little evidence that the slopes of schools' individual effects on examination results cross over. The same schools are most successful with more *and* the less able pupils, 'but a more able pupil gains a greater advantage than a less able one from going to a good school' (p. 273). The findings for mathematics were similar to those for English.

Nuttall *et al.*'s (1989) and Nuttall's (1990) secondary-school analyses also report evidence that schools' performance varies differentially, some schools narrowing the gap between students of high and low attainment on entry. The results suggest that variability in high-ability pupils between schools is much larger than that of low-ability students. Thomas and Nuttall's (1993) analysis of AMA data also found that the correlations between schools' value-added results for pupils in VR bands 1 and 3 were 0.73 for the total GCSE score, r = 0.76 for English and r = 0.73 for mathematics, indicating the existence of some differential effectiveness for pupils of different ability on entry to secondary school. These studies were limited, however, by inadequate statistical adjustment because the only prior attainment data available was the crude categorization of three VR bands.

In the Scottish context, Willms and Raudenbush (1989) also report some evidence of differential school effectiveness for pupils of different prior attainment (VRQ) levels. However, in an earlier study of Scottish secondary schools Willms (1986) concluded 'the *within* school relationships between outcomes and pupil characteristics did not vary much across schools' (p. 239).

Jesson and Gray (1991) investigated the issue of differential school effectiveness for pupils with different levels of prior achievement at the secondary level. These authors suggest that there is no conclusive evidence for the existence of differential slopes. Their research provides evidence of modest differential slopes but, although, 'Pupils of different prior attainment levels did slightly better in some schools than in others ... schools which were more effective for one group of pupils were generally speaking more effective for other groups as well' (p. 46). This conclusion is broadly in line with that of Smith and Tomlinson (1989). Jesson and Gray (1991) suggest a number of possible reasons for the difference between Nuttall *et al.*'s (1989) and their own results. They draw particular attention to the high degree of social differentiation in inner-city areas and to the crude measure of prior attainment in the ILEA research. They conclude that the use of a crude grouped measure rather than a finely differentiated measure of prior attainment may affect findings about the nature and extent of differential school effectiveness.

Most of the evidence concerning differential school effectiveness and prior attainment has been conducted at the secondary level. The original analyses for the *School Matters* (Mortimore *et al.*, 1988a) study did not re-examine differential effectiveness for pupils with different levels of prior attainment. The subsequent reanalysis, however, did address this issue. Sammons *et al.* (1993a) found some evidence of differential school effectiveness for pupils with different levels of prior attainment, although this was less notable for reading than for mathematics where some evidence of crossing of school slopes was found. Nonetheless, the general conclusion was that although significant, differential effects were fairly modest and that schools which were effective for low attaining pupils also tended to be effective for those with high prior attainment also.

Research in the Netherlands by Brandsma and Knuver (1989) at the primary level also investigated the extent of differential effectiveness in language and arithmetic progress. No evidence of equity differences, as these authors entitle such effects, were found in relation to pre-test scores for mathematics. However, for language 'the effect of language pre-test on post-test differs slightly between schools' but 'these differences are very small' (p. 787).

Gender

A few studies have pointed to the existence of differential school effects related to pupil gender (after taking account of the impact of gender at the level of the individual level). For example, Nuttall et al.'s (1989) study of examination results over three years in inner London points to the existence of such differential effects in terms of total examination scores 'some schools narrowing the gap between boys and girls ... and some widening the gap, relatively speaking' (p. 774).

However, in the Scottish context Willms and Raudenbush (1989) who noted differential effects for prior attainment did not identify any differential effects for other background characteristics, including gender.

At the primary level the study by Mortimore et al. (1988a) produced no evidence of differential school effectiveness related to gender for reading or mathematics progress and the more detailed reanalysis supports the earlier conclusions (Sammons et al., 1993a).

In the Netherlands, Brandsma and Knuver (1989) found no evidence of differential school effects related to gender for mathematics and only very small equity differences for the Dutch language. 'The influence of gender (overall positive for girls), does differ somewhat between schools' (p. 787) but the authors note that these differences are very small and cannot be explained by the school or classroom factors investigated in their study.

In Scotland Bondi's (1991) cross-sectional study of reading attainment (rather than of progress) at the primary school also produced some evidence of differential school effectiveness for the two sexes.

Ethnicity

Several studies at the secondary level point to the existence of differential school effects for students of different ethnic backgrounds. Nuttall et al. (1989) reported within school Caribbean–English, Scottish, Welsh (ESW) differences in effectiveness and comment that other ethnic differences vary across schools even more than the Caribbean–ESW differences: 'the Pakistani–ESW differences has a standard deviation of some 3 score points across schools' (p. 775). However, the authors draw attention to the lack of individual-level data about the socio-economic level of students' families which could confound ethnic differences with socio-economic differences.

Elsewhere in the UK Smith and Tomlinson's (1989) study also produced evidence of differential school effectiveness for children of different ethnic groups although these differences were found to be 'small compared with differences in overall performance between schools' (p. 268). The authors make a general conclusion about schools in their sample: 'the ones that are good for white people tend to be about equally good for black people' (p. 305).

At the primary level neither the original Mortimore *et al.* (1988a) analyses nor the reanalysis by Sammons *et al.* (1993a) found evidence of significant differential school effectiveness for specific ethnic groups. Brandsma and Knuver (1989) likewise found no indications of the existence of differential school effectiveness according to ethnic group in their study of Dutch primary schools.

These inconclusive results point to the need for further research into ethnic differential school effectiveness using data sets which contain adequate individual-level socio-economic as well as ethnic data. Exploration of the possible reasons for the apparent primary–secondary school differences in differential effectiveness are also called for.

Age

In two studies analysing the results of Key Stage 1 assessments (Thomas and Nuttall, 1992, 1993) from 1991 and 1992 it was found that there were differential school effects according to age (in months). However, in both these studies a measure of prior attainment for entry to infant school was not available. Therefore, given that age and prior attainment are related, further research concerning the issue of differential school effectiveness according to the age of pupils is required to establish whether age effects are of importance in value-added analyses.

Socio-economic Indicators

The importance of taking into account relevant socio-economic factors in studies of school effectiveness has been noted earlier (e.g. Mortimore *et al.*, 1988a, 1988b; Willms, 1992). In addition to effects at the level of the individual pupil, compositional or contextual effects related to the proportion of pupils from particular social-class groups or of low family income have been identified in some studies (see Contextual Effects). Few studies have examined the extent of within-school differential effects related to socio-economic factors. Willms and Raudenbush (1989) report compositional effects related to SES, but no within-school differences related to such characteristics.

At the primary level Mortimore *et al.*'s (1988a) study found no evidence of differential effectiveness related to non-manual versus manual social-class background. Sammons *et al.*'s (1993a) reanalysis confirmed this earlier conclusion. These authors also tested for differential effects related to low family income but found no evidence to support their existence. Interestingly, the Mortimore *et al.* research found no case in their sample of schools where students from manual backgrounds performed markedly better on average than those from non-manual groups. Schools were unable to overcome the powerful effects of social class. However, it was found that students from manual groups in the most effective schools on average outperformed those from non-manual groups in the least effective schools. The school was the unit of change rather than the social class group within it. The Mortimore *et al.* (1988a) sample was fairly small (just over 1,100 students and 49 schools) and it would be of interest to establish whether, with a larger sample, the negative findings concerning differential effects at primary level would be maintained.

Overall, it appears that, at the secondary level, there is some evidence of important contextual effects related to schools' pupil composition in terms of SES and ability or prior attainment in UK and Scottish studies, but less evidence for such effects in studies of younger age groups. For differential school effects (within school differences) again, secondary studies suggest that gender, ethnicity and prior attainment may all be relevant. However, for prior attainment, it is important that the control measure adopted is adequate (finely differentiated). Less evidence for differential effects exists at the primary stage.

CONCLUSIONS

In this section we have reviewed the evidence from a variety of school effectiveness studies conducted in different countries and contexts of consistency in schools' effects. We have examined consistency on different outcomes, on the same outcomes over time, across different phases of schooling, and across differing school memberships. No simple answers can be given to the four questions we raise, although some conclusions can be drawn, the least surprising of which is the need for further research using carefully designed longitudinal studies in different phases of schooling to investigate these issues in more depth.

In terms of different outcomes there is evidence, particularly on the academic/cognitive front, of modest (but by no means perfect) positive associations between effects on different areas. Relatively less attention has been paid to the affective or social (non-cognitive) outcomes of education. At the secondary level some evidence of links between the effectiveness in examination results and in aspects such as behaviour and attendance has been found. However, the evidence is by no means conclusive and at the primary level research to date suggests that the two domains are relatively independent.

Greater consistency in school effects over time for the same outcome appears to exist, at least in the short to medium term for secondary schools, although greater stability is evident for total examination scores than for performance in particular subjects. Evidence at the primary level is limited but also suggests stability, although correlations tend to be lower.

Evidence of significant differences between schools in their effectiveness has been identified for all phases of schooling. Nonetheless, there is some indication that effects may be stronger for primary than for secondary schools and for particular school subjects (which may be less likely to be taught at home such as mathematics and science than others e.g. language, reading). In addition, evidence for the existence of schools' effects has been identified by studies in a wide variety of countries. Very little attention has been paid to the issue of continuity of schools' effects over the long term (e.g. across phases), however.

Finally, there is inconclusive evidence about the extent to which schools perform consistently across differing school memberships. Overall, there appears to be some evidence of modest differential effectiveness for pupils of differing levels of prior attainment both from primary and from secondary studies. In addition, some contextual compositional effects have been reported related to SES and balance of high-ability students at the secondary level.

The evidence for the existence of differential effectiveness related to pupil gender varies as does that for ethnic differences. Some studies identify effects (which tend to be quite small for gender though not necessarily small for ethnicity) and others produce negative findings. Again, such effects are more commonly noted in secondary studies.

Methodological and Conceptual Issues

A wide variety of methodological and conceptual issues concerning research into consistency in schools' effects is highlighted by our review. A number of those which appear to be of particular importance are briefly noted, but the list is by no means exhaustive.

Absolute differences versus progress   There is now fairly general acceptance that studies of school effectiveness in cognitive areas require adequate control for prior attainment at the level of the individual pupil (McPherson, 1992; Cuttance, 1992; Reynolds, 1992; Scheerens, 1992). Ideally such measures should be collected at the point of entry to school at the beginning of a relevant phase (infant, junior or secondary). The use of baseline attainment or ability data collected after a period of years in the same school is likely to lead to a reduction in the estimate of school effects. For example, control of GCSE scores at 16 and for ability at age 17 is likely to lead to reduced estimates of departmental differences at A level. Yet GCSE and arguably ability scores are themselves likely to have been influenced by earlier secondary school (or departmental) effects. Ideally, the measures of prior attainment used should be finely differentiated rather than crude categorizations such as VR band and related to the outcome areas under investigation.

Control for prior attainment may also be relevant for studies of schools' effects on non-cognitive outcomes such as self-concept, behaviour and attendance, especially at the secondary level. The value of utilizing a baseline measure of the relevant outcome at intake in addition to prior attainment (e.g. behaviour at entry for studies of behaviour) should also be considered.

Controlling for intake   In addition to control for prior attainment levels, there is evidence that control for the background characteristics of pupil intakes is also important. There is evidence that a variety of student background characteristics affect later attainment even after control for prior attainment has been made. The availability of individual level data concerning socio-economic factors, sex, ethnicity and language fluency is therefore important to ensure that comparisons do not unfairly reflect on schools serving disadvantaged communities. Such data are also necessary for the exploration of possible differential within school effects for particular pupil groups. Aggregate whole-school or year-group data concerning pupil composition especially related to ability and SES are also necessary to enable exploration of possible contextual or compositional effects.

Range of outcome measures   The results of school effectiveness studies are heavily dependent upon the choice of outcome measures used. In the main, research has focused on a narrow range of measures of academic outcomes (e.g. basic skill attainment in primary schools, total examination scores at secondary level). Further work on a wider variety of academic measures is required to examine stability and consistency over time in different aspects of academic attainment (e.g. writing, science, technology). Oracy at primary school, subject differences at GCSE or attainment in 'core skill' areas at secondary level might prove fruitful areas for further investigation.

In addition, relatively little attention has been paid to the affective/social outcomes of education. The evidence from studies which have examined both affective/social and academic aspects suggests that schools' effects on the two domains can vary considerably, especially for younger age groups. It is also conceivable that school effects may be more marked for some of these outcomes (e.g. behaviour, attendance) whereas teacher (for primary) or departmental (for secondary) effects may be relatively more influential for academic outcomes.

Further investigations are required as Mortimore (1992) notes, 'the adoption of a broad range of outcome measures is essential if studies are to address, adequately, the all-round development of students, and if they are to be used to judge the effectiveness of schools' (p. 156). Longitudinal, multilevel studies are required to examine the size, consistency and interrelationships between school and classroom/departmental effects for different kinds of outcomes and for different phases of schooling.

Continuity of effects over time Very little work has been conducted to establish the long-term impact of schools across phases (e.g. primary to secondary or secondary to post-school). Scheerens (1992) provides a brief review of the evaluation of compensatory programmes (rather than school effects). 'Long-term effects of compensatory programmes cannot usually be established although studies and meta-analyses give a somewhat divided picture. For instance, researchers belonging to the Consortium for Longitudinal Studies report sustained effects of early intervention programmes like Project Head Start (Lazar et al., 1982), while Mullin and Summers (1983) conclude from a meta-analysis of 47 studies that the evidence is fairly strong that early gains are not sustained' (p. 38).

Work by Rutter et al. (1979) suggests that the post-school work records of students from more effective schools were better than those of their counterparts from less effective schools. Sammons et al. (1993b) provide some evidence for continuity of primary-school effects at GCSE. Further long-term longitudinal research is required using studies specially designed to investigate the overall impact of early as well as later school attended on students' subsequent educational careers and employment patterns.

Sampling A major limitation of many studies of school effectiveness is related to the nature of the sample of schools utilized for the analyses. Most studies have focused on inner-city schools serving disadvantaged intakes (often with a substantial ethnic mix). Further research is required using more diverse samples of schools to establish to what extent existing findings of school effectiveness research (e.g. concerning the relative size of school/class/departmental effects for different kinds of outcomes and different phases of schooling, and of stability of effects over time) apply to schools in other locations and serving different kinds of communities. In addition, further clarification of the relative size and importance of school effects for particular kinds of students is needed. For example, are school effects relatively greater for those of low compared with those of high level of prior attainment, or for those of low in comparison with those of high SES groupings?

Processes related to school effectiveness   Our review has focused on consistency in the effects of schools across outcomes and areas. However, the question of what factors and processes (school and classroom) relate to effectiveness is clearly of major interest. Less attention has been paid, particularly in multilevel studies, to testing process data. Despite methodological weakness in studies which have attempted to examine aspects of process, recent reviews of the relevant literature (e.g. Reynolds, 1992; Scheerens, 1992; Levine, 1992) suggest that a fair degree of consistency in major findings has emerged.

Hallinger and Murphy (1987) for example report that, in general, effective schools had similar characteristics regardless of the kind of intakes they serve (low, middle or upper-middle income). 'A safe and orderly environment; a clear mission; capable instructional leadership; high expectations; a well coordinated curriculum; monitoring of student progress and structure of staff development' (Hallinger and Murphy, 1986 cited in Levine and Lezotte, 1990, p. 5). Scheerens (1992) has also drawn attention to the extent of consistency in school and classroom process factors identified in a range of studies of school or teacher effectiveness.

Nonetheless, this is clearly an area which requires much further investigation. As Mortimore (1992) and Reynolds (1992) have noted research on *which* school and classroom processes are associated with greater effectiveness, *how* school organizational factors have an effect on student outcomes, and what mechanisms create the organizational factors is needed. Reynolds suggests that, in addition to large-scale quantitative studies, in-depth qualitative case studies of individual schools may have a key role to play in promoting our understanding of effective school and classroom practices and the processes of school change. Studies which utilize qualitative case-study approaches to supplement multilevel investigations may prove particularly fruitful.

Theory development   Related to the process issue noted above, there is an urgent need for more coherent and developed theories of school effectiveness. Despite a fair degree of consistency in findings concerning school and classroom processes, 'The causal status of the relationships found between school characteristics and effect measures is relatively small because of the correlative nature of the research, a lack of theory and insufficiently sharp-edged conceptualization' (Scheerens, 1992, p. 76). It is to be hoped that the next generation of school effectiveness studies will be able to build on and test out existing findings concerning the processes of school effectiveness and to assist in the construction of a more coherent and developed theoretical body of knowledge concerning the ways schools influence their students' outcomes.

OVERVIEW

In this chapter we have endeavoured to lay out the evidence on a series of issues concerned with the consistency of school effects. In particular, we have sought to ascertain how consistently schools perform on different outcomes, over time, across different phases of schooling and across different school memberships. We have drawn on the available literature – from the USA and from mainland Europe as well as from the UK – but are conscious that we may be unaware of other relevant studies in this fast-burgeoning area of research. We conclude that the answers to the questions that we pose in the Introduction are complex. No simple answers can be given. We have, however, indicated where the relationships are strong and have noted any inconsistencies and unexpected findings. The detailed literature search that we have carried out has illuminated – as we have noted – the complexity of the issues but, nevertheless, supports our belief in the validity of school effects. What we have shown is that these effects are more complex than have sometimes been assumed to be the case. It is, of course, common for researchers to advocate further work. In this case, we are glad to be able to report that some of this further work is in hand. Subsequent studies will no doubt spell out further complexity but it is only through carefully designed empirical studies which build on the findings that have been established to date that this important area will be fully illuminated.

REFERENCES

Bondi, L. (1991) 'Attainment in primary schools', *British Educational Research Journal*, **17** (3), 203–17.

Bosker, R. J. (1989) 'Theory-development in school effectiveness research: in search for stability of effects'. Paper presented at the multilevel conference, Nijmegen.

Bosker, R. J., Guldemond, H., Hofman, R. H. and Hofman, W. H. A. (1988) *Kwaliteit in het voortgezet oriderwijs*. Groningen: RION.

Bosker, R. J. and Scheerens, J. (1989) 'Issues in the interpretation of the results of school effectiveness research', chapter 4 in *International Journal of Educational Research*, special issue *Developments in School Effectiveness Research*, **13** (7), 741–51.

Brandsma, H. P. and Knuver, J. W. M. (1989) 'Effects of school and classroom characteristics on pupil progress in language and arithmetic', chapter 7 in *International Journal of Educational Research*, special issue *Developments in School Effectiveness Research*, **13** (7), 777–88.

Brookover, W., Beady, C., Flood, P., Schweitzer, J. and Wisenbaker, J. (1979) *School Social Systems and Student Achievement: Schools can make a difference*. New York: Prager.

Coleman, J., Hoffer, T. and Kilgore, S. (1982) *High School Achievement*. New York: Basic Books.

Crone, L. J., Lang, M. H. and Franklin, B. J. (1994) *Achievement Measures of School Effectiveness: Comparison of consistency across years*. Paper presented at the annual meeting of the American Educational Research Association, New Orleans, 4–8 April.

Cuttance, P. (1987) *Modelling Variation in the Effectiveness of Schooling*. Edinburgh: CES.

Daly, P. (1991) 'How large are secondary school effects in Northern Ireland', *School Effectiveness and School Improvement*, **2** (4), 305–23.

Fitz-Gibbon, C. T. (1991) 'Multilevel modelling in an indicator system', chapter 6 in Raudenbush, S. W. and Willms, J. D. (eds) *Schools, Classrooms and Pupils: International Studies of Schooling from a Multilevel Perspective*. San Diego: Academic Press.

Goldstein, H. (1987) *Multilevel Models in Educational and Social Research*. London: Charles Griffin.

Gray, J., McPherson, A. and Raffe, D. (1983) *Reconstructions of Secondary Education*. London: Routledge & Kegan Paul.

Hallinger, P. and Murphy, J. (1987) 'Instructional leadership in the school context', in Greenfield, W. (ed.) *Instructional Leadership*. Boston, Mass: Allyn & Bacon.

Husen, T., Tuijnman, A. and Halls, W. (1992) *Schooling in Modern European Society*. Oxford: Pergamon.

Jesson, D. and Gray, J. (1991) 'Slants on slopes: using multi-level models to investigate differential school effectiveness and its impact on pupils' examination results', *School Effectiveness and School Improvement*, **2** (3), 230–47.

Knuver, J. W. M. and Brandsma, H. P. (1993) 'Cognitive and affective outcomes in school effectiveness research', *School Effectiveness and School Improvement*, **4** (3), 189–204.

Lazar, I., Darlington, R. B., Murray, H. W. and Snipper, A. S. (1982) 'Lasting effects of early education: a report from the Consortium for Longitudinal Studies', *Monograph of the Society for Research in Child Development*, **47** (2–3).

Levine, D. (1992) 'An interpretative review of US research and practice dealing with unusually effective schools' in Reynolds, D. and Cuttance, P. (eds) *School Effectiveness Research, Policy and Practice*. London: Cassell.

Luyten, H. (1994) *Stability of School Effects in Secondary Education: The impact of variance across subjects and years*. Paper presented at the annual meeting of the American Educational Research Association, New Orleans, 4–8 April.

McPherson, A. (1992) 'Measuring added value in schools', *National Commission on Education Briefing No. 1*, February.

Madaus, G. F., Kellagham, T., Rakow, E. A. and King, D. (1979) 'The sensitivity of measures of school effectiveness', *Harvard Educational Review*, **49**, 207–30.

Manderville, G. K. and Anderson, L. W. (1986) *A Study of the Stability of School Effectiveness Measures across Grades and Subject Areas*. AREA paper, San Francisco.

Manderville, G. K. (1987) 'The stability of school effectiveness indices across years'. NCME paper, Washington.

Martini, R., Mortimore, P. and Byford, D. (1985) 'Some O-levels are more equal than others', *The Times Educational Supplement*, 28 June, 17.

Mortimore, P., Sammons, P., Stoll, L., Lewis, D. and Ecob, R. (1986) *The Junior School Project* (4 volumes) Research and Statistics Branch Reports. London: ILEA.

Mortimore, P., Sammons, P., Stoll, L., Lewis, D. and Ecob, R. (1988a) *School Matters: The Junior Years*. Wells: Open Books.

Mortimore, P., Sammons, P., Stoll, L., Lewis, D. and Ecob, R. (1988b) 'The effects of school membership on pupils' educational outcomes', *Research Papers in Education*, **3** (1), 3–26.

Mortimore, P. (1991) 'Effective schools from a British perspective: research and practice', in Bliss, J. and Firestone, W. (eds) *Creating Effective Schools*. London: Prentice Hall.

Mortimore, P. (1992) 'Issues in school effectiveness', in Reynolds, D. and Cuttance, P. (eds) *School Effectiveness Research, Policy and Practice*. London: Cassell.

Mullin, S. P. and Summers, A. A. (1983) 'Is more better? The effectiveness of spending on compensatory education', *Phi Delta Kappan*, **64**, 339–47.

Nuttall, D. L., Goldstein, H., Prosser, R. and Rasbash, J. (1989) 'Differential school effectiveness', chapter 6 in *International Journal of Education Research*, special issue *Developments in School Effectiveness Research*, **13** (7), 769–76.

Nuttall, D. L. (1990) *Differences in Examination Performance*, RS 1277/90. London: Research and Statistics Branch, ILEA.

Nuttall, D. L., Sammons, P., Thomas, S. and Mortimore, P. (1992) *Differential School Effectiveness: Departmental Variations in GCSE Attainment*. ESRC award R000234130, Institute of Education, University of London.

Preece, P. (1988) 'Misleading ways of expressing the magnitude of school effects', *Research Papers in Education*, **3** (2), 97–8.

Raudenbush, S. W. (1989) 'The analysis of longitudinal, multilevel data', chapter 3 in *International Journal of Educational Research*, special issue *Developments in School Effectiveness Research*, **13** (7), 721–40.

Reynolds, D. (1976) 'The delinquent school', in Woods, P. (ed.) *The Process of Schooling*. London: Routledge & Kegan Paul.

Reynolds, D., Sullivan, M. and Murgatroyd, S. (1987) *The Comprehensive Experiment*. Lewes: Falmer Press.

Reynolds, D. and Cuttance, P. (eds) (1992) *School Effectiveness Research, Policy and Practice*. London: Cassell.

Reynolds, D. (1992) 'School effectiveness and school improvement: an updated review of the British literature', in Reynolds, D. and Cuttance, P. (eds) *School Effectiveness Research, Policy and Practice*. London: Cassell.

Roeleveld, J. and de Jong, U. (1989) 'Evaluating effectiveness of secondary schools in the Netherlands: models and stability', in Creemers, B. P. M. and Reynolds, D. (eds) *The Proceedings of the Second International Congress for School Effectiveness*. Rotterdam.

Rutter, M., Maughan, B., Mortimore, P., and Ouston, J. (1979) *Fifteen Thousand Hours*. London: Open Books.

Sammons, P., Nuttall, D. and Cuttance, P. (1993a) 'Differential school effectiveness: results from a reanalysis of the ILEA's Junior School Project data', *British Educational Research Journal*, **19** (4), 381–405.

Sammons, P., Nuttall, D., Cuttance, P. and Thomas, S. (1993b) *Continuity of*

School Effects: a longitudinal analysis of primary and secondary school effects on GCSE performance. Revised version of a paper presented to the annual meeting of the International Congress of School Effectiveness and Improvement, Norrköping, January 1993.

Sammons, P., Thomas, S. and Mortimore, P. (1995) *Differential School Effectiveness: Departmental Variations in GCSE Attainment*. ESRC End of Award Report, R000234130, Institute of Education, University of London.

Scheerens, J. (1992) *Effective Schooling: Research, Theory and Practice*. London: Cassell.

Sime, N. and Gray, J. (1991) *The Stability of School Effects Over Time*. Paper presented to the British Educational Research Annual Conference, Nottingham Polytechnic, August.

Smith, D. J. and Tomlinson, S. (1989) *The School Effect: A Study of Multi-Racial Comprehensives*. London: Policy Studies Institute.

Stringfield, S., Teddlie, C., Wimpleberg, R. K. and Kirby, P. (1992) 'A five-year follow-up of schools in the Louisiana school effectiveness study', in Baslin, J. and Sass, Z. (eds) *School Effectiveness and Improvement Proceedings of the Third International Congress for School Effectiveness*. Jerusalem: Magness.

Thomas, S., Nuttall, D. and Goldstein, H. (1992) 'The Guardian Survey (of A-level examination results) October 1992', *Guardian*, 20 October.

Thomas, S., Nuttall, D. and Goldstein, H. (1993) 'The Guardian Survey (of A-level examination results) November 1993', *Guardian*, 30 November.

Thomas, S. and Nuttall, D. (1993) *An Analysis of 1992 Key Stage 1 Results in Lancashire – Final Report: a multilevel analysis of total subject score, English score and mathematics score*. London: ISEIC, Institute of Education, University of London.

Thomas, S., Nuttall, D. and Goldstein, H. (1993) *Report on Analysis of 1992 Examination Results*. Association of Metropolitan Authorities.

Tizard, B., Blatchford, P., Burke, J., Farquhar, C. and Plewis, I. (1988) *Young Children at School in the Inner City*. Hove: Lawrence Erlbaum.

Willms, J. D. (1985) 'The balance thesis – contextual effects of ability on pupils' O-grade examination results', *Oxford Review of Education*, **11** (1), 33–41.

Willms, J. D. (1986) 'Social class segregation and its relationship to pupils' examination results in Scotland', *American Sociological Review*, **51**, 224–41.

Willms, J. D. (1987) 'Differences between Scottish education authorities in their examination attainment', *Oxford Review of Education*, **13** (2), 211–32.

Willms, J. D. and Raudenbush, S. W. (1989) 'A longitudinal hierarchial linear model for estimating school effects and their stability', *Journal of Educational Measurement*, **26** (3), 209–32.

Willms, J. D. (1992) *Monitoring School Performance: A Guide for Educators*. London: Falmer Press.

Yelton, B. T., Miller, S. K. and Ruscoe, G. C. (1994) *The Stability of School Effectiveness: Comparative Path Models*. Paper presented at the annual meeting of the American Educational Research Association, New Orleans, 4–8 April.

Chapter 2

Towards a Theory for School Improvement

David Hopkins

INTRODUCTION

One of the most encouraging recent developments in the area of school effectiveness and school improvement is the seriousness with which the confluence of these two streams of enquiry is being taken. The rather bland exhortations that each 'should learn from the other' now appear to be a thing of the past as practitioners and researchers are rethinking in a fundamental way the connections between theory and practice in effectiveness and improvement (Reynolds *et al.*, 1993). This radical reorientation of the field has not come a moment too soon. School effectiveness studies are in a period of stagnation and the ability of the research base to fundamentally effect practice has been seriously questioned. Although the interest in school improvement strategies has burgeoned of late, even the best of current practice has been likened to the work of surgeons some 200 years ago, when they attempted complex operations with rudimentary technique and little knowledge of physiology and anatomy!

The links between the two areas of enquiry, despite goodwill between the two communities, are not however to be forged easily. There are substantive differences between the two approaches that are difficult to reconcile. For example, as John Gray and his colleagues (1995) have pointed out, school effectiveness research is predicated on stable conceptions of schooling, whereas strategies for school improvement are based on assumptions that schools can change. This key difference has profound implications for policy, practice and research, most of which have yet to be articulated in any systematic and coherent way. One of the main problems, it seems to me, is a lack of commitment by researchers and practitioners in both areas of enquiry to the generation of theory or the development of models. Much conceptual work in both traditions remains to be done.

School effectiveness research, apart from a rather superficial dalliance by Rutter and his colleagues (1979), has studiously avoided using its increasingly refined technology to develop models of schooling. The so-called 'effectiveness correlates' however sophisticatedly defined are no substitute for models or theories of how schools function. Without this knowledge it is difficult to see how the field can progress. Indeed, Murphy (1992) one of the leading American effectiveness researchers has also commented on the cul-de-sac in which school effectiveness research currently finds itself. He has helpfully proposed that we look more at the 'legacy' of school effectiveness studies as a means of informing policy and the practical work of school improvement.

Those working within the school improvement tradition find themselves in a similar impasse. Despite the increase of practical work in this area, the level of discourse about how school improvement 'works' remains disturbingly low. The analogy of the 18th-century surgeons is unerringly and frighteningly apt. Even the best of school improvement work has failed to elaborate *theories of school development* or begun in any sustained way to develop and evaluate a range of *models of school improvement intervention*. Without serious reflection on these two key elements it is unlikely that strategies for school improvement will contribute to the enhancement of student achievement that its rhetoric heralds.

The initial thesis of this chapter is that if the current efforts to integrate work in the areas of school effectiveness and school improvement are to result in the 'paradigm shift' the field requires, then more attention needs to be given to establishing theories and models of schools, how they change and develop, and what interventions assist the improvement process. Without such conceptual development, the field, despite recent advances, will remain moribund. Paradoxically, irrespective of the commitment to the transformation and unification of the two areas, this stage of theorizing needs initially to be accomplished for each individually, as a precursor to the radical reshaping of the field that we all aspire to.

This chapter is an attempt to address this agenda, by initiating a debate on the theories of school development and models of intervention that underlie the work of school improvement practitioners, policy-makers and researchers. In doing so I draw heavily on our own recent attempts to practise, research and theorize about school improvement, rather than attempt a more comprehensive review, a task which would unnecessarily duplicate other recent work (Hopkins *et al.*, 1994). What follows is therefore a highly personal, and at times idiosyncratic, view of how work in the area of school improvement could develop. In the chapter:

- First, I set the scene by briefly defining school improvement.
- Second, I outline the elements of an emerging theory of how schools develop in times of change.
- Third, I review the main strategies for school improvement at the policy level, describe a generic school improvement strategy, and suggest a framework for assessing the impact of school improvement on school effectiveness.
- Finally, I conclude by raising a series of questions about the main issues emerging from this discussion and the implications for research, policy and practice.

DEFINING SCHOOL IMPROVEMENT

There are two senses in which the phrase *school improvement* is generally used. The first is the common-sense meaning which relates to general efforts to make schools better places for pupils and students to learn. This is a sensible interpretation of the phrase and its most common usage. In this chapter however, I am principally concerned with a second more technical or specific definition. I regard *school improvement as a strategy for educational change that enhances student outcomes as well as strengthening the school's capacity for managing change.* In this sense school improvement is about raising student achievement through focusing on the teaching–learning process and the conditions which support it. It is about strategies for improving the school's capacity for providing quality education in times of change (Hopkins, 1987).

This approach leads to some liberating ways of thinking about change. Schools, and those who live out their daily lives within them, are no longer the victims of change, but can take more control of the process. By using the opportunity of external change as a stimulus, they can subject the specificities of change to their own professional scrutiny and judgement. They do this by finding ways of enhancing student outcomes through specific changes in teaching approaches and the curriculum, and through strengthening the school's organizational ability to support the work of teachers.

In summary, this approach to school improvement regards it as:

- a vehicle for planned educational change; but it is also accepted that educational change is necessary for school improvement;
- particularly appropriate during times of centralized initiatives and innovation overload when there are competing reforms to implement;
- usually involving some form of external support;
- having a dual emphasis on strategies for strengthening the school's capacity for managing change; whilst
- raising student achievement (broadly defined); through
- specifically focusing on the teaching–learning process.

Our recent analysis of the school improvement literature (Hopkins *et al.*, 1994, chapter 5), suggests that few commentators have fully explored the potential of this approach as an alternative means of educational change. Most have been content to use the term as a collective noun under which to group a variety of strategies for innovation and change that pay scant attention to the organizational context in which they intervene, or to how they do intervene. In particular they fail to address the two key questions which need answering if we are to obtain any operational or conceptual purchase on the terms: How do schools develop? What are the key elements of a school improvement initiative? It is these two issues that provide the substance of the rest of the chapter.

TOWARDS A THEORY OF SCHOOL DEVELOPMENT

I suppose one should begin by saying what one means by 'school development'. My starting point is a simple one. It is this – schools that are developing are those that are able to 'survive with integrity' in times of change. Development and change are inextricably linked – 'successful' schools use the opportunity of change for developmental purpose. In other words, schools that are developing continue to keep abreast with innovation within the context of a pervasive political reform agenda, whilst remaining true to the educational futures they desire for their students. This implies that the school has a capacity to innovate and change as well as having some clarity over the educational values that inform its work. This is a basic definition of a developing school. It is however a dynamic concept because schools in our 'post-modern' age are always in a state of change. It is dynamic in another sense because the definition allows for schools who are aspiring to 'survive with integrity' in changing times as well as those that are. School development then is the process through which schools adapt external changes to internal purpose. When successful, this leads to enhanced outcomes for teachers and students, and ultimately affects the culture of the school, as well as its internal organizational structures.

As our work on school development at Cambridge continues, we are finding some common patterns to the way in which this process unfolds. The experience of the 'Improving the Quality of Education for All' project (IQEA) is particularly pertinent (Hopkins, 1994c). Although the following account of the developmental process (adapted from Hopkins *et al.*, 1994, chapter 14) is empirically grounded, it is presented here as a secular parable that has heuristic power, and from which a series of more formal questions pertaining to the developmental process can be deduced.

Most schools as the recent HMI document *Improving Schools* (OFSTED, 1994) attests, are now familiar with the school development planning process that encourages them to express their developmental aspirations in the form of *priorities*. The school's development plan consists of a series of priorities which ideally are supported by action plans. These are the working documents for teachers. In them the priority is subdivided into *targets* and *tasks*, responsibilities are allocated, a time frame established, and evaluation or progress checks are identified. This approach to development planning generally follows the advice given by the DES-sponsored *Planning for School Development* project (Hargreaves *et al.*, 1989; Hargreaves and Hopkins, 1991).

This approach to planning places great importance on implementation where priorities are formulated within a coherent *strategy*. A strategy typically involves teachers in some form of collaborative classroom-based action. The exact nature of the strategy, or combination of strategies, is peculiar to each school. Strategies need to take account of the priorities that have been agreed, existing conditions and the resources that are available. So for example, the *priority* in one of our secondary schools was developing 'resource-based learning', one of the strategies they used to implement this priority was classroom observation amongst the members of the working group.

Many schools are now used to establishing working groups for developmental tasks. But it is as they move into action that problems tend to arise. Beginning to work on something new, to change, inevitably creates some difficulties, both for individuals and the institution. Teachers are faced with acquiring new teaching skills or mastering new curriculum material; the school is often faced with new ways of working that are incompatible with existing organizational structures. So with the example of resource-based learning, teachers had to work out what it meant to them, to their teaching styles, and the curriculum content. They then had to adapt their classroom practice to match this understanding. The school, for its part, had to provide time on the timetable for classroom observation, and to give increased responsibility to relatively junior members of staff.

Such changes are inevitably disruptive. This phase of 'internal turbulence', however, is as predictable as it is uncomfortable (Huberman, 1992). Many research studies have found that without a period of destabilization successful, long-lasting change is unlikely to occur (Huberman and Miles, 1984). This is the 'implementation dip' to which Fullan (1991) so graphically refers to; but it is important to note that the phenomena exists at the institutional as well as the individual level. It is at this point that most change fails to progress beyond early implementation. In these cases, when the change hits the 'wall' of individual learning or institutional resistance, internal turbulence begins to occur and developmental work begins to stall. The working group usually continues to meet for a while, but it generally backs off from focusing on classroom practice and requesting organizational modifications, and eventually progress slows. Fortunately in our change-rich environment, another priority is soon found for them or another group to focus on! The change circles back on itself and nothing much is achieved – so we start something new. This is the cycle of educational failure, the predictable pathology of educational change, so well documented by Robert Slavin (1989).

Many of the schools that we have been working with have survived this period of destabilization by either consciously or intuitively adapting or accommodating the *internal conditions* in the school to meet the demands of the agreed on change or priority. In order to overcome the 'wall', we encourage schools to diagnose their internal conditions in relation to their chosen change *before they begin developmental work* (see Anscow et al., 1994, chapter 9). They can then begin to build these modifications to the school's internal conditions into the strategies they are going to adopt. So in the running example, time was found for the classroom observation, staff training days were devoted to discussing the definitions that various curriculum groups had of resource-based learning and the wall was successfully breached.

When this happens, we begin to see changes occurring to the *culture* of the school. In the example, as a result of the staff training day and the classroom observation, teachers began to talk more about teaching, collaborative work outside the particular project became more commonplace, and management structures were adapted to support this and future changes. When taken together, these changes in attitudes and structure created a more supportive environment within the school for managing change. The school's 'change capacity' was increased and the groundwork was laid for future change efforts. Instead of rebounding against the wall, a virtuous cycle of change began to be established. Schools who have been through similar 'change cycles' either experience less internal turbulence, or are able to tolerate greater levels of turbulence, because they have progressively enhanced their capacity to change as a result of this developmental process.

One can summarize this process using the following notation: P stands for the priority the school sets itself, S the chosen strategy, the wavy line the period of destabilization, Co the school's internal conditions that are modified in order to ameliorate the destabilization, and Cu the resulting change in culture.

P>	*S>*	*{}*	*Co>*	*Cu*
Priority	*Strategy*	*Turbulence*	*Conditions*	*Culture*

Real life of course is not as simple or as linear as this formula suggests, but this way of describing the process of development resonates with the experience of many of those that we talk to and work with. The process of cultural change is also not a 'one off' as implied by the notation, but evolves and unfolds over time. Often many sequences have to be gone through before a radically different culture emerges in a school.

Many of the heads and school leaders we have interviewed, adopt, albeit intuitively, such an approach to the management of change. They seem to agree with Schein (1985, chapter 2) when he wrote, 'that the only thing of real importance that leaders do is to create and manage culture'. They realize that the impact of successful change needs to be on the culture of the school, for it is culture that sustains change and consequently enhances the achievement of students. Many of them appear to focus on culture first. It is almost as if they begin by asking 'What cultural changes are required?' and then, 'What priorities, strategies and changes in conditions can bring this about?' The link between setting priorities and the culture of the school is therefore of some importance. Sequencing priorities over time can help the successive shaping of school culture. In recognition of this many school leaders 'start small and think big' in their planning for development. They also sequence priorities in such a way that they build on initial good practice and then on subsequent success. As they lay the basis for each other, successive priorities assume a character of increasing depth and sophistication. These heads manipulate priorities, strategies and conditions in order to affect culture, in the pursuit of enhancing the quality of educational outcomes and experience for all pupils. The process often unfolds as seen in the sequence below.

P1>	*S1>*	*{}*	*C1>*	*Cu1*
Priority	*Strategy*	*Turbulence*	*Conditions*	*Culture*
P2>	*S2>*	*{}*	*C2>*	*Cu2*
Priority	*Strategy*	*Turbulence*	*Conditions*	*Culture*
P3>	*S3>*	*{}*	*C3>*	*Cu3*
Priority	*Strategy*	*Turbulence*	*Conditions*	*Culture*

When the process of cultural change is embarked on, it may be that *Culture 3* is the ultimate goal. To move there too quickly is impossible, so the various intermediate stages have to be traversed first. There are a number of interesting paradoxes here. Although real life is not as rational as this, we often need to have strategic maps in our minds as we begin and sustain the journey of improvement (Fullan and Miles, 1992). Also there is rarely any clarity about the nature of subsequent priorities or the cultural change they affect at the start of the journey. Priorities unfold almost organically as progress is made. This is not to say that everything is *ad hoc*. There is often a concomitant clarification of values within the school as the process unfolds that provides a framework for, and maintains the integrity and consistency of, the development work. In this sense the notion of 'vision' which is so popular nowadays, is more about the clarification and articulation of a set of values that occurs throughout the development work, than a concrete image given by the head at the outset. It also appears in our experience that the process unfolds unevenly. There are *always* highs and lows, peaks and troughs. Even in the most successful schools development accelerates then levels off. When a new priority is set, energy flows once again. Sustaining momentum over time and appreciating the inevitability of such plateaux, is consequently very important. This is especially the case as the process often takes two years to work through, and consequently does not conform to neat planning cycles.

We have also found that something similar operates at the level of the teacher and the student. For the *teacher*, although the conditions may be eased and the internal turbulence reduced at the school level, the pressure of *individual learning* on their part often remains the same. The conditions in, and the culture of, the school are however increasingly supportive of their developmental efforts. As teachers experience a more supportive environment within the school, so they are more able to endure the threat of new learning. As they adapt the teaching and learning practices in their classrooms, they begin to see that the learning of their pupils is enhanced and this evidence gives them confidence in the change and increases their commitment to the new approach.

Similarly *students* will experience dissonance as a teacher provides new and sometimes strikingly different classroom experiences. As a result students too will have to make an adjustment to their conditions of learning before there is a pay-off in 'outcomes'. This emphasizes the point that in order to reduce the internal turbulence for pupils they should become equal partners in development activities.

It is possible, at least theoretically, to see this process operating at the three levels of school, teacher and student, with each complementing and supporting the other. In the following diagram the priorities are consistent, although the strategies may well vary across the three levels. If the destabilization is to be coped with, then alterations to the conditions have to occur at the organizational, teaching and learning levels. Ideally, this will result in modifications to the culture of the school, the quality of the teaching process on the part of teachers, and to the learning outcomes of students. It is in this way that the process of cultural change supports the learning of students.

School	P> Priority	S> Strategy	{} Turbulence	O Co> Organizational conditions	Cu Culture of the school
Teacher	P> Priority	S> Strategy	{} Dissonance	T Co> Teaching conditions	T & L Teaching and learning
Student	P> Priority	S> Strategy	{} Dissonance	L Co> Learning conditions	S O Student outomes

If this account has any validity it would appear that the process of development in schools is contingent on a dialectic between what on the one hand is called here 'conditions', and 'culture' on the other. The notion of conditions is akin to what sociologists term structures. So to put it more formally, the proposition contained in this account is that *schools continue to develop by adapting external change to internal purpose through a process of structural and cultural accommodation*. Innovations by themselves are insufficient; attention also needs to be given to the organizational conditions or school work cultures within schools that allow them to manage and sustain change over time. In his presentation to the seminar series, David Hargreaves (1995) elaborated on the theme of school culture and its relationship to school change, effectiveness and improvement. It was this conceptualization that laid the basis for some of the methodological techniques for *Mapping Change in Schools* that we subsequently developed (Cambridge University, 1994).

Unfortunately, as we note in the introduction to *Development Planning for School Improvement* (Hargreaves and Hopkins, 1994), there is still substantial ignorance about how structures generate or influence cultures and cultures generate or influence structures. We doubt whether a school culture is readily changed by teachers talking about it or as a result of exhortations by the school leader. But significant structural changes, especially ones that bring teachers into working more closely together, will affect how teachers talk to one another and define their professional relationships. It is through the new relationships and the content and style of talk arising from structural changes that the culture begins to shift; in turn, the emerging culture then stabilizes, legitimizes and even routinizes the structural conditions which form the essential foundations for the new culture.

In much of our recent research we have been preoccupied with the internal conditions of schools that support development. Much of this has focused on the *structural* aspects of schools. In the work on development planning for example, the term *management arrangements* was used to emphasize that the content of management is a set of arrangements which are *chosen* by the school to help it conduct its affairs and realize its aims (Hargreaves and Hopkins, 1991, chapter 3). There are a wide variety of possible arrangements, they can be changed or adapted according to circumstances and preferences. There is an endless possible variety of management arrangements and we doubt whether there is an ideal set of arrangements, a recipe which all schools should follow. There are however some *dimensions* shared by all management arrangements, whatever the particular set that is chosen by any individual school.

There appear to be three main dimensions common to all sets of management arrangements: *frameworks, roles and responsibilities* and *ways of working*. Of these, frameworks which guide the actions of all who are involved in the school – policies, systems and strategies – provide the structures within which action for change takes place. They are the guides to action, the scaffolding that supports the educational work of the school. Clear frameworks give direction and purpose to development planning and support its management. Examples of frameworks are the school's aims and policies, and the systems for decision-making and consultation. Without clear frameworks, the school would soon lapse into confusion and conflict. Secondly, the management arrangements clarify roles and responsibilities. All who are involved in the school need to have a shared understanding of their respective roles and of *whom* is taking responsibility for what. Well-designed frameworks are useless without clear roles and responsibilities. To build the confidence and security of those involved with development planning, roles and responsibilities need to be clarified. These too are largely structural. Ways of working however are mainly cultural.

The division of the management arrangements into three analytically distinct dimensions was a limited first attempt at simplifying the structure-and-culture complex that underpins school organization and so also development and improvement. Subsequent experience enabled us to understand more fully another dimension introduced in *The Empowered School* – the distinction between a school's development and maintenance activities (Hargreaves and Hopkins, 1991, chapter 3). It was suggested in *The Empowered School* that it was the school's management arrangements that were crucial in achieving the correct balance between these two fundamental activities. Although this is still sound advice, it is becoming increasingly apparent from current work that the most successful schools are deliberately creating contrasting but mutually supportive structural arrangements to cope with the twin pressures of development and maintenance.

As is also argued in the introduction to *Development Planning for School Improvement* (Hargreaves and Hopkins, 1994), maintenance structures established to organize teaching, learning and assessment cannot also cope with developmental activities which inevitably cut across established hierarchies, curriculum areas, meeting patterns and timetables. The innovative responses required for sustained development, e.g. delegation, task groups, high levels of specific staff development, quality time for planning, collaborative classroom activity are inimical to successful maintenance. Maintenance structures, however well developed, often do not cope well with development. In our experience, structures that attempt to do both, usually do neither satisfactorily. What is required are complementary structures each with their own purpose, budget and ways of working. Obviously the majority of a school's time and resources will go on maintenance; but unless there is also an element dedicated to development then the school is unlikely to progress in times of change.

The distinction between development and maintenance also helps to clarify the process of prioritization in development planning. Often the stricture that a school should only select a very small number of priorities for development at any one time is met with derision by teachers and school leaders. What they do not recognize is that an external change does not inevitably have to become a development priority. There are at least three general ways in which an external change can be dealt with. In the first instance, a school will embrace some changes immediately and place them directly into the maintenance structure. This will be because the school either has no other legal option, or because it has a particular expertise or penchant for that change. Secondly, other changes, initially having been put into maintenance, are subsequently selected as development priorities and sequenced over time. Thirdly, some centralized initiatives, however, are resisted, because they are incompatible with the school's central purpose.

In addition, the development and maintenance distinction should allow the school to make more coherent decisions about what it is to devote its developmental energy to, irrespective to some extent of the external reform agenda. By placing all, even desirable, changes into maintenance first, allows for a more considered decision to be made about what constitutes development. It is becoming apparent from recent interviews with teachers and students in schools that we are working with, that the more 'generic' yet focused a priority for development is, the more impact it will have on the maintenance system. Paradoxically, and excitingly, it appears that the more focused the priority the more diffuse yet powerful is its impact on the teaching–learning process in general.

We therefore feel that one of the criteria for a developmental priority should be its ability to affect a range of maintenance activities. Although some external changes need to become developmental priorities in their own right, more often it is better to select priorities that cut across a range of external or curriculum changes. A priority on teaching and learning, for example, will inevitably spread across a school's curriculum activities to the darkest realms of its maintenance activities when teachers realize that this approach 'works' and can be used in another unit of study or scheme of work. Similarly if a particular way of working for example, collaborative teaching is found to be effective in development work, it will not be long before teachers begin using that approach in other areas of their teaching.

It is in this way that the development structure acts as a support system for the maintenance activities. What is vitally important however is that after the allocated period of development the priority is returned to maintenance. And that any competing practices within the maintenance structure are removed. Experience suggests that schools have some difficulty in 'letting go' of development priorities and find it even more difficult to erase practices that in many ways contradict new developments. Many schools for example still retain summative assessment schemes long after more formative modes of student evaluation become part of accepted practice in the school. Obviously the cycle should also continue; after any particular development phase another aspect of maintenance is selected and so on. Over time therefore most aspects of the school are subject to some form of development activity.

We have also been exploring the structure/culture dimension within the IQEA project, where we have been able to elaborate a series of conditions that underpin the work of successful schools (Ainscow and Hopkins, 1992; Hopkins and West, 1994). Although the following list represents our best estimate, rather than a definitive statement, of what the important conditions are at present, we believe that there is both research-based and practical evidence to support them. Broadly stated the conditions are:

- attention to the potential benefits of *enquiry and reflection*;
- a commitment to *collaborative planning*;
- a commitment to *staff development*;
- the *involvement* of staff, students and the community in school policies and decisions;
- effective *coordination* strategies;
- effective *leadership*, but not just of the head; the leadership function is spread throughout the school.

Two points of clarification need to be entered about this list. The first is that the list is not definitive. It is more than likely that over the next year we will expand and embellish our view of the 'conditions' as we explore more systematically the conditions necessary for classroom as well as school improvement. The second caveat is more germane to this argument. It is that the conditions as formulated within the IQEA project form a specific set of management arrangements that relate more explicitly to the school's *development* rather than the school's *maintenance* structure. In bolder moments I have tentatively suggested that the conditions are a form of development structure within the school.

In this section of the chapter I have attempted to outline in the form of a 'parable' a description of how schools develop in times of change. The key dynamic necessary for effective and sustained development is the interrelationship between structure and culture. Based on our research and development work over the past five years two interpretations of 'structure' have been described, one relating to the way in which schools balance their maintenance and development activities, i.e. the school's management arrangements; the other, the 'conditions supporting school improvement' being a more specific description of a school's development structure. This account of, and reflection, on the process of development in schools can be regarded as an extended hypothesis about how schools develop in times of change. The next step is to translate this account into a series of more precise questions or propositions amenable to testing. Before doing this however, we need to look more closely at the ways in which school improvement initiatives can support this process.

THE EFFECTIVENESS OF SCHOOL IMPROVEMENT INITIATIVES

The previous discussion leads inevitably to the question, can centralized policy change by itself result in school development? I would suggest not. A fundamental problem of centralized change initiatives as a strategy for school improvement is that it is almost always the case that there is an implicit assumption that implementation is an event rather than a process: that change proceeds on 'auto pilot' once the policy has been enunciated or passed. This perspective ignores the critical distinction between the *object of change*, for example, the contents of the Education Reform Acts, and the *process of changing*, i.e. how schools and local agencies put the reforms into practice.

The pathology of policy implementation, has recently been described by Milbrey McLaughlin (1990) in her reanalysis of the large-scale Rand Change Agent study undertaken in the USA in the mid late-seventies. She found that many of the conclusions from the study still hold true today, and commented that (McLaughlin, 1990, p. 12):

> A general finding of the Change Agent study that has become almost
> a truism is that it is exceedingly difficult for policy to change
> practice, especially across levels of government. Contrary to the one-
> to-one relationship assumed to exist between policy and practice, the
> Change Agent study demonstrated that the nature, amount and pace
> of change at the local level was a product of local factors that were
> largely beyond the control of higher-level policy makers.

According to McLaughlin (1990) this general observation has three specific implications:

- policy cannot mandate what matters;
- implementation dominates outcomes;
- local variability is the rule; uniformity is the exception.

Although polices set directions and provide a framework, they do not and cannot determine student outcomes. It is implementation, rather than the decision to adopt a new policy, that determines student achievement. It is also the case that the most effective school improvement strategies seem to be internal rather than external to the school and relate to the types of organizational conditions described in the previous section. What is needed is 'implementation-friendly' policy, that is concerned with the process as well as the substance of change at the teacher and school level.

In many countries, schools are now faced with a number of innovations – self-evaluation, development planning, changes in staff development policy and practice and teacher appraisal – that are 'content free'. Although they all have a carefully specified process or structure, the *substance* of each is for the teacher and school to decide. In combination, these strategies can form an 'infrastructure' at the school level that facilitate the implementation of specific curriculum changes or teaching methods that can have a direct impact on student achievement.

Centralized policies can and do *create the conditions* for student achievement, but by themselves they have *little direct* impact on the progress of pupils (Hopkins, 1994a). They are a necessary, but not sufficient condition for enhancing student achievement. As is seen in the following section they have to be integrated with, or lead to, specific modifications in curriculum or teaching if the result is to be enhanced student outcomes.

A GENERIC FRAMEWORK FOR SCHOOL IMPROVEMENT

Elsewhere we have outlined a theoretical model, 'A framework for school improvement' that informs our work with schools (Hopkins *et al.*, 1994). In these terms, school improvement is the process through which schools adapt external changes to internal purpose (Hopkins, 1994b). When successful, this leads to enhanced outcomes for teachers and students, and ultimately affects the culture of the school, as well as its internal organizational structures. The framework (see Figure 2.1) provides the setting for a series of assumptions upon which this generic approach to school improvement is based. There are essentially three major components to the framework – the 'givens', the 'strategic dimension' and the 'capacity-building dimension'.

The 'givens' are those aspects of the educational change process that are not amenable to alteration within the short term. First there is the *external impetus for change* which can be of three types – the national reform agenda, recommendations emanating from reviews and inspections of the school, and local needs or demands. Although they will change over time, at any one point in time these forces provide a set of parameters within which the school has to work. The other 'given' is the school's *background, organization and values*. Unfortunately most school improvement efforts address background and organizational factors, which are often the main inhibitors of change, as only explanatory factors. It is also interesting to note that a school's organizational structure is inevitably a reflection of its values, which may be at the same time a force for, a barrier against, and the object of, change.

The 'strategic dimension' reflects the vertical links in the diagram between priorities, strategy and outcomes. Most schools are becoming more competent at establishing a clear and practical focus for the development effort. The school's 'priorities' are normally some aspect of curriculum, assessment or classroom process which the school has identified from the many changes that confront it. In this sense, the choice represents the school's interpretation of the current reform agenda. Although the balance of activities varies from school to school, we find that more successful schools set priorities for development that:

- are few in number – trying to do too much is counterproductive;
- are central to the mission of the school;
- relate to the current reform agenda;
- link to teaching and learning;
- lead to specific outcomes for students and staff.

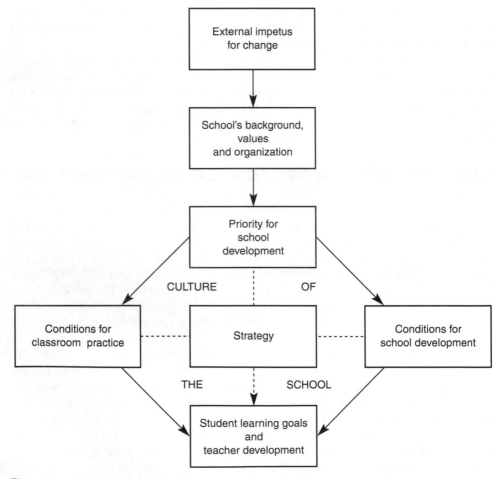

Figure 2.1 *A framework for school improvement*

The school improvement *strategy* is the deliberate actions or sequence of actions taken by a school staff in order to implement identified curriculum or organizational priorities. The strategy will need to be more or less powerful depending on the relative strength of the other factors. As was argued earlier, in some cases the school's organizational structures will have to be modified as part of the development process.

There is usually an assumption that such school improvement efforts will result in enhanced *outcomes* for students and staff. Outcomes are defined broadly, and will obviously vary according to the focus of the improvement effort. For students, outcomes could be critical thinking, learning capacity, self-esteem and so on, as well as improved examination and test results. For staff they could be increased collegiality, opportunities for professional learning and increased responsibility.

Most schools quite logically regard the sequence that I have just described as the appropriate way to plan their school improvement activities, and in many ways it is. Some schools however, and those that appear to be more successful than most at managing school improvement, begin at the other end of the sequence – with student-learning goals. It is as if they say what changes in student performance do we wish to see this year? Having decided that, they then devise a strategy for so doing and establish a priority which they can then link to some external change, preferably one that has resources attached to it! It is in this way I believe that the most successful schools pursue their improvement efforts.

The third dimension is *capacity building*. The key finding from the first phase of the IQEA school improvement work was 'that school improvement works best when a clear and practical focus for development is linked to simultaneous work on the internal conditions within the school' (Ainscow and Hopkins, 1992, p. 79). Without an equal focus on conditions, even priorities that meet the above criteria can quickly become marginalized. We have also found that when circumstances exist that are less supportive of change, it is necessary to concentrate much more in the initial stages on creating the internal conditions within the school which facilitate development. Work on the priorities is limited until the conditions are in place; and as I noted earlier there are conditions that relate both to classroom practice and school improvement.

The final element in the framework is *school culture*. A key assumption is that school improvement strategies can lead to cultural change in schools through modifications to their internal conditions. It is the cultural change that supports the teaching–learning process which leads to enhanced outcomes for students. The types of school cultures most supportive of school improvement efforts appear to be those that are collaborative, have high expectations for both students and staff, exhibit a consensus on values (or an ability to deal effectively with differences), support an orderly and secure environment, and encourage teachers to assume a variety of leadership roles.

This framework for school improvement is highly consistent with Joyce's analysis of the characteristics of effective large-scale school improvement initiatives (Joyce *et al.*, 1993, p. 72):

- All have focused on specific student-learning goals. None has had only general goals of the 'to make exam results go up' variety.

- All have employed strategies tailored to their goals and backed by rationales grounded in theory or research or a combination of these.

- All have measured learning outcomes on a formative and summative basis, collecting information about student gains on a regular basis and not leaving evaluation to a yearly examination.

- All have employed substantial amounts of staff development in recognition that the initiative involved teacher and student learning.

In the quest for student achievement, centralized policy changes are by themselves insufficient. To impact directly on student achievement more specific and focused interventions of the type described here are required. Experience, as well as the available research, suggests that more systematic approaches to teaching provide the link to enhanced student performance. Changes in teaching behaviour cannot however be acquired or sustained without, in some cases dramatic and in every case some, modification to the culture of the school. There is potential in this approach to school improvement to create the conditions within which specific changes to student learning can take root and flourish. Enhanced student achievement is therefore the result of a constellation of factors interacting in subtle but self-conscious and meaningful ways that create school cultures in which both teachers and students learn and grow.

TOWARDS A MORE COMPREHENSIVE FRAMEWORK FOR CONSIDERING SCHOOL IMPROVEMENT STRATEGIES

This description of a generic school improvement strategy is fine as far as it goes, but important questions still remain. The strategy has still for example to be tested empirically. It is also far from certain whether this approach requires external support or whether schools can 'go it alone'. Similarly we know little about how different school improvement strategies affect different schools. On reflecting on these questions I have found it helpful to organize my thoughts by using a framework provided by the research on school effects. A typical representation of the results from the research on school effects is given in Figure 2.2.

The diagonal (regression) line represents the level of achievement one would expect from a student based on their prior attainment on entry to a school, having controlled for background variables. Data sets from LEA and school district studies where such individual student scores are available suggest that on average most schools cluster around the line, as in B on the diagram (see for example Teddlie and Stringfield, 1993; Rosenholtz, 1989). These data sets also tend to contain a few schools, such as those at A, which consistently 'add value' to their students in comparison with what one would expect from measures of these students' prior attainment. Unfortunately these data sets often also contain schools, such as those at C, that consistently reduce the levels of student achievement one would expect. All this is well established in the school effects literature. What is of central importance for those interested in school development and improvement is how do schools at C assume the characteristics of those schools at A and so produce higher levels of achievement for their students?

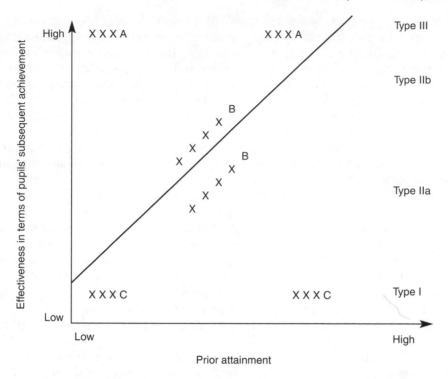

Figure 2.2 *A framework for considering school improvement strategies*

The research base on the effects of school improvement strategies is unfortu-nately very weak. It is sensible to assume however that the same strategy will not move a school directly from C to A. I would suggest that a strategy for moving a school from position C to position B would be qualitatively different from a strategy that would move a school from position B to position A. I would further suggest that a strategy that helps to keep a school at A is different again. For the purposes of this chapter I have called these strategies Type I, Type II and Type III.

Type I strategies are those that assist failing schools become moderately effective. They need to involve a high level of external support. Failing schools cannot improve themselves. These strategies have to involve a clear and direct focus on a limited number of basic curriculum and organizational issues in order to build the confidence and competence to continue (Hopkins, 1994b). Two examples of this directive, externally initiated approach to school improvement would be the IBIS scheme developed by David Hargreaves and his colleagues in the then ILEA (Hargreaves, 1990), or the Schenley High School experiment in school improvement in Pittsburgh (Wallace *et al.*, 1990).

Type II strategies are those that assist moderately effective schools become effective. In line with the argument of this chapter these schools need to refine their developmental priorities to focus on specific teaching and learning issues and to build the capacity within the school to support this work. I suggest that the approach to school improvement described earlier in this section of the chapter would in general be appropriate here. These strategies usually involve a certain level of external support, but it is theoretically possible for schools in this category to 'improve' by themselves. It may therefore be more helpful to differentiate between *Type IIa* and *Type IIb* strategies. Type IIa strategies are characterized by a strategic focus on innovations in teaching and learning that are informed and supported by external knowledge and support. Examples of such school improvement strategies would be Slavin's *Success for All* project (Slavin *et al.*, 1992; 1994), Joyce's *Models of Teaching* approach (Joyce *et al.*, 1992; 1993). Type IIb strategies rely less on external support and tend to be more school initiated. Strategic school improvement programmes such as the Cambridge-based Improving the Quality of Education for All (IQEA) project referred to earlier (Hopkins, 1994c; Hopkins *et al.*, 1994), and the 'improvement through planning' approach recently described by OFSTED (1994), are pertinent examples.

Type III strategies are those that assist effective schools remain so. In these instances external support although often welcomed is not necessary as the school searches out and creates its own support networks. Exposure to new ideas and practices, collaboration through consortia or 'pairing'-type arrangements seem to be common in these situations. Examples of these types of school improvement strategies would be those described recently by Kate Myers and Louise Stoll (1993) and school improvement projects such as the League of Professional Schools (Glickman, 1990) or the Coalition of Essential Schools (Sizer, 1992).

As work in this area progresses it will hopefully be possible to describe more specifically these types of school improvement interventions and strategies. Even at present it is feasible to classify types on criteria such as: range and number of priorities addressed; focus, i.e. curriculum, instruction, school organization; research knowledge/school-generated knowledge; external directives/internal purpose; level of capacity building, and so on. Such a classification would allow us to move a step closer to a full conceptualization of school improvement by linking 'type' of strategy to various stages of school development. It is this iterative approach to theory building through linking conceptual development to action research, in its true Lewinian sense, that holds as I note in the final section of the chapter, the most promise for future work in this area.

A THEORY FOR SCHOOL IMPROVEMENT?

Although it is inappropriate to draw conclusions from an exploratory chapter such as this, the discussion does raise a series of questions that need to be debated, and suggests a broad agenda for research, policy and practice in the area of school improvement.

The account of the *process of development in schools* gives rise to a series of questions which with further refinement may be amenable to empirical testing and so contribute to the generation of a theory of school development (some of these questions are further elaborated in the introduction to Hargreaves and Hopkins (1994)):

> How plausible is this extended hypothesis about how schools develop in times of change?
>
> What is the impact (intended or unintended) of the selection and

sequencing of a particular set of priorities and chosen strategies on the deeper level of school structures and culture?

Can measurable links be made between the impact of development work on a priority and changes in (i) student outcomes, and (ii) school culture?

How far does the chosen strategy for development work itself effect the dialectical relationship between changing structures and cultures?

How are those forms of social organization that generate and sustain certain values and belief systems (from structure to culture) and vice versa (from culture into structure) created?

Do successful leaders begin by asking what cultural changes will generate the new structures that are needed to make the school more effective or do they ask what structural changes will stimulate new cultures? If they do both, under what circumstances and in relation to what issues do they adopt the one tactic rather than the other?

The discussion on the *effectiveness of school improvement initiatives* was informed by a series of questions about how the process of school development is best facilitated. Is the presence of a centralized reform agenda in most Western countries a sufficient strategy for school improvement? Is school development a naturally occurring phenomenon? Or does it require some form of external support? If it does are different support strategies required for different schools at different stages of development? What is the relative effectiveness of centralized implementation strategies? These are the sorts of questions that come to mind when thinking about school improvement strategies. They give rise to others:

Is the analysis of school improvement polices and strategies (the response to my first two rhetorical questions) sensible, does it resonate with the experiences of others?

Is the description of a framework for school improvement as generic as is implied?

Is it true that schools at different stages of development require different school improvement strategies?

Does the 'effectiveness framework' provide the basis of a helpful typology for considering various school improvement initiatives? How can it be tested empirically? How would one form hypotheses based on it?

What existing school improvement strategies fit into the typology? Does the typology suggest that we need to create new, or modify existing, school improvement strategies?

There are also more general issues to be considered related to research, policy and practice, which in concluding I would briefly like to raise.

As regards research I would make one general exhortation and two suggestions. The exhortation is that in the area of school improvement we have for too long been content with anecdotal evidence and perceptual data collected unsystematically. If we are to be true to our rhetoric we must ask serious questions about theory and strategy, and be prepared to test them empirically. As to the suggestions, the first is to echo David Hargreaves' (1994) call in his DEMOS pamphlet for the need to develop experimental (or in the argot quasi-experimental) designs for educational research in this case, amongst other things, the effectiveness of school improvement interventions. In particular to track the relationship between 'independent' or process variables, and 'dependent' or outcome variables in the school improvement (Hopkins, 1995). The second suggestion is to develop methodologies for exploring the process of change in schools. At present the range of research methods open to those who take school improvement seriously are very limited and much more work needs to be done. Mel Ainscow, David Hargreaves and myself have recently made a small contribution to this endeavour by developing six innovative techniques for 'mapping the process of change in schools' (Ainscow *et al.*, 1995; Cambridge University, 1994).

I have two suggestions as regards to policy. Neither is original but both are profound. The first is to incorporate within policy some of the insights developed from the work on school change, effectiveness, and improvement which regard change as more of a 'process than an event'. Although this sounds trite, if our politicians had taken this suggestion seriously in 1988 then our 'era' of reform would perhaps by now be producing unequivocally positive results. The second suggestion is to recentre the discussion of innovation and reform on student outcomes. Unless we do this then the whole debate on educational change, school improvement and social equity will remain ideological, semantic and vacuous. Recent methods for evaluating school effectiveness and pupil progress using authentic assessment (see, for example, the work of Peter Hill and his colleagues at the University of Melbourne, e.g. Rowe *et al.*, 1993), and meta-analysis techniques which allow us some operational purchase on the 'effect size' of various strategies for improvement (for a discussion of how this applies to teaching models see Joyce *et al.*, 1992), would if they became part of the public debate fundamentally transform the ways in which we as a society view education.

Finally practice. There are two practical issues which complement and overlap the previous suggestions on research and policy. The first is to become clearer in an operational sense about what school improvement actually is, and to clarify the distinction between 'naturally occurring', internally driven and externally supported school improvement. Second, to become far more sensitive to the 'growth states' or 'performance cycles' of schools. Do, for example, failing schools respond in different ways to school improvement initiatives than more successful schools?

More clarity on these three sets of issues would go a long way to transforming the 18th-century medical image of school improvement. It would also give it the maturity to enter a full and mutually supportive partnership with school effectiveness; assuming of course that those working in that tradition do likewise. It is the argument of this chapter that unless such discussion and conceptual work is done, the integration between school effectiveness and school improvement will remain at the level of aspiration.

REFERENCES

Ainscow, M. and Hopkins, D. (1992) 'Aboard the moving school', *Educational Leadership*, **50** (3), 79–81.

Ainscow, M., Hopkins, D., Southworth, G. and West, M. (1994) *Creating the Conditions for School Improvement*. London: Fulton.

Ainscow, M., Hargreaves, D. H. and Hopkins, D. (1995) 'Mapping the process of change in schools', *Evaluation and Research in Education*, **9** (2) 75–90.

Cambridge University (1994) *Mapping Change in Schools: The Cambridge Manual of Research Techniques*. Cambridge: University of Cambridge Institute of Education.

Fullan, M. (1991) *The Meaning of Educational Change*. London: Cassell.

Fullan, M. and Miles, M. (1992) 'Getting reform right: what works and what doesn't', *Phi Delta Kappan*, **73** (10), 745–52.

Glickman, C. (1990) 'Pushing school reforms to a new edge: the seven ironies of school empowerment', *Phi Delta Kappan*, **72** (1), 68–75.

Gray, J. *et al.* (1995) 'The statistics of school improvement', in Gray, J. and Wilcox, B. *'Good School, Bad School: Evaluating Performance and Encouraging Improvement*. Buckingham: Open University Press.

Hargreaves, D. H. (1990) 'Accountability and school improvement in the work of LEA inspectorates: the rhetoric and beyond', *Journal of Education Policy*, **5** (3), 230–39.

Hargreaves, D. H. (1994) *The Mosaic of Learning: Schools and Teachers for the Next Century*. London: DEMOS.

Hargreaves, D. H. (1995) 'School culture, school effectiveness and school improvement', *School Effectiveness and School Improvement*, **6** (1), 23–46.

Hargreaves, D. H. *et al.* (1989) *Planning for School Development*. London: DES.

Hargreaves, D. H. and Hopkins, D. (1991) *The Empowered School*. London: Cassell.

Hargreaves, D. H. and Hopkins, D. (eds) (1994) *Development Planning for School Improvement*. London: Cassell.

Hopkins, D. (1987) *Improving the Quality of Schooling*. Lewes: Falmer Press.

Hopkins, D. (1994a) 'Institutional self evaluation and renewal', in Husen, T. and Postlethwaite, N. (eds) *The International Encyclopaedia of Education*. New York: Pergamon.

Hopkins, D. (1994b) 'Process indicators for school improvement', in Bottani, N. and Tuijman, A. (eds) *Making Education Count*. Paris: OECD.

Hopkins, D. (1994c) 'The Yellow Brick Road', *Managing Schools Today*, **3** (6), 14–17.

Hopkins, D. (1995) 'Towards effective school improvement', *School Effectiveness and School Improvement*, **6** (3), 265–74.

Hopkins, D., Ainscow, M. and West, M. (1994) *School Improvement in an Era of Change*. London: Cassell.

Hopkins, D. and West, M. (1994) 'Teacher development and school improvement', in Walling, D., *Teachers as Learners*. Bloomington, Ind: PDK.

Huberman, M. (1992) 'Critical introduction', in Fullan, M., *Successful School Improvement*. Milton Keynes: Open University Press.

Huberman, M. and Miles, M. (1984) *Innovation Up Close*. New York: Plenum.

Joyce, B., Showers, B. and Weil, M. (1992) *Models of Teaching* (4th edn). Englewood Cliffs, NJ: Prentice-Hall.

Joyce, B., Wolf, J. and Calhoun, E. (1993) *The Self-Renewing School*. Alexandria, Va: ASCD.

McLaughlin, M. (1990) 'The Rand Change Agent Study revisited: macro perspectives, micro realities', *Educational Researcher*, **19** (9), 11–16.

Murphy, J. (1992) 'School effectiveness and school restructuring contributions to educational improvement', *School Effectiveness and School Improvement*, **3** (2), 90–109.

Myers, K. and Stoll, L. (1993) 'Mapping the movement', *Education*, **182** (3), 51.

OFSTED (1994) *Improving Schools*. London: HMSO.

Reynolds, D., Hopkins, D. and Stoll, L. (1993) 'Linking school effectiveness knowledge and school improvement practice: towards a synergy', *School Effectiveness and School Improvement*, **4** (1), 37–58.

Rowe, K., Holmes-Smith, P. and Hill, P. (1993) 'The Link between School Effectiveness Research, Policy and School Improvement'. Paper presented at the 1993 annual conference of the Australian Association for Research in Education, Fremantle, Western Australia, November 22–25.

Rutter, M., Maugham, B., Mortimore P. and Ouston, J. (1979) *Fifteen Thousand Hours*. London: Open Books.

Schein, E. (1985) *Organization Cultures and Leadership: A Dynamic View*. San Francisco: Jossey-Bass.

Sizer, T. (1992) *Horace's School*. New York: Houghton Mifflin.

Slavin, R. (1989) 'PET and the pendulum: faddism in education and how to stop it', *Phi Delta Kappan*, **70** (10), 752–8.

Slavin, R. *et al.* (1992) *Success for All: A Relentless Approach to Prevention and Early Intervention in Elementary Schools*. Arlington Va: Educational Research Service.

Slavin, R. *et al.* (1994) '"Whenever and wherever we chose" the replication of "Success for All"', *Phi Delta Kappan*, **75** (8), 639–47.

Wallace, R. C. *et al.* (1990) 'The Pittsburgh experience', in Joyce, B. (ed.) *Changing School Culture Through Staff Development* (1990 ASCD Year Book). Alexandria Va: ASCD.

Chapter 3

Linking School Effectiveness and School Improvement: Issues and Possibilities

Louise Stoll

INTRODUCTION

In an effort to make their schools more effective, educators often ask two related but distinct questions: 'Which of the many activities that we do have greater benefits for pupils?' and: 'How can we make our school better than it is now?' The first question focuses specifically on the impact of schools on pupil outcomes and the characteristics of effective schools, and the second on the implementation of change and school improvement.

Over the past two decades, two different groups of educational researchers have attempted to answer these questions. School effectiveness researchers have examined the quality and equity of schooling in order to find out why some schools are more effective than others in promoting positive outcomes, whether schools perform consistently over time, across outcomes and areas, and what characteristics are most commonly found in schools that are effective for all their pupils (for example, see reviews in Reynolds *et al.*, 1989a; Cotton, 1995; Sammons *et al.*, elsewhere in this volume). Over the same period, school improvement researchers have focused their studies on the processes that schools go through to become more successful and sustain this improvement (for example, van Velzen, 1987; Fullan, 1991). Caught in the middle have been practitioners engaged in attempts to improve their schools. These people have wanted high-quality, practical information to support their efforts. Thus, they have taken the pieces of research from both traditions that have made most sense to them and, albeit unknowingly, have linked the two areas through their improvement efforts. Sometimes their adoption of ideas from research has been somewhat uncritical; for example, attempts to apply findings from one specific context to another entirely different context when research has demonstrated significant contextual differences (e.g. Hallinger and Murphy, 1985; Teddlie *et al.*, 1989). At other times, they have an understanding of what makes a school effective, but not how to translate this into action, or they have a clear sense of how people need to work together, but have no framework or road map that tells them key areas on which to focus their attention.

If practitioners can see and make links between school effectiveness and school improvement, surely it is time for researchers studying the two areas to do the same and to work with schools to develop a deeper and more meaningful understanding of the research and its implications for practice. Still, however, there appears to be a reticence to join forces and, particularly in Britain, there continues to exist an 'intellectually and practically unhealthy separation between the effectiveness and improvement communities' (Reynolds, 1993).

In this chapter I shall briefly review the two paradigms to examine some of the key issues underlying this separation. I shall then highlight the features that both traditions could bring to a merger. Five action research projects that illustrate attempts to link school effectiveness and school improvement will be outlined. Finally, some unresolved issues that arise out of such 'possibilities' will be discussed.

ISSUES WITHIN THE RESEARCH LITERATURE

In looking at school effectiveness and school improvement, some similarities, but more differences, can be found within their definitions, origins and aims, preferred research designs, key findings, and models and theory.

Definition

Levine and Lezotte's (1990) basic definition of 'effectiveness' is the production of a desired result or outcome. Effectiveness, therefore, forces choices to be made among competing values. Some researchers take a narrow approach with a basic skills emphasis, while others perceive schools' aims to be more diverse. There is also a division between those who believe the chief focus should be students 'at risk' while others are committed to quality for all children. Recent research has broadened the definition of effectiveness to focus on progress in relationship to background and initial attainment (Mortimore, 1991a), as well as progress for all children across many outcomes over time (Stoll and Fink, 1996).

In addition, some researchers are moving towards a broader definition of effectiveness to encompass process and teacher outcomes (Rosenholtz, 1989; Richards, 1991). This process orientation has more in common with school improvement research. Interestingly, at the same time, the definition of school improvement is moving closer to those of school effectiveness in its more recent acknowledgement of outcomes. Unlike school effectiveness, school improvement did not until recently suffer from a wide array of definitions. The most frequently quoted definition emanates from the International School Improvement Project (ISIP), where van Velzen et al. (1985) incorporated research findings into a comprehensive statement:

> a systematic sustained effort aimed at change in learning conditions
> and other related internal conditions in one or more schools, with the
> ultimate aim of accomplishing educational goals more effectively (p. 48).

In this definition, it is clear that there is an intricate relationship between school improvement and change. Indeed, all school improvement is change, although it cannot be assumed that all change is improvement (Hopkins, 1994).

Origins and Aims

The school effectiveness movement in both Britain and the USA developed in response to findings of studies that suggested that home background, including social class and economic status, had a far greater influence on a child's development than did the school they attended (for example, Coleman *et al.*, 1966; Plowden, 1967). The title of the study *School Matters* (Mortimore *et al.*, 1988), was one illustration of the intent of school effectiveness researchers to demonstrate that schools, indeed, made a difference. Ultimately, school effectiveness research aims to describe what an effective school looks like and to 'search for ways – both adequate and reliable – to measure the quality of the school' (Mortimore, 1991b, p. 214).

In contrast, school improvement researchers aim to understand the processes and stages of change that lead to successful outcomes. A key goal is to improve the competencies of the school itself to analyse problems and develop and manage change. Thus, Firestone (1991) suggests, school improvement researchers tend to be applied rather than pure researchers in their more specific orientation to understand the processes that will support the service concerns of educators. However, it is not only researchers who engage in school improvement. Educators, themselves, are the fundamental backbone of school improvement and many, while engaged in such efforts, also monitor these efforts internally. Thus, there has been a difference within the traditions between the research, development and dissemination approach of the researchers, and school-based improvement projects developed and carried out by practitioners.

Research Design

Within the scope of this chapter it is not possible to discuss the analysis methods and detailed research designs of the two traditions. That is the focus of other chapters by members of this seminar series. Interestingly, however, as Clark *et al.* (1984) argue, the two approaches share many input and process variables although, both in their outcome orientation and investigation methods, these are treated differently. The school improvement paradigm predominantly favours a qualitative approaches in contrast to the quantitative slant of school effectiveness research, although the mixed methodological approaches of the Louisiana School Effectiveness Study (Teddlie and Stringfield, 1993) and of the Improving School Effectiveness Project (MacBeath and Mortimore, 1994) hopefully herald greater convergence. While classrooms have been a focus of a few major school effectiveness studies, many others have neglected attention to them. The inclusion of classroom process data is particularly important given that recent studies demonstrate that most of the variation among schools is due to classroom variation (Scheerens, 1992).

Key Findings

While the key findings of school improvement research are orientated more towards the change process, the two traditions concur on many areas which, Clark *et al.* (1984) note 'justifies a comparative analysis of these bodies of literature' (p. 42). It would seem that more than a comparative analysis is required, given the clear attempts of people within both fields to incorporate features of both into lists (Purkey and Smith, 1983; Levine and Lezotte, 1990), processes (Fullan, 1985) and projects that link the two paradigms (for example, Reynolds *et al.*, 1989b; McGaw *et al.*, 1992; Ouston *et al.*, 1991), albeit not always successfully.

Models and Theory

The evolution of models and theories of school effectiveness and school improvement captures elements of the definition, aims and purpose, research design and
key findings outlined thus far, and further reflects their different orientations.

Given the large number of studies of school effectiveness and their applications, there is surprisingly little theory on 'why things work in education'
(Scheerens and Creemers, 1989). The simplistic 'five-factor' model consisting of
Edmonds' (1979) original correlates of achievement was replaced, in Britain at
least, by a context-input–process-output model, exemplified in the longitudinal
studies of Rutter *et al.* (1979) and Mortimore *et al.* (1988). More recently,
Scheerens (1992) has further refined the analytic systems model to incorporate
situational and contextual situations, and Teddlie and Stringfield (1993) in their
contingency-stage theory, give further emphasis to context and process. Theirs is
the first school effectiveness theory to suggest movement: that is, that schools go
through states of effectiveness. Mortimore (1991b) notes the controversy that
surrounds theory and offers an alternative, in the form of a set of postulates to be
tested empirically.

In the field of school improvement and change, while models exist, there
appears to be a preference for frameworks, processes and guidelines. House
(1981) outlines three perspectives, or screens, through which any innovation can
be viewed: technological, political and cultural. The technological perspective
focuses on the innovation itself, the political perspective on the innovation in
context, and the cultural perspective on the context. In reality, any change
attempts need to be aware of and attend to ramifications of all three perspectives,
for it would seem unlikely that a comprehensive improvement effort would not
involve them all. Other school improvement processes and guidelines outlined
here all tend to blend at least two of the perspectives, although one may be dominant.

The school-based development process can be seen in various guises, and had
its British origins in school self-review. Foremost among these, and a prototype for
many others, are the *Guidelines for Review and Internal Development in
Schools* (GRIDS) (McMahon *et al.*, 1984). Britain's school development plan
(Hargreaves *et al.*, 1989; Hargreaves and Hopkins, 1991) differs slightly in its
attention to budgeting as a phase within the cycle, in response to the realities of
local management of schools reform.

Purkey and Smith (1983) prefer to outline organization-structure and process
variables of school effectiveness, then speculate on the improvement strategies
necessary to mobilize these variables. Fullan's (1985) model of the school
improvement process goes even further in that it links eight organization factors
and four process factors to improvement, which he defines as achievement of
goals, sense of community and meaning and capacity for improvement. His 'model'
begins to blend school effectiveness and school improvement findings.

In another school improvement framework, Joyce (1991) describes five different doors offered by proponents of school improvement: collegiality, research
findings, site-specific information, curriculum initiatives and instructional initiatives. Traditionally, he believes, schools have selected one door through which
they will enter into 'a passageway into the culture of the school' (p. 59). Joyce

54

argues that adherence to one approach alone is inadequate and that major school improvement efforts need to open all the doors. Hopkins (1991) cautions, however, the opening of any of these doors without attention to the deeper culture and organization conditions of the school 'leads only into a cul-de-sac' (p. 60).

Thus, while school effectiveness research demonstrates a greater orientation to model formation to represent its theoretical underpinnings, the school improvement researchers tend towards processes and guidelines that reflect its more practical orientation.

FEATURES OF THE TWO PARADIGMS NECESSARY FOR A MERGER

It seems from the preceding review that, while there are some basic differences, the two research traditions complement each other, and shortcomings of each approach can be counterbalanced by the strengths of the other. Indeed, Reynolds *et al*. (1993) point out that school effectiveness and school improvement persons need each other. School effectiveness researchers can provide knowledge for school improvers about factors within schools and classrooms that can be changed to produce higher-quality schooling, whereas school improvement strategies provide the ultimate test for many of the theories posited by school effectiveness researchers. In order for closer links to be made between the two paradigms, it is necessary to examine what each can bring to a union.

School Effectiveness

A focus on outcomes   In this increased age of accountability, it is necessary for schools to demonstrate both to themselves and the wider community that what they do makes a difference to student outcomes. A focus on enhancing performance in the basic skills, as advocated by some of the earlier American school effectiveness studies, will not be adequate. We are becoming increasingly aware that children may have many intelligences (Gardner, 1983). Researchers, therefore, need to develop valid instruments to measure growth in a broad range of academic and social areas of students' development that match these intelligences and are seen by educators to be important.

An emphasis on equity   Many schools in their current school improvement efforts still do not pay sufficient attention to ensure that disadvantaged students in their schools make as much progress as their more affluent peers. Edmonds (1979) brought the issue of equity to the forefront of school effectiveness research. His legacy has been continued worldwide, and now there is a considerable knowledge base from which schools can draw (for example, Teddlie and Stringfield, 1985; Scheerens, 1987; Nuttall *et al*., 1989; Bashi and Sass, 1989). Researchers of school improvement also need to be aware of the background of the student population in a school before they assess the value added by the school's change effort over and above what the students might be expected to learn given their background, prior knowledge and attitudes.

The use of data for decision-making   Because school effectiveness research is based on measured outcomes, it offers a database to help schools in their planning. Schools need to gather information that relates to their current situation, and to determine from it where their needs lie. Through the disaggregation of student data, schools can also establish whether they are meeting the needs of different groups of students, for example females versus males, and students of different ages, social class or ethnic backgrounds.

A knowledge of what is effective elsewhere   Although not every study of school effectiveness has come up with an identical list of the characteristics of effectiveness, there is sufficient overlap of several of these elements to believe that there must be some consistency of impact across situations. It is important that schools gain access to these findings, that researchers help to bring these to them in a meaningful form, and explain important contextual differences and areas where it is possible to generalize, so that they can become the basis for whole-school discussion and part of a school's assessment process.

An understanding that the school is the focus of change   Goodlad (1984), in a study of school effectiveness, stressed that change must be school-based. Early applications of school effectiveness research in various American districts also demonstrated that a top-down approach did not work (Lezotte, 1989). If each school has a unique population and context, as discussed above, it is clear that individual schools need to take responsibility for their own change efforts.

Quantitative research methodology   With the increased sophistication of research techniques, in particular multilevel modelling (for example, Goldstein, 1995; Raudenbush, 1989), it is now possible to examine precisely differential effects and to establish the real value added by schools. This kind of information can feed directly into improvement efforts and highlight specific issues for school improvement researchers to study. The larger sample sizes associated with quantitative studies also leads to greater confidence in terms of the generalizability of findings. In addition, researchers have studied differential effects using quantitative methodology (for example, Sammons et al., 1996). The implication of their findings is that whole-school strategies may not be as appropriate as programmes targeted towards certain groups (Reynolds et al., 1993).

School Improvement

A focus on process   There are a wealth of theoretical and practical studies that have helped advance our understanding of the initiation, implementation and institutionalization of change (for example, Crandall et al., 1982; Huberman and Miles, 1984; Fullan, 1991). Change in schools is not an event or 'one-shot deal'. Rather, it is a process that takes time and considerable patience, as proponents of 'quick fix' solutions have found to their cost. School effectiveness researchers need to learn more about this process and its interplay with the characteristics identified by their own research. Although the Louisiana School Effectiveness Study (Teddlie and Stringfield, 1993) has made some headway in this area, further work remains to be done. As Gray et al. (1995) note, ineffective schools that are improving represent a particularly important focus for study.

An orientation towards action and ongoing development   School improvement approaches do not tend to be imposed solutions. Rather, 'they embody the long-term goal of moving towards the vision of the "problem-solving" or "thinking" or "relatively autonomous" school' (Hopkins, 1994). As Hopkins points out, this approach underpinned the work of the OECD's International School Improvement Project (ISIP), in itself a changing and evolutionary project. Schools do not stand still and wait to be measured by researchers. They are dynamic institutions, subject to frequent change. Only by studying this process of change and its impact, can we really understand schools.

An emphasis on school-selected priorities for development   School improvement research emphasizes the importance of teacher involvement in change efforts, and ownership for the process. Consequently, it is important that staff members be involved in the selection of priorities for future development. British school self-evaluation efforts in the 1970s and 1980s (Clift et al., 1987; McMahon et al., 1984) emphasized the need to establish priorities or goals. This has now been incorporated into the school development planning process (Hargreaves et al., 1989; Hargreaves and Hopkins, 1991). Similar processes are found in other countries (for example Loucks-Horsley and Hergert, 1985; Caldwell and Spinks, 1988; Stoll and Fink, 1992).

An understanding of the importance of school culture   In recent years, researchers have become much more aware of the powerful impact of school culture on change efforts (for example, Fullan and Hargreaves, 1992; A. Hargreaves, 1994; Siskin, 1994; D. Hargreaves 1995; Stoll and Fink, 1994). Hargreaves and Hopkins (1991) explain:

> Successful schools realize that developmental planning is about
> creating a school culture which will support the planning and
> management of changes of many different kinds. School culture is
> difficult to define, but is best thought of as the procedures, values
> and expectations that guide people's behaviour within an
> organization (pp. 16–17).

In short, a culture that promotes norms of collaboration, trust, the taking of risks, and a focus on continuous learning for students and adults, appears to be a key feature of school improvement efforts (Stoll and Fink, 1996).

The importance of a focus on teaching and learning   The greatest effects on student achievement have been demonstrated at classroom level (Scheerens, 1992). Change efforts have to have a focus and, above all, must have meaning for teachers if they have the chief responsibility to implement changes and make them work (Fullan, 1991). An understanding of school organization and its underlying processes may not be sufficient to engage teachers' interest or commitment. Furthermore, collaboration or collegiality for its own sake may have little impact on the culture of the school. Teachers need a focus for their collaborative efforts; an opportunity to engage in 'joint work' around topics related to the classroom (Little, 1990).

A view of the school as the centre of change   As a result of the 1988 Education Reform Act, there is increasing impetus for schools to be autonomous. School improvement, however, not only views the school as the focus of change but as its centre, in that it cannot be isolated from the context around it (Sirotnik, 1987). Indeed the LEA has traditionally been seen as key to school improvement, provided that it offers appropriate support to schools and is also engaged in a process of ongoing learning. Schools need to be a part of a wider system, networking with other schools as well as the LEA, community, higher education institutions and business.

Qualititative research methodology   Exemplified in the in-depth case-study approach, qualitative data-gathering and analysis techniques (for example, Miles and Huberman, 1984) have enabled school improvement researchers to get below the surface of improvement, which is essential to the study of its processes. More case studies are needed in this country of effective or even ineffective schools that paint the fine-grained reality of school and classroom processes.

POSSIBILITIES ARISING OUT OF THE RESEARCH LITERATURE

Several possibilities arise out of the outline above. In the remainder of this chapter I will focus on one that I believe is a fruitful area for applied researchers who wish to link school effectiveness and improvement: school effectiveness and improvement projects with an action research orientation, where researchers work to a greater or lesser degree with schools and LEAs to help them develop and monitor their projects and to gain further understanding of the processes of improvement that lead to effectiveness. Five such projects are now outlined, one Canadian, the other four British. I am, or have been, directly involved in three of these projects.

Action Projects that Arise out of the Blended Research Literature

Halton's Effective Schools Project   The Effective Schools Project in the Halton Board of Education in Ontario started, in 1986, as an attempt to bring the results of school effectiveness research carried out within Britain (Mortimore *et al.*, 1988) into the schooling practices of Canada, but it soon became clear that potential difficulties involved in the project's implementation could only be resolved by the adoption at school and system level of organizational and planning arrangements from the school improvement literature. Essentially, 'top-down' mandates to schools to address the characteristics of effectiveness failed because they did not engender ownership and commitment, nor did they pay attention to the process and impact of change on those who worked through it.

A search of the international effectiveness literature was carried out by members of a task force, and a model of the characteristics of effectiveness produced. Visits to school districts where change was known to have occurred successfully, and meetings with Michael Fullan, convinced task-force members that improvement was more likely to occur if the school was seen as the focal point of change. A school growth planning process was developed, largely based on British models (McMahon *et al.*, 1984; ILEA, 1986) and similar to the school development plan that is now a feature of many countries, states and territories.

Where do the effective schools' characteristics fit in? Within the assessment, or audit, phase, when the school is trying to get a picture of its current successes and areas for improvement, it examines Halton's model of characteristics as it relates to its own context. Questionnaires for teachers, students and parents focus on where the respondents think the school is in relation to a set of indicators, and how important each indicator is in order to create a more effective school. Through analysing the gap between where the school is and where it should be, the school can identify areas of need. Furthermore, the information from the three sources provides triangulation. Clearly, this is not the only information schools examine during the assessment phase; they also look at current curricula and instructional practices, initiatives coming out of the school board and the Ontario Ministry of Education, and also a variety of information related to their students' progress and development. In line with the emphasis on equity in school effect-iveness research, schools are encouraged to disaggregate student data: that is, to look for any differences in achievement, progress or development between subsets of the population. Work has been in progress to create a profile for schools that would contain key student information in summarized form.

Further understandings about school improvement have been gained during the project. The school growth-planning process is very different from traditional forms of planning in Halton. Increased staff involvement in decision-making has necessitated greater understanding on the part of principals of the processes involved in working with groups. In the more successful schools attention has been paid early on to the development of clear decision-making structures and organ-izational processes that will reduce later problems. In short, in these schools a climate has been built within which a more dynamic and ongoing planning process can occur. More important, time has been spent building a collaborative culture within the school, in which teachers continue to learn and feel valued, and risk-taking is encouraged. Finally, people are encouraged to articulate their values and beliefs such that a shared vision for the school's future can be developed. In essence, the growth-planning process has shown that the creation of an effective school depends on more than the knowledge of what has been successful and effective elsewhere, although that can be a useful starting point.

Further important characteristics of this project have been the importance of the school district's role in the process. Halton created a strategic plan that emphasized three key directions. One of these was the growth planning process itself. The second was a focus on instruction, in recognition of the central role in the determination of school outcomes of what actually goes on in the classroom; the teaching and learning process. The third direction supported the other two: that is, an emphasis on staff development. Thus the system provided a framework within which growth planning could occur, and offered support for the process. This support came in the form of voluntary workshops for school teams on all aspects of growth planning, a variety of instructional strategies and assessment, and for entire staffs on their chosen instructional goals. Support was also offered through regional consultants who worked with individual teachers or whole staffs, and area consultants and special education staff assigned to particular schools. Thus the school was not seen as an isolated unit of change but as the centre of change, connected to a wider system. This system also has to continue to grow, and in 1993, through a collaborative process involving representatives from the entire system as well as the local community, the three original directions were re-endorsed and a new one added, to highlight the importance of the school system's relationship with its community.

The effective schools questionnaires have also been used throughout the system to look at the impact of the project on attitudes. Student retention data has been collected, and shows a decrease in drop-outs over a five-year period since the project began. Halton continues to perform above average on Ministry curriculum reviews, and individual schools have demonstrated improvements in student attitudes and attendance, as well as other indicators related to their specific growth plans.

Institutionalization of school growth planning in Halton, another outcome of the project, has resulted from the weaving together of a variety of initiatives; the development of a shared language around school effectiveness and school improvement; incorporation of existing aspects of Halton's culture, such as the teacher evaluation process, and a strong commitment to collaboration; strategic directions that acknowledge the importance of the process; and an emphasis on well-coordinated leadership and staff development (Stoll and Fink, 1994).

This project was developed by practitioners and policy-makers. I aided and advised these people, in my capacity as school-board researcher. The roles I played in the project were diverse, as necessitated by the occasion: conveyer of research findings, participant in the task force, leader, provider of staff development, facilitator, supporter to schools in their self-evaluation and monitoring efforts, and evaluator of the project at system level. University personnel were also involved in this project, largely in training and advisory roles, through Halton's participation in *The Learning Consortium*, a school board/university partnership (Fullan *et al.*, 1990). In the next projects described, researchers play slightly different roles.

Lewisham School Improvement Project The Lewisham School Improvement Project commenced in the spring of 1993. It arises out of a partnership between Lewisham schools, Lewisham local education authority (LEA) and the London Institute of Education. It had four aims: (1) To enhance pupil progress, achievement and development; (2) to develop the internal capacity of schools for managing change and evaluating its impact at whole-school level, classroom level and pupil level; (3) to develop the capacity of the LEA to provide data to schools that will strengthen their ability to plan and evaluate change; and (4) to integrate the above with the system's ongoing inservice and support services to form a coherent approach to professional development.

The project began with four dimensions, although these overlap to some extent:

1. A series of voluntary workshops ('Leaders Together') with headteachers and deputy headteachers across the borough, who work with a partner during and between sessions. Topics covered include and emphasize school effectiveness and school improvement. Almost all the schools have now attended these sessions.

2. More intense work with a core group of ten schools (primary, secondary and special schools are represented), the heads and deputies of whom participated in the initial workshops. These schools identified a teaching and learning focus for improvement, and cross-role project teams attended several sessions in which they worked with Institute facilitators to refine their focus areas through analysis of school-based data. They were also introduced to the school effectiveness and school improvement research findings, with a special emphasis on their role as change agents within their schools. The title of the workshop series, 'Moving Together', reflects the impact on school improvement of teachers learning together (Rosenholtz, 1989). Accreditation is offered for course and project work.

There are nine 'ground rules' for participation in this part of the project, based on findings of school effectiveness and school improvement research.

- A focus on achievement in its broadest sense – to ensure that the core of the project emphasizes outcomes for pupils, and teaching and learning. Examination of school effectiveness findings and the notion of value-added (McPherson, 1993) helps schools to focus their efforts.

- Start small, think big – that the focus of the project should be manageable and linked to the school's development plan, in recognition that school development and classroom development go hand in hand (Fullan and Hargreaves, 1992; Hargreaves and Hopkins, 1991).

- Teams of people – the importance of shared leadership and teacher ownership in school improvement.

- Composition of teams – that teams who coordinate the project in their school and attended workshops should represent the entire staff in their composition, and may also include other stakeholders.

- Teams are agents of change – while the school improvement teams are not responsible for change in their school, they need to facilitate that change, and therefore must understand the change process and its impact on people.

- School-managed project – it is the school's responsibility to establish and maintain their project's focus, to manage the change process and to monitor and evaluate the project (van Velzen *et al.*, 1985).

- Systematic monitoring and evaluation – the importance of setting success criteria, gathering and evaluating evidence, and using the knowledge and information gained.

- Support from outside – that ongoing support is available from the LEA in the form of advisory services, tailor-made staff development programmes, access to present programmes, resourcing, and help with measurement of indicators of achievement and development. Support from the Institute of Education focused on strengthening the school's capacity to manage change effectively, through accredited training and visits to individual schools.

- Dissemination – project schools are involved in disseminating their findings to colleagues throughout the school system.

3. Work with a voluntary group – containing teachers, headteachers and a variety of LEA staff – to identify and develop whole system indicators of change, achievement and development.

4. Monitoring and evaluating this project at school and system level are an important feature. Schools have been given training and support in the areas of data collection, developing and measuring success criteria and ongoing evaluation of their project, its process and progress. LEA people are also monitoring the progress and impact of the project. Baseline data have been gathered for the ten core schools, against which progress will be measured. Institute staff carry out interviews in the ten schools at various time points to elicit insights into the change process. Dissemination of findings throughout the LEA is an important part of the project. A steering group is overseeing the process.

One of the ten schools involved in the more detailed project work is a special school that caters for students who have severe learning difficulties and are between the ages of 11 and 19 years. The school reported that 'Leaders Together' provided them with the impetus to work as a whole staff to write curriculum group schemes of work. For their project they are focusing on recording and assessment, to develop accessible, useful and informative linked systems to support National Curriculum attainment-target recording and allow for differentiation, given the wide range in students' age and ability. Every teacher has chosen to be a member of one of four working groups: recording and assessment for students with profound and multiple learning difficulties; individual action planning for 16–19 year olds; reporting to parents and home–school communication; and national Records of Achievement and accreditation. A limited amount of non-contact time has been arranged for group meetings, although teachers also meet more frequently informally. A core team, consisting of the deputy head, a member of the senior management team and another teacher attended 'Moving Together' and coordinate the activities. Each of these is a member of a different working group, and the headteacher is also a member of one of these groups. Only one group, therefore, does not have representation from people involved in either 'Leaders Together' or 'Moving Together'. Part of the cultural conditions of the school that underpin their four focus areas is the greater involvement of non-teaching staff.

A primary school also involved in the project decided to concentrate on writing, the curriculum focus from the school's development plan. The staff as a whole initially spent time articulating their vision for the school and aims, and the improvement team began to explore and coordinate a variety of strategies that included: analysis of the school's own statistics on achievement, using relevant research findings to inform practice; paired classroom observations; staff development sessions; yearly targets for individual teachers related to the aims of the project; and the development of a commonly known and agreed monitoring scheme that is being used by the headteacher and language post-holder when they visit classrooms and give feedback to teachers.

In this project, LEA research staff are providing data for the ten core schools from their ongoing data bank, and participate in the indicators group. Institute staff both work with schools to help them examine, work on and evaluate their own efforts, and carry out separate monitoring of the project.

Schools Make a Difference (SMAD)   In early 1993, Hammersmith and Fulham LEA established the Schools Make a Difference project to help the borough's eight secondary schools raise student levels of attainment, achievement and morale (Myers, 1996). While affiliation to the project was optional, all eight schools chose to participate. The project's guiding principles were based on school effectiveness research findings. These principles are:

- that students need to believe that schooling can be worthwhile and relevant;
- that learning must be challenging and relevant, to encourage students to develop their capabilities as responsible, thoughtful and active citizens;
- that students' intellectual, personal and technical abilities, aptitudes and capabilities are recognized and valued, and that expectations of progress and performance are high;
- that good behaviour is a necessary condition for effective learning, and that students take responsibility for their own behaviour and display a high level of engagement in a well-structured learning process;
- that parental involvement is vital and should be sought;
- that all staff in the schools are involved in, and committed to the school's development;
- that schools and the community work towards a shared vision and that a professional learning community is created within schools;
- that headteachers have a vital role to play in providing a climate where this can occur;
- that a 'plan, do and review' approach is systematically and rigorously applied.

Hammersmith and Fulham appointed a project manager to work with schools and LEA personnel to establish the structures and procedures for the project. Within her role she made regular visits to the schools and took the schools' senior management teams to visit schools of interest around the country. In conjunction with headteachers and higher education staff, she also organized inservice meetings for the coordinators, headteachers, senior management teams and various other staff members.

The schools all appointed project coordinators, who were awarded 30 half-days' cover in order to carry out work associated with the project in their schools, attend inservice and visit other schools. Coordinators received accreditation for their course and project work through the Institute of Education. The coordinators established project working parties in their schools with representation from a wide range of teaching and support staff and in some schools, students, parents and governors.

Each school produced a project plan based on criteria agreed by the head-teachers for expenditure of the budget. The plan was developed as a result of wide consultation, and included a project focus based on the school's development plan. Several schools chose as a focus flexible learning strategies, and have been engaged in a variety of forms of staff development to help introduce new teaching and student study methods to staff. In one school, for example, the eight voluntary members of the SMAD Development Group decided to pair up with a partner to engage in classroom observation and act as each other's 'critical friend'. Supply cover for this was incorporated within the school's project plan. The project also funded school-based revision centres during the Easter vacation, that helped increase student engagement.

Early findings demonstrated that coordinator enthusiasm and an emphasis on action, and pupil and teacher learning and involvement were having a positive impact. As in so many other studies, time was also an issue. Nine months into the project, the coordinator in one school that purchased computers and arranged for two teachers and one pupil to receive training, observed little change in information technology in the school. She reflected, 'I thought once we had the ideas it would happen, but it's a development process.' External events proved to have an impact on the implementation of the project in some schools. In particular, schools undergoing the OFSTED inspection process often found it extremely difficult to focus their attention on school improvement issues, especially those that did not receive positive inspection reports. The impact of the inspection process is not isolated to Hammersmith and Fulham. In schools in at least two of the other examples presented here, similar reactions have been demonstrated, in some cases virtually paralysing the development work of schools for a period of time.

An external evaluator was appointed to the project. He worked in conjunction with the LEA's research staff, who already collected data on examination results, attendance and delinquency. Attitudinal data were also collected from students. Additionally, the schools were all involved in self-evaluation. As part of their project plans the schools developed their own success criteria and performance indicators. Dissemination of project findings also occurred.

Improving the Quality of Education for All (IQEA)   The overall aim of IQEA is 'to strengthen the school's ability to provide quality education for all its pupils by building upon good practice. In so doing, we are also producing and evaluating a model of school development, and a programme of support' (Ainscow *et al.*, 1994). In the project, approaches and methods from the improvement and effectiveness paradigms are blended; in particular, use of and work on improvement and change processes with input on school and classroom effectiveness and measurement of outcomes.

On the basis of their previous work in school improvement from this study, Hopkins and Ainscow (see chapter 2 in this volume for a fuller description of the project) describe six assumptions on which they have based the project:

1. School improvement will result in enhanced student and staff outcomes.
2. School culture, a blend of the values, beliefs and norms of the people who work in the school, is vital to the improvement process.
3. The school's background and organizational structure are key factors in the school improvement process.
4. School improvement is most successful when there is a clear and practical focus for development.
5. The school needs to work on certain conditions at the same time as the curriculum or other priorities. These include staff development, student involvement, enquiry and reflection, leadership, coordination and planning.
6. A school improvement strategy needs to be developed to link priorities to these conditions.

The project, which began with only nine schools in 1991, has grown each year, and currently involves approximately 30 schools in East Anglia, North London and Yorkshire. A contract is agreed between school staff, the local education authority and a team from the University of Cambridge Institute of Education. All staff of a school have to agree that the school will participate, and at least 40 per cent receive release time to engage in specific project-related activities in their own and each other's classrooms, although all staff participate in certain IQEA-focused staff development events. Two staff members are designated as coordinators and attend ten days of training and support meetings, for which accreditation is offered by the Cambridge Institute. The school selects its own priorities for development and its own methods to achieve these priorities. It also participates in the evaluation of the project and has to commit itself to share findings with other participants in the project.

Emerging findings suggest that schools that are more successful in bringing about improvement-related changes have done so by working on or incorporating the school's internal conditions, and thereby changing the culture of the school (Hopkins *et al.*, 1994). Those schools that recognize the social complexity of change are also finding its implementation to be easier. Hopkins and Ainscow have identified five aspects of this complexity; teacher learning, opportunities for staff to take leadership roles, student involvement, an overall school vision and the celebration of success.

In this project, as in the Halton and Lewisham ones, the researchers take an interventionist role. While it proves a dilemma for them in a pure research sense, they emphasize the increased understanding of school improvement and change for themselves as a consequence of this kind of relationship with practitioners. From the school's perspective, support is received from outsiders, 'critical friends', who can give them an unbiased view of their work.

Quality Development Initiative (QDI)   Somewhat different from the previous projects in that there is no direct input of effective schools research findings is the Quality Development Initiative introduced by Birmingham local education authority and evaluated by the Centre for Education Policy and Management Studies at the University of Birmingham (Ribbins and Burridge, 1994). The approach is based on the concept of school self-evaluation, and is intended to address three purposes: to improve learning and teaching (*improving*), to respond proactively to accountability demands (*proving*), and to support the development of schools as learning communities for everyone connected with them (*learning*).

Nine principles underpin Quality Development:

1. A direct impact on learning and teaching.
2. Building on actual school needs and embedded into development planning.
3. Monitoring and evaluation through a collaborative, participative process.
4. School ownership and responsibility.
5. Introduction through staff training.
6. Open management, a responsive organizational structure and whole-school commitment.
7. Allocation of clear roles and responsibilities.
8. Resource allocation, especially time for monitoring and evaluation.
9. Involvement of all stakeholders: pupils/students, teaching and non-teaching staff, parents, employers and governors.

In the essence of a blended school effectiveness and school improvement approach, there is significant emphasis on the incorporation of both formative and summative review mechanisms, generation of qualitative and quantitative information, collection of evidence to be judged against agreed criteria, and interpretation of evidence in context.

Nineteen schools participated in a pilot study in 1991. By 1994, approximately 200 schools were involved. Schools take part in an accredited training programme provided by the university in which they identify a common set of principles and working practices that will enable them to build self-evaluation processes into the school's working life. Birmingham's Education Committee supported a three-year extension of the Initiative, a resource centre has been set up, and 'Investors in People' has been incorporated. The latter is a national scheme designed to give public recognition to organizations' commitment to quality.

One participating school described the impact of QDI:

> *Before QDI*: Evaluation was rather unsystematic. Many teachers were uneasy about sharing concerns and classroom practice with others. Staff morale had been low.
>
> *Since QDI*: The staff ... work very much as a cohesive team, sharing their successes and difficulties, teaching across the phases within the school and productively in curriculum working parties. Self-evaluation and observation skills have improved, as have staff attitudes towards children's involvement in their own evaluation and planning ... We have begun to use the QD process for developing our assessment and recording throughout the school ... the processes of auditing, evaluating and planning for progress are becoming very much a part of everyone's approach to managing change within the school.

As a consequence of these and other similar projects, some issues arise that require consideration.

Unresolved Issues

Are the effectiveness characteristics relevant for schools of the 1990s?

It has been suggested that the school effectiveness characteristics might have outlived their usefulness given a changing world and its impact on education (Reynolds and Packer, 1992; Murphy, 1992). To some extent this is true, and improvement schemes in the 1990s need to be based on knowledge that reflects the characteristics of schools in the 1990s, not the 1970s and 1980s (Reynolds *et al.*, 1993). Nonetheless, ongoing school effectiveness research and Halton's experience suggest that there are many constants among the characteristics of effectiveness; for example, teacher involvement, high expectations, forms of leadership, frequent monitoring of progress, and praise and recognition, to quote a few. In essence, these appear to be the foundations for school growth. Although they may represent a first wave of reform (Holly, 1990), they cannot just be equated with 'doing the same but more of it' (Banathy, 1988). They are fundamental to further reform. They could be seen as the roots that enable the branches to grow (Hargreaves and Hopkins, 1991). This does not mean that schools and researchers should not be future-orientated in the areas they choose to develop or study, but that these areas may well not grow without prior and ongoing attention to their foundations. Cetainly, school improvers would also benefit from current knowledge about effective teaching and learning techniques and the impact of the role of the headteacher and of other educational institutions, arrangements and layers above the level of the school.

Can the effectiveness characteristics be implemented?

Rutter *et al.* (1979) demonstrated that the combination of all of the effectiveness characteristics into an overall concept of 'ethos' was more powerful than the impact of any individual characteristic. This might suggest that it is necessary for a school to work on all the characteristics at one time. It is clear from the experience of schools in the examples already cited, and from many other studies of school improvement that it is necessary to focus improvement efforts on a few key goals at one time. It would be useful if school effectiveness researchers could help to isolate the direction and strength of the influences that link school process variables together. It should be noted, however, that schools deal in multiple innovations of their own (Fullan, 1991; Wallace, 1991) and a 'plethora of external innovations' (Wallace and McMahon, 1994) which makes it very hard to separate different influences. In addition, with external pressure for less variability between schools, it may become more difficult to discover the characteristics that make a difference.

A further issue arises out of this question. Many educators find themselves working in historically ineffective settings. The knowledge base within school effectiveness may not be easily applicable to those settings. In Halton, it took some schools several years to build the climate, structures and collaborative norms described earlier. Further studies of ineffective but improving schools would be useful, as would those of schools with a particularly large percentage of students traditionally viewed as 'at risk'.

What is the best way to measure the impact of such projects?   The evaluation of school improvement projects poses a problem, particularly those initially generated at system level. There is a desire to know that such a project has made a difference, and pressure from those who have committed funding to see early evidence of enhanced student outcomes, usually in the form of achievement scores. As Gray *et al.* show later in chapter 9, however, gains in one year may only be minimal. How, therefore, does a school assess early impact? Furthermore, when a school has chosen a particular focus, for example the writing process, is it appropriate to measure its progress in comparison to other schools in terms of GCSE mathematics results? Student outcomes must be measured, but it may be more appropriate for each school to determine its own success criteria and performance indicators based on its chosen focus areas. A way forward may be the development of assessments of cross-curricular skills, for example problem solving, that should be enhanced no matter what subjects the school selects as its particular targets.

There is also the change process itself. Analysis of the process and progress of an improvement project is as important as evaluation of its outcomes. If development of a learning community that includes teachers as well as students is a goal, the process by which this is achieved needs to be monitored and evaluated. While progress and enhanced student outcomes should be the ultimate aims and measures of school improvement, improved teaching quality is an important intermediate goal, the measurement of which should be undertaken. Considerable work remains to be done in this area.

What is the impact of the researcher on the project?   The role of the researcher in many of these projects, as already described, was multifaceted. In pure research terms, this may be seen as questionable. It is fair to suggest that researchers who play such a role do influence the course of a project. This has to be weighed up against potential improvement benefits that may accrue as a result of the knowledge the researcher brings and her/his desire to make research findings accessible to practitioners and to facilitate their school's development as a problem-solving, self-evaluating institution. Increasingly, researchers such as myself are finding ourselves in the role of 'critical friend'; an objective but supportive outsider who can act as a mirror, ask probing questions and provide feedback.

While school improvement researchers want to see schools succeed, it should not be forgotten that it is also important for them to know what does and does not work, and that an understanding gained about an ineffective process is equally as significant as that gained about an effective one. This continues to be a dilemma for those of us engaged in such projects.

CONCLUSION

Despite significant differences in orientation, methodology and aims, the separate traditions of school effectiveness and school improvement possess many complementary features that have been harnessed by practitioners engaged in school improvement efforts. While there continues to be a major role for 'pure' researchers to play, many facets of which have been articulated elsewhere in this seminar series, there is also a key role for 'applied' researchers to work closely with schools, introduce the research findings to them in the action research mode; in short, in partnership with schools, to try out, reflect on and evaluate the findings in projects tailored to schools' unique contexts. Through their improvement endeavours, effectiveness knowledge can be tested and further understanding about improvement gained. Clearly, unresolved issues remain. It is hoped that school effectiveness and school improvement researchers, working together and with practitioners, can resolve them.

REFERENCES

Ainscow, M., Hopkins, D., Southworth, G. and West, M. (1994) *School Improvement in an Era of Change: an Overview of the 'Improving the Quality of Education for All' (IQEA) Project*. Paper presented at the annual meeting of the American Educational Research Association, New Orleans.

Banathy, B. (1988) 'Improvement or transformation?', *Noteworthy*. Denver, Co: McREL.

Bashi, J. and Sass, Z. (1989) 'Factors affecting stable continuation of outcomes of school improvement projects', in Creemers, B., Peters, T. and Reynolds, D. (eds) *School Effectiveness and School Improvement*. Amsterdam: Swets & Zeitlinger.

Caldwell, B. and Spinks, J. (1988) *The Self-Managing School*. Lewes: Falmer Press.

Clark, D. L., Lotto, L. S. and Astuto, T. A. (1984) 'Effective schools and school improvement: a comparative analysis of two lines of inquiry', *Educational Administration Quarterly*, **20** (3), 41–68.

Clift, P. S., Nuttall, D. L. and McCormick, R. (eds) (1987) *Studies in School Self-Evaluation*. Lewes: Falmer Press.

Coleman, J. S., Campbell, E., Hobson, C., McPartland, J., Mood, A., Weinfeld, F. and York, R. (1966) *Equality of Educational Opportunity*. Washington: National Center for Educational Statistics.

Cotton, K. (1995) *Effective School Practices: A Research Synthesis (1995 Update)*. Portland, Oregon: Northwest Regional Educational Laboratory.

Crandall, D. *et al.* (1982) *People, Policies and Practice: Examining the Chain of School Improvement* (vols. 1–10). Andover, Ma: The Network.

Edmonds, R. R. (1979) 'Effective schools for the urban poor', *Educational Leadership*, **37** (1), 15–27.

Firestone, W. A. (1991) 'Educators, researchers, and the effective schools movement', in Bliss, J. R., Firestone, W. A. and Richards, C. E. (eds), *Rethinking Effective Schools: Research and Practice*. Englewood Cliffs, NJ: Prentice Hall.

Fullan, M. G. (1985) 'Change processes and strategies at the local level', *Elementary School Journal*, **85** (3), 391–420.

Fullan, M. G. (1991) *The New Meaning of Educational Change*. New York: Teachers College Press.

Fullan, M. G., Bennett, B. and Rolheiser-Bennett, C. (1990) 'Linking classroom and school improvement', *Educational Leadership*, **47** (8), 13–19.

Fullan, M. and Hargreaves, A. (1992) *What's Worth Fighting For in Your School?* Milton Keynes: Open University Press.

Gardner, H. (1983) *Frames of Mind*. New York: Basic Books.

Goldstein, H. (1995) *Multilevel Models in Educational and Social Research*. London: Charles Griffin, 2nd edn.

Goodlad, J. I. (1984) *A Place Called School: Prospects for the Future*. New York: McGraw-Hill.

Gray, J., Jesson, D., Goldstein, H., Hedger, K. and Rasbash, J. (1995) 'The statistics of school improvement: establishing the agenda', in Gray, J. and Wilcox, B. (eds), *'Good School, Bad School': Evaluating Performance and Encouraging Improvement*. Milton Keynes: Open University Press.

Hallinger, P. and Murphy, J. (1985) 'Assessing the instructional leadership behaviour of principals', *Elementary School Journal*, **86** (2), 217–48.

Hargreaves, A. (1994) *Changing Teachers, Changing Times: Teachers' Work and Culture in the Postmodern Age*. London: Cassell.

Hargreaves, D. (1995) 'School culture, school effectiveness and school improvement', *School Effectiveness and School Improvement*, **6** (1), 23–46.

Hargreaves, D. H., Hopkins, D., Leask, M., Connolly, J. and Robinson, P. (1989) *Planning for School Development: Advice to Governors, Headteachers and Teachers*. London: DES.

Hargreaves, D. H. and Hopkins, D. (1991) *The Empowered School: The Management and Practice of Development Planning*. London: Cassell.

Holly, P. (1990) '"Catching the wave of the future": moving beyond school effectiveness by redesigning schools', *School Organisation*, **10** (2 and 3), 195–212.

Hopkins, D. (1991) 'Changing school culture through development planning', in Riddell, S. and Brown, S. (eds) *School Effectiveness Research: Its Messages for School Improvement*. Edinburgh: HMSO.

Hopkins, D. (1994) 'School improvement in an era of change', in Ribbins, P. and Burridge, E. (eds) *Improving Education*. London: Cassell.

Hopkins, D., Ainscow, M. and West, M. (1994) *School Improvement in an Era of Change*. London: Cassell.

House, E. R. (1981) 'Three perspectives on innovation', in Lehming R. and Kane, M. (eds) *Improving Schools: Using What We Know*. Beverly Hills, Ca: Sage Publications.

Huberman, A. M. and Miles, M. B. (1984) *Innovation Up Close*. New York: Plenum.

ILEA (1986) *Primary School Development Plans: A Support Booklet*. Primary Management Studies, Inner London Education Authority.

Joyce, B. R. (1991) 'The doors to school improvement', *Educational Leadership*, **48** (8), 59–62.

Levine, D. U. and Lezotte, L. W. (1990) *Unusually Effective Schools: A Review and Analysis of Research and Practice*. Madison, WI: National Center for Effective Schools Research and Development.

Lezotte, L. W. (1989) 'Base school improvement on what we know about effective schools', *Amercian School Board Journal*, **176** (8), 18–20.

Little, J. W. (1990) 'The persistence of privacy: autonomy and initiative in teachers' professional relations', *Teachers College Record*, **91** (4), 509–36.

Loucks-Horsley, S. F. and Hergert, L. F. (1985) *An Action Guide to School Improvement*. Alexandria, Va: Association for Supervision and Curriculum Development and The Network.

McGaw, B., Piper, K., Banks, D. and Evans, B. (1992) *Making Schools More Effective*. Victoria: ACER.

McMahon, A., Bolam, R., Abbott, R. and Holly, P. (1984) *Guidelines for Review and Internal Development in Schools* (Primary and Secondary School Handbooks). York: Longman/Schools Council.

McPherson, A. (1993) 'Measuring added value in schools', *The Paul Hamlyn Foundation National Commission on Education Briefings*. London: Heinemann.

Miles, M. B. and Huberman, M. (1984) *Qualitative Data Analysis*. London: Sage.

Mortimore, P. (1991a) 'The nature and findings of research on school effectiveness in the primary sector', in Riddell, S. and Brown, S. (eds) *School Effectiveness Research: Its Messages for School Improvement*. Edinburgh: HMSO.

Mortimore, P. (1991b) 'School effectiveness research: which way at the crossroads?' *School Effectiveness and School Improvement*, **2** (3), 213–29.

Mortimore, P., Sammons, P., Stoll, L., Lewis, D. and Ecob, R. (1988) *School Matters: The Junior Years*. Wells: Open Books (Reprinted in 1994 by Chapman.)

Murphy, J. (1992) 'School effectiveness and school restructuring: contributions to educational improvement', *School Effectiveness and School Improvement*, **3** (2), 90–109.

Myers, K. (1996) *School Improvement in Practice.* London: Falmer Press.

Nuttall, D. L., Goldstein, H., Prosser, R. and Rasbash, J. (1989) 'Differential school effectiveness', *International Journal of Educational Research*, **13** (7), 769–76.

Ouston, J., Maughan, B. and Rutter, M. (1991) 'Can schools change? II: practice in six London secondary schools', *School Effectiveness and School Improvement*, **2** (1), 3–13.

Plowden Committee (1967) *Children and Their Primary Schools.* London: HMSO.

Purkey, S. D. and Smith, M. S. (1983) 'Effective schools: a review', *The Elementary School Journal*, **83** (4), 427–52.

Raudenbush, S. (1989) 'The analysis of longitudinal multilevel data', *International Journal of Educational Research*, **13** (7), 721–40.

Reynolds, D. (1993) *School Effectiveness: The International Perspective*. Paper presented to ESRC Seminar Series on School Effectiveness and School Improvement, Sheffield.

Reynolds, D., Creemers, B. P. M. and Peters, T. (eds) (1989a) *School Effectiveness and Improvement: Proceedings of the First International Congress, London 1988*. Cardiff, University of Wales College of Cardiff and Groningen, RION.

Reynolds, D., Davie, R. and Phillips, D. (1989b) 'The Cardiff programme: an effective school improvement project based upon school effectiveness research', *International Journal of Educational Research*, **13** (7), 801–14.

Reynolds, D. and Packer, A. (1992) 'School effectiveness and school improvement in the 1990s' in Reynolds, D. and Cuttance, P. (eds) *School Effectiveness: Research, Policy and Practice.* London: Cassell.

Reynolds, D., Hopkins, D. and Stoll, L. (1993) 'Linking school effectiveness knowledge and school improvement practice: towards a synergy', *School Effectiveness and School Improvement*, **4** (1), 37–58.

Ribbins, P. and Burridge, E. (1994) *Improving Education: Promoting Quality in Schools*. London: Cassell.

Richards, C. E. (1991) 'The meaning and measure of school effectiveness', in Bliss, J. R., Firestone, W. A. and Richards, C. E. (eds) *Rethinking Effective Schools: Research and Practice*. Englewood Cliffs, NJ: Prentice Hall.

Rosenholtz, S. J. (1989) *Teachers' Workplace: The Social Organization of Schools*. New York: Longman.

Rutter, M., Maughan, B., Mortimore, P. and Ouston, J. (1979) *Fifteen Thousand Hours: Secondary Schools and Their Effects on Children*. London: Open Books.

Sammons, P., Thomas, S. and Mortimore, P. (1996) 'Differential School Effectiveness: departmental variations'. Paper to AERA Conference, New York.

Schereens, J. (1987) *Enhancing Educational Opportunities for Disadvantaged Learners: A Review of Dutch Research on Compensatory Education and*

Educational Development Policy. Amsterdam/Oxford/New York: North-Holland Publishing Co.

Scheerens, J. (1992) *Effective Schooling: Research, Theory and Practice*. London: Cassell.

Scheerens, J. and Creemers, B. P. M. (1989) 'Conceptualizing school effectiveness', *International Journal of Educational Research*, **13** (7), 691–706.

Sirotnik, K. A. (1987) *The School as the Center of Change (Occasional Paper No. 5)*. Seattle, Wa: Center for Educational Research.

Siskin, L. S. (1994) *Realms of Knowledge: Academic Departments in Secondary Schools*. London: Falmer Press.

Stoll, L. and Fink, D. (1992) 'Effecting school change: the Halton approach', *School Effectiveness and School Improvement*, **3** (1), 19–41.

Stoll, L. and Fink, D. (1994) 'Views from the field: linking school effectiveness and school improvement', *School Effectiveness and School Improvement*, **5** (2), 149–77.

Stoll, L. and Fink, D. (1996) *Changing Our Schools: Linking School Effectiveness and School Improvement*. Buckingham: Open University Press.

Teddlie, C. and Stringfield, S. (1985) 'A differential analysis of effectiveness in middle and lower socio-economic status schools', *Journal of Classroom Interaction*, **20** (2), 38–44.

Teddlie, C. and Stringfield, S. (1993) *Schools Make a Difference: Lessons Learned From a Ten-Year Study of School Effects*. New York: Teachers College Press.

Teddlie, C., Stringfield, S., Wimpelberg, R. and Kirby, P. (1989) 'Contextual differences in models for effective schooling in the USA', in Creemers, B. P. M., Peters, T. and Hopkins, D. (eds) *School Effectiveness and School Improvement: Proceedings of the Second International Congress, Rotterdam 1989*. Amsterdam: Swets & Zeitlinger.

van Velzen, W. (1987) 'The International School Improvement Project', in Hopkins, D. (ed.) *Improving the Quality of Schooling: Lessons from the OECD International School Improvement Project*. Lewes: Falmer Press.

van Velzen, W., Miles, M., Ekholm, M., Hameyer, U. and Robin, D. (1985) *Making School Improvement Work: A Conceptual Guide to Practice*. Leuven: Belgium, ACCO.

Wallace, M. (1991) 'Coping with multiple innovations in schools', *School Organisation*, **11** (2), 187–209.

Wallace, M. and McMahon, A. (1994) *Planning for Change in Turbulent Times: The Case of Multi-racial Primary Schools*. London: Cassell.

Chapter 4

Monitoring School Effectiveness: Simplicity and Complexity

Carol Fitz-Gibbon

INTRODUCTION

Educational research has been too ready to leap from correlation to causation, too ready to neglect, after the epidemiology, the necessary clinical trials. The hope has been that finding 'the correlates of effectiveness', i.e. features common to 'effective schools', would enable researchers to guide 'ineffective schools' towards improvement (Figure 4.1a).

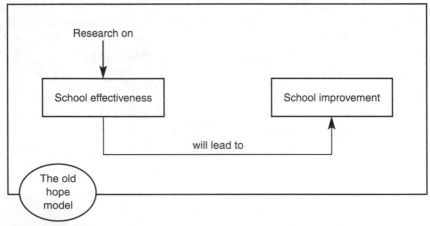

Figure 4.1a *Effectiveness focus*

But correlations only generate hypotheses which then need testing, ideally by well-designed multi-site field trials, the sort of replicated experiments which provided evidence for the effectiveness of pre-school education in highly deprived inner cities in the USA (Lazar and Darlington, 1982). Furthermore a correlate such as 'a safe and orderly environment' is of little use. There are few campaigners for unsafe and disorderly environments and the question which faces schools is how to create the safe and orderly environment. What actions are needed? This requires experimental efforts at school improvement. Indeed, it is likely that careful monitoring of school improvement efforts would be a faster route to a knowledge of effective actions than further surveys attempting to find correlates of effectiveness by comparing schools deemed effective or ineffective (Figure 4.1b). To know which actions work it is actions which must be studied.

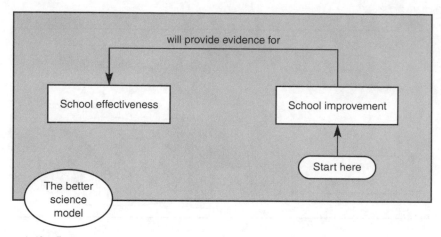

Figure 4.1b *Improvement focus*

Yet either approach – testing and validating hypotheses or collecting evidence of effective school improvement efforts – would take years of research to arrive at reliable, generalizable findings and would require a level of funding which is unlikely. Furthermore after adopting this approach of 'normal science', i.e. pursuing valid research strategies to find strong nomothetic rules, there would then follow the problems of dissemination and uptake, both of them fraught and lengthy processes. Set against this long time horizon we have to recognize a sense of urgency which is based on perceptions of serious problems in schools (particularly in the USA more so than in the UK). If children feel afraid, fail to learn, stay away from school, disrupt when they are in school, then teachers cannot wait for validated research findings to seek improvements; they cannot wait for evaluators to find the dream programme which applies to their particular patch of the educational pastiche.

Another major problem with the 'science as normal' RD&D (research, development and dissemination) approach to school effectiveness is more fundamental: there may be very few nomothetic rules or generalizable findings, very few 'laws' which are locally applicable. This is not to assert that phenomenology rules and we must all retreat into qualitative studies along with our one-legged friends, the illogical negativists. The point here is that we may be dealing with a system which is so complex as to be fundamentally unpredictable in a way which is only just beginning to be understood in science proper. If this is the case we have to rethink how to approach the vital task of school improvement.

THE EMERGING SCIENCE OF COMPLEXITY

Science itself is currently undergoing a sea change, possibly even a paradigm shift. P. C. W. Davies, the famous cosmologist and professor of physics has described the change as 'nothing less than a brand new start in the description of nature' (Davies, 1987, p. 23). In the next few paragraphs an attempt is made to trace the ideas which have led to the present mix of models and beliefs reflected in Figure 4.1c.

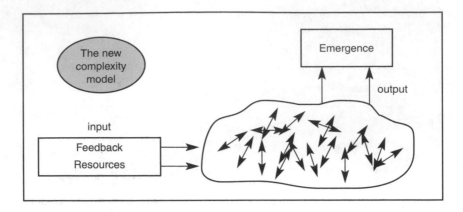

Figure 4.1c *Feedback focus*

Some Key Events

To select a few major currents from the rapid and turbulent flow of human affairs is a difficult if not distressing activity. As historians must be painfully aware, what is represented in a few pen sketches, however long, is but a fraction of what has gone before us. However, just as science looks for broad and simple outlines, which are, to some extent, only an approximation, so must anyone attempting to give a view of the years which have preceded our own.

Although 'complexity' as an area of study is a new development, there were already hints around in physics and mathematics. As long ago as 1908 Henri Poincaré wrote, 'It may happen that small differences in the initial conditions produce very great ones in the final phenomena. A small error in the former, will produce an enormous error in the latter. Prediction becomes impossible, and we have the fortuitous phenomenon' (cited in Davies, 1987, p. 53). Decades later, notions of unpredictable systems, non-linear dynamics, cellular automata, emergence, sensitivity to initial conditions and all the delights that you can enjoy by reading Waldrop's 1992 book on *Complexity: the Emerging Science at the Edge of Order and Chaos* are providing a new set of mental models for how we can approach science, the universe, and everything. How did this transformation occur?

We could divide science into two phases: the first phase could be called the discovery of simplicity, and the second the understanding of complexity. The first phase of science is well illustrated by Fourier analysis. French mathematician and physicist Jean G. Fourier, showed that highly complex signals such as are carried on the radio or emerge from outer space, although they seem formless and random, can, if they are periodic, be broken down into a series of sine waves (simple up and down waves) and all the original complexity can be reconstructed by simply combining the pure sine waves. This possibility of adding up simple parts to get complex wholes has made enormous advances in science possible. The whole as a simple sum of parts applies not only to periodic waves as proved mathematically by Fourier, but also to electric and magnetic fields, stresses and strains in many materials, heat flow, diffusion of gases and liquids, and many other phenomena (Davies, 1987, p. 94). Social scientists will recognize this 'additivity' as underpinning statistical models such as analysis of variance. Systems which can be decomposed and analysed by linear models, multilevel models or 'hierarchical linear' models are called linear; in these systems the whole is simply the sum of the parts.

The second phase of science arises with the study of non-linear systems:

> In a non-linear system a whole is much more than the sum of its parts, and it cannot be reduced or analysed in terms of simple sub-units acting together. The resulting properties can often be unexpected, complicated and mathematically intractable (Davies, 1987, p. 25).

Mathematically intractable! This seems to sound the death knell for science as normally conducted. If systems are chaotic, full of discontinuities, catastrophes, unevenness and unpredictability, science cannot construct mathematical laws that will predict the future. Mathematical modelling meets its limits. Are we then left with nothing but a complexity that we are unable to analyse? Not at all, but the tools of analysis become a kind of modelling using computers, a method which is different from the highly successful previous work in science resting on mathematical equations. Computer modelling can attempt to simulate events in a direct fashion, by rules and procedures, incorporating feedback, rather than by equations (see Tymms in this volume, chapter 6). For example, the universe (scientists are nothing if not willing to consider the big questions) is modelled by a clock ticking away, which is time, and a lattice of cells which can interact according to certain rules. The lattice defines space. Instead of the compelling logic of numbers, the compelling logic of a computer simulation is sought. If a few simple rules are implemented for the interactions of the cells in the lattice and certain patterns emerge, then there is a compelling logic that those few rules are sufficient to produce the emergent patterns. This does not mean they are necessarily the only way to produce the emergent patterns but, since they have done so once, the sufficiency is demonstrated.

These kinds of interactions are called 'cellular automata'. Chris Langton, who had become interested in computing when undertaking alternative military service in a hospital in preference to participation in the Vietnam war, did a literature search on the key words 'self-reproduction'. Von Neumann's *Theory of Self-Reproducing Automata* and a piece of work called *Cellular Automata* by Ted Codd (who had invented relational databases) caught his attention. Langton knew that, in dynamical systems, whether the outcomes were simple or chaotic was often a function of a single parameter; as the parameter increases, the outcomes pass through a chaotic phase. (This interesting behaviour of non-linear systems can be very simply demonstrated on a spreadsheet using the equation:

$$X_n = p^* x_{(n-1)} [1 - X_{(n-1)}]$$

and putting in the values $X_0 = 0.2$ and $n = 1, 2, \ldots 17$ and for successive computation series using these kinds of values for the parameter: $p = 1, 2, 2.5, 3, 3.5, 3.57, 3.7, 4$ and 5.) Langton set out to look for such a parameter in the systems of cellular automata. Eventually, he hit on a simple parameter which could be embodied in the rules for the computer program, the probability that any given cell would be alive in the next generation. Exploring values of this parameter, he found, for low values, simple frozen patterns or periodic repeating patterns. With slightly larger values there was a transition phase and then, with even larger values, there was chaos. Langton was aware of the work of a British mathematician, John Conway, who had created, on computers, a program called the *Game of Life*. It too was a 'cellular automaton' program simulating evolution. With a few simple rules the program would run and create successful species, predator species, extinctions, patterns which were pictured on the screen as coloured cells and which mimicked biological evolution. Langton recognized the *Game of Life* as being in the transition part between the frozen, periodic, ordered phase and the completely chaotic phase. It seems that life emerges, self-reproduction occurs, patterns evolve, compete, cooperate and behave in a lifelike manner *on the edge of chaos*, in a region of 'complexity'.

The ideas of the evolution of effectiveness in open interacting systems are now being applied in many fields: economics, biology, archaeology and speculations on the stock market. Perhaps we are seeing the development of newly discovered laws of nature, laws about how complex systems manage to develop effectiveness – survival, success. One message is that the systems are often *locally organized*. They are not told what to do but they do get regular feedback. Can these ideas apply to schools?

In 1979, in an article entitled 'Policy for the unpredictable', Gene Glass (1979) suggested that it might not be possible to evaluate schools or create widely applicable research findings. Education was so complex that we might simply have to be content with 'fire-fighting': having monitoring systems in place which could alert us when untoward events were happening. This was a prescient article and fits well with modern theories of complexity.

SCHOOLS AS COMPLEX SYSTEMS

Schools are nothing if not complex systems subject to feedback such as examination results and enrolment patterns. They are very likely, then, to show the kind of behaviours to be expected in complexity. Furthermore, they contain within themselves further self-organizing units such as departments and classrooms.

The *flow of information* plays a key role in any complex system. However, it is important to note that in all the writings on complex systems scientists do not seem to be considering the possibility of *disinformation as opposed to valid information*. This is quite understandable in that in the evolution of cells in response to the availability of food sources, light, other cells etc., the feedback to the cell is veridical, uncorrupted, actual. The light is there where the light intensity is greatest; the organism that is eaten provides nourishment, or if it poisons, that poison feeds back into the survival mechanism. There is little in natural systems as clearly corrupted as in human information systems; a point to which we shall return later in asking how schools as complex systems can be effective.

There is a reason why the information flow back to humans or to groups of humans in complex systems is not as accurate as that in the natural systems which have been subject to the greatest amounts of modelling and investigation. The feedback which is needed from a complex activity may be very difficult to acquire.

Take teaching as an example, the teacher gets immediate feedback from pupils about their levels of enjoyment and cooperation, and teachers generally learn class control with practice. The immediacy of the feedback and its lack of ambiguity make it useful for the teachers' learning. *But some feedback, such as how effectively they have enabled pupils to learn, is very difficult to acquire.* The pupils' final learning level can be measured, but a vital piece of information is needed if this final level is to be interpreted: what would it have been if the pupils had been taught some other way? If teachers were always assigned randomly selected, representative groups of pupils then the simple end achievement levels would be interpretable by simple comparisons between teachers. But schools are not like that. Teachers face classes which are exceedingly different from each other, even in the same subject, even, possibly, in the same school. (Vague notions of general correction factors as suggested by the politicians and the Office of Standards in Education make no sense. For example, in one inner-city school, every pupil taking A-level mathematics was highly able and from a professional home background. Schools are not homogeneous and classes within schools can vary substantially in their intake.) Only pupil-by-pupil information interpreted against a large database can sort out what kind of results should be expected from a class. In other words, without access to data on the performance of similar pupils in other schools, it is exceedingly difficult for teachers to evaluate how effective they have been. This lack of clear, unambiguous, accurate information is typical of many of our complex social systems. Until recently this has been an inevitable situation but now the growth of computing has finally made the management of very large and complex data sets economically feasible.

We are moving into an era in which information can be made available in great detail at every level of complex systems. The impact of such information needs investigating, but first the quality of the information and its availability needs to be developed. In other words, we need monitoring systems. Whether we are looking at sentencing policies for juveniles, welfare policies, reward structures for directors of companies, productivity, truancy, satisfaction levels, health or school effectiveness, extensive monitoring is needed and is indeed developing in many areas of activity.

Few would set their face against the provision of information although we get some researchers more concerned with the second decimal place than with the method of collection of the data. What I am arguing here is that the growing understanding in the hard sciences of how complex systems function emphasizes the need for the flow of feedback into the system. With new insights provided by what is coming to be called 'complexity theory', our mental models of how the world functions need some adjustment. *In short, education is a complex, adaptive system which can probably become self-improving if given better data.*

Two Illustrations of Complexity

Since the complexity of education is not strongly questioned, just two illustrations will be given. One is an artefact: a list, drawn up by just one school for one lunch-time meeting, of factors which might be affecting their examination results. More than 100 factors were listed, most of which are shown in Table 4.1. None of these factors could be ruled out as unimportant for some students in some classes.

Table 4.1   *An Artefact: part of the list discussed by a Senior Management Team*
(Figures in the margin show that more than one person suggested this factor)

'Student' Factors

Part-time jobs	11
'Unrealistic' students admitted to courses	
Unrealistic parental demands/expectations	
(Parents and pupils) lack of real understanding of what A level entails	3
Too many extra-curricular activities	2
Insufficient involvement in life of school/ community	2
Students need to know what they are aiming for	
Casual approach after easy ride to 16+	
Marital/family break-ups	
Student absence	2
Attitudes of students to school	
Drugs and alcohol	
Student responsibility	
Career/job prospects	
Instrumental approach to being a sixth-form student	
Student–teacher relationship	
Teachers' reaction to attendance & punctuality	
Social activities in sixth form	
Total demand made of students	

'Teaching/Learning' Factors

Teaching and learning strategies/range of styles (some outmoded)	3
No structured teaching of study skills (e.g. note-taking)	5
Quality of teaching	
Resources for teaching and learning (see separate list)	
Time for 1:1 discussions (teacher/student)	2
Lack of 'bridging course' induction programme	3
Inadequate concentration on *process* of learning	
Inconsistent expectations re marked written work	
Lack of exam practice/revision techniques	
Importance of homework in students' eyes	
Teaching approaches not responsive enough to needs of *all* students	
Teacher-pairs not communicating sufficiently	
Students not encouraged to read widely enough	
Student self-assessment	
Progress not reviewed often enough	
Number and use of study periods	
Lack of common deadlines within and between departments	
Teacher expectations of students	

GCSE and the Transition to A Level

Cumulative effects of GCSE on students' study habits	
GCSE as preparation for A level	3
Transition to A level is difficult	
Transition to A level needs planning	
Good GCSE grades give false confidence to students	
Relevance of GCSE teaching strategies	
Students used to coursework demands dislike courses with final exam only	
Subjects seen as 'easy' or 'difficult'	
Choosing subjects which are inappropriate	

Policy Factors

Open-entry policy	
Negotiated time out	6
Paired sharing of classes (= diminished teacher responsibility)	2
Inadequate *range* of courses	
Poor/old-fashioned syllabus – choice which ignores changes at GCSE	
Too many A levels on offer – resources too thinly stretched	
Too many A levels on offer – poor *selection* of courses	
No credible alternative for the many students who can manage only two (or even one) A level	
Inadequate resourcing of vocational courses (e.g. low staffing priority) leads to too many choosing A level inappropriately	
Homework policy?	3
Quality of information in Y11	
Quality of guidance in Y11, 12, 13	
Approach of subject choice at A level (several aspects of this noted, e.g. 'wrong' choices, inappropriate combinations, influence of teachers on subject choice)	5
Lack of academic emphasis in school development	
Perceived management indifference to exam results	

School Organization

Structure of school day since 1990	
Use of registration and tutorial time	
Assemblies	
Leave of absence: timing and *use* of	
Inadequacy of previous pastoral system: inadequate monitoring	
Inadequacy of arrangements when staff miss lessons	4

Amount or use of 'free' time
Visits/fieldwork, etc.
Ethos of school

Lack of debate on A-level teaching
Diversion of SMG attention from essentially
curricular matters

Problems
Too many interruptions to a 5-term course
Too much time wasted between June and
September
We have given too much football during lesson
time
Staff turnover   2
Retirements, resignations, illnesses, maternity
leave
Total sustained demands on staff time and
energy in non-academic directions
Instability: many changes since 1988
Complacency: our results seemed OK
General teacher demoralization
Diversion of teachers'/departments'/school's
energy towards   2
• GCSE
• National Curriculum
• LMS
• Pastoral reorganization
• Appraisal
• Parent's Charter
• etc., etc.

Questions
Is our 'performance' as implied by national
statistics distorted by the proportion of those
statistics which emanate from:
• independent sector (massively better
resourced)?
• sixth-form college sector: not distracted by
KS3 and KS4 planning?
Are we losing more quality sixth-form students:
• from the state education altogether?
• to neighbouring schools/colleges?

Resources and Facilities
Teaching environment   2
Availability (or not) of study areas especially
silent areas and supervised areas   6
General decline in funding for teaching
materials – inadequate resourcing   3
Books get (and look) older
Poor, largely book-based, study facilities
(library stock; IT resources and facilities)   2

The second illustration of this assertion of the complexity of the system with which we are dealing is due to Ibrahim (1992) and based on data from the A-Level Information System (ALIS), supported by many hours of classroom observation and interviews with teachers and pupils. In Figure 4.2, the Y-axis represents residuals (what is left over after we have taken account of the best single predictor of achievement at A level – the average achievement score two years earlier). Positive residuals indicate performance above that which would be expected on the basis of prior achievement, negative residuals represent achievement below what would be expected on the basis of the prior-achievement measure. Ibrahim divided the sample into high and low ability according to their scores on the International Test of Developed Abilities (Ottobre and Turnbull, 1987). As can be seen from the graph, the amount of individual help given by the teacher was associated with quite different outcomes, according to the ability category of the pupils. More able pupils appeared to do better when not receiving individual help, and less able pupils seemed to need an extensive amount of individual help to achieve at a level consistent with their prior achievement. Interestingly, in discussion, a number of able pupils stated explicitly that, in mathematics, if they could work it out, they liked to work it out for themselves rather than seek help from the teacher because that way they understood it better and remembered it better (Ibrahim, 1992, p. 298). This is correlational data so the direction of cause (if cause there is) cannot be assumed from the data. It serves to illustrate, however, that teaching is directed at individuals and different individuals may need different styles of teaching. Furthermore each action will have consequences and reactions. Giving help

81

Apparent effects of help from the teacher: mathematics A-level

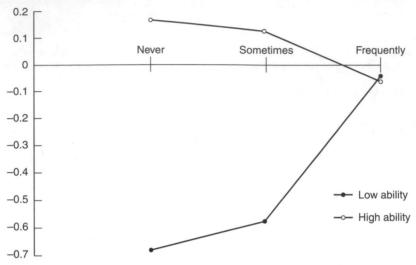

Figure 4.2 *Residuals associated with various amounts of help from the teacher (after Ibrahim, 1992)*

contains the message that help is needed – a message of incompetence. Help can be harmful. Whether or not it is may depend upon many subtle factors of interpretation, style of help, personalities. Here, in Ibrahim's work, we see the effect of help *apparently* dependent upon the ability of the student.

In summary, even if we confine our attention to just one simple, central outcome of education, namely pupils' cognitive achievement, the numerous factors affecting this outcome, and the contingencies in patterns of interactions, are possibly so locally determined as to be *un*amenable to much in the way of general rules which say 'this is good practice'. The specification of good practice may be as difficult to catch hold of as the end of the rainbow.

It is not just the presence of many factors which makes the discovery of rules for action unlikely. If the factors acted consistently, in a linear, additive fashion, and could all be measured, the mathematical modelling and the normal procedures for establishing 'research has shown'-type findings could yield results. We might manage to 'explain' more variance simply by measuring more factors. It is the feedback loops (the non-linearity) in the system which make for predictable unpredictability.

COMPLEXITY – HOW DO WE RESPOND?

How then, if we cannot pursue research as normal and locate the principles of good practice and pass on these rules to teachers, can we improve the complex system of education?

The question that we must ask in pursuit of school improvement is how do complex adaptive systems become most effective? Not an easy question, but it is the essential question at the heart of trying to influence a social system as complex as education. To answer this question requires that we return to the sea changes taking place in science and social science disciplines, driven forward by the fascination with computers as a tool for the simulation of complex information processing.

Perhaps the first thing to learn is to think in terms of systems rather than picking out pieces of a system. To think in terms of getting the whole system to work, not all at once, not in some distant future when we finally understand some fundamental laws. What can we do now, for the entire educational system, to improve its effectiveness?

Emergence

One relevant construct is that of emergence – the emergence of complexity and order. Many of the studies in complexity have been concerned with the nature of life, its characteristics and its emergence. The work is getting very close to explanations as to how disordered systems can become self-organizing in local areas, using local laws with feedback, selection, adaptation, conflict and cooperation. The emergence of organization when there are simple local laws is a highly important concept for it suggests that complex systems *are* locally organized and perhaps *have to be* locally organized, with their sub-units making independent decisions, not governed by some Great Plan from higher in the system. What do these ideas suggest about management? The ideas seem to fit well with LMS – the local management of schools which has devolved large proportions of LEA budgets to schools. Whatever the problems, there is a widely held impression that local management has been strongly welcomed, at least by secondary schools and colleges. Classrooms have always enjoyed a good deal of independence – a situation sometimes bemoaned by management but, it would seem from complexity theories, highly important.

The Flow of Information

What, then *is* the role of management? As Davies (1987) says, complex systems are 'describable by a web of informational interactions' (p. 159). If schools evolve like organisms they do so in response to information about their students, their potential students, external requirements and internal information about resources, human and material. Self-organizing units can only respond effectively if they have the necessary information. Management must provide the information infrastructure which enables local problem-solving to be effective.

What if disinformation is introduced? Presumably this can distract attention and effort from more valid information which could have led to more useful activities. If inspectors, for example, declare that teachers' expectations are too low, what are teachers to do about this? Feel bad? Does this help? After 25 years of developing this deeply flawed research (Elashoff and Snow, 1971) we are no wiser as to its implications for action and recent work continues to cast doubt on its validity (Goldenberg, 1992; Raudenbush, 1984).

If inspectors demand written development plans (in this unpredictable world) does this lead to endless hours of writing and discussion? Is there any evidence that written development plans are beneficial for any activity other than satisfying inspectors? These issues need evidence. Inspection itself, and the efforts schools put into responding to inspection, represent enormous amounts of time and effort diverted from teaching. Were this misdirected it would have a negative cost–benefit ratio. One task of management for improvement is to remove or discount poor information.

Prediction and Feedback

> An adaptive agent is constantly playing a game with its environment.
> ... What actually has to happen to game-playing agents to survive
> and prosper? Two things ... prediction and feedback (Holland,
> quoted by Waldrop, 1992, p. 282).

In order to make effective decisions for school improvement we need values (to know in which directions we wish to move) and information. To thrive on the edge of chaos, the system needs the capacity to act in multiple self-organizing, adequately informed, local units, i.e. the capacity to act on the basis of feedback. (Indeed the Hawthorne Effect has been reanalysed to show it to have been largely due to feedback (Parsons, 1974).)

Monitoring systems enable schools to make accurate predictions where these are possible and provide a constant flow of feedback. Thus monitoring systems fit in with the model of a school as an evolving complex system.

SIMPLICITY – THE NEED TO KNOW THE MAJOR PATTERNS IN DATA

Although it has been argued above that the educational enterprise is exceedingly complex it can also be shown that stable features can be derived from monitoring data. Just as the *weather* is variable and unpredictable – a frequently cited example of a non-linear, open system, determined by the laws of physics but essentially unpredictable – and yet the *climate* is a fairly reliable guide to the range of weather to be expected, so there are broad features in the system which adequate monitoring can clarify and, by so doing, can inform the interpretation of data and the feedback into the system.

The major point which needs emphasis, and which it is the intention in this section to illustrate, is the extent to which *mistakes can be made if the broad features which pertain throughout a system are not known and/or are not taken into account*. In other words there will be variations in outcomes which are seen throughout the system ('noise') and there will be some stable broad features. Four examples will be drawn from the ALIS monitoring system.

Are some teachers to blame for inaccurate predictions? David Elsom, a former college vice-principal, draws on his experience to portray a scenario which he has frequently encountered: complaints against the English department for being unable to predict accurately their pupils' A-level grades. Anyone thinking to blame individual English department staff needs to recognize that the prediction of grades in English is a problem throughout the system and may have more to do with the nature of the A-level English examination, and its lack of discrimination, than with the competence or otherwise of individual A-level English teachers. Appeals against grades are more frequent in English than in other subjects.

This is an important illustration of two principles: that the broad features of the system must be known before individuals are judged and that the competencies of teachers can only be considered in comparison with similar teachers *teaching the same subject* to similar pupils.

Subject differences are substantial and should not be neglected. Indeed *school effectiveness may need to be reconceptualized, if not for every subject then certainly for broad bands of subjects such as the foreign languages, the sciences, mathematics, the humanities, practical or vocational subjects. What applies in one curriculum area may not apply in another.*

Can examination results be fairly contextualized by SES data? Rarely is socio-economic status a good predictor of achievement in the UK – which is perhaps a tribute to the UK system of education. SES is not the most important covariate so that comparisons which rely on SES comparisons will be less fair than comparisons of pupils' achievements based on cognitive measures. In general SES may explain about 9 per cent of the variance whereas any prior achievement measure would generally explain about four times as much. Furthermore, within schools the composition of classes varies from year to year and this variation will itself vary from school to school depending perhaps on the 'pulling power' of various departments (Fitz-Gibbon, 1984). If one inner-city French department had recruited all the highly able students it would be an error to adjust its results for the average SES of the school, or even the average achievement level of the school.

Are A-level subjects 'level' in difficulty? Rhodes Robson is an accountancy firm. It has written to schools offering to work out residuals for A-level subjects. How does it compute the predicted/expected grade for a student? By assuming that all subjects are equally difficult at A level and therefore if your student has 24 UCAS points the 'predicted' grade in each of three subjects can be taken as 24/3 or 8. The fact is that A-level subjects differ in difficulty on any reasonable definition (Fitz-Gibbon, 1988). Consequently the approach suggested will lead to unfair chastisement of teachers teaching difficult A levels: maths, sciences and foreign languages. Do trading standards apply in social science?

Table 4.2 shows subjects rank ordered according to their intercept as calculated using ordinary least squares (OLS) regression. We see physics as having the lowest intercept. It appears to have been, that year, the most difficult subject and history was at the other end of the rank order appearing to have been the easiest subject in the 1989 sample. A second method of calculating difficulty (Kelly–Lawley adjustments) gave similar results (Kelly, 1976; Fitz-Gibbon, 1991).

Table 4.2 *The relative difficulty of the 1989 A-level examinations*

Subject	Intercept from OLS regression[1]	Difficulty rank OLS	Difficulty rank Lawley[2]	Lawley correction factors	N
Physics	−9.8	1	1	0.58	867
French	−8.5	2	5	0.12	371
Chemistry	−8.0	3	4	0.28	853
Maths	−7.4	4	3	0.31	1,357
General Studies	−7.4	5	2	0.36	1,087
Biology	−6.7	6	9	−0.54	667
Geography	−6.0	7	8	−0.66	630
Economics	−5.7	8	7	−0.18	606
English	−4.6	9	10	−0.75	831
History	−4.1	10	6	−0.15	674

[1] Based on 1989 ALIS data.
[2] Based on the subset of candidates taking 2 or more subjects.

There is no excuse for the use of untenable assumptions demonstrated by the accountancy firm. The differences illustrated here have been a consistent feature of the data for years and apply to Scotland's Highers as well as to English/Welsh A levels. If these differences in difficulty are not (a) recognized and (b) monitored accurately from year to year then unfair comparisons are likely to be made in schools and colleges trying to assess the performance of departments by means of comparing the grades pupils achieve in one subject as compared with another. Such errors can demoralize teachers or even, in a harsher world, cost them their jobs.

Are departments differentially effective to a substantive degree? Note that the question posed above is not 'Are departments differentially effective to a *statistically significant* degree?' The sizes of differences which are important to schools cannot be determined *a priori* by reference to levels of statistical significance habitually employed in other studies, but will come to be understood over the years as people work with the data. Statisticians should not mindlessly adopt significance testing in novel situations without justifying their weighting of Type I and Type II errors. (A touching faith in the 0.05 level is not science but habit.)

We can use regression lines to look at differences in effectiveness and try to get some handle on the *substantive* difference that effective and ineffective departments make to A-level grades. Departments can be rank ordered on the average residual obtained by the pupils on the examination in a particular subject, for example, biology. If we select, from this rank-ordered league table of average residuals, the top quarter and the bottom quarter and plot the regression lines, we get the graph shown in Figure 4.3. There appears to be a difference of more than one and a half grades across the range of GCSE scores. Thus, for a given average GCSE score, those pupils who were in departments in the top quarter

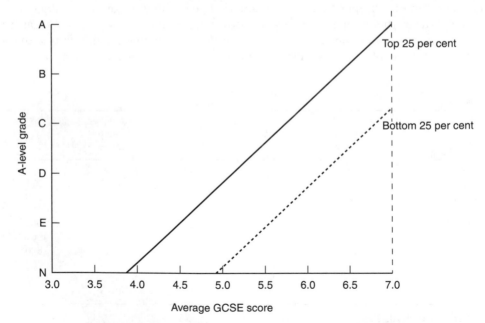

Figure 4.3 *Biology 1992: regression lines for top and bottom 25 per cent of institutions in ALIS*

generally obtained substantially better grades in biology than pupils of similar prior achievement in departments in the bottom quarter. What are we to make of these differences? Are they just noise or can they be altered? Only repeated efforts to alter the residuals will inform us as to whether they are alterable or just noise or features of particular student bodies, or schools, in ways that we have not measured. In other words, we can only establish what is or is not alterable by monitoring the outcomes of attempts at alteration, preferably in the framework of an experimental design (Campbell and Stanley, 1966). As Willms (1992) has pointed out, experimentation is greatly facilitated by being set up in the framework of a monitoring system.

SUMMARY AND PROPOSALS

We argue frequently by metaphor and with underlying mental models. I have tried to give some flavour of the sea change taking place in science as physicists, mathematicians and those who can follow in their footsteps tackle not the simple, predictable systems of stars and galaxies (not so simple and not always predictable), but complex systems of economies, living organisms and the complexities of organizations. One can certainly draw the conclusion from much recent work on complexity that the number of connections in a system (who talks to whom, where information flows, how many people receive the information, the amount and quality of information) have to be crucial variables in the functioning of any system, and are probably the variables which should be manipulated in order to improve the functioning of the system, although in what direction and by how much will be a matter of trial-and-error learning. These are not answers we can dream up; we have to run the programs and see what happens.

As already noted, current writing on complex systems seems to pay no attention to the effects of feedback which is false. I would like to suggest the hypothesis that an important way to improve education is to *increase the amount of valid feedback and to decrease the amount of misleading feedback; increase fair comparisons and decrease disinformation such as the overinterpreted generalizations and opinions offered by inspection and the disinformation of inadequate models, illustrated by the offer from an accountancy firm.*

The validity of the judgements made by inspectors has been called into question many times (Bennett, 1978; Gray and Hannon, 1986; Fitz-Gibbon, 1994) yet it appears that the system which has operated for more than 100 years has made no effort to have independent checks made on its reliability or validity, let alone value for money.

In this chapter an attempt has been made to show that monitoring in a complex system like post-16 education can draw attention to some broad, simplifying features in the data and that lack of knowledge of these features can leave people open to unjust criticisms and can mislead people into trying to take actions on the basis of inadequate information. Misinformation can cause pain and can distract the system from working towards the outcomes it values.

The setting up of systems of *monitoring with feedback* is the most vital task of the next decade – and we have only just begun. Whilst we must increase the amount and quality of feedback, all the while monitoring the effect of feedback – monitoring the monitoring – we also need to be concerned to eliminate from the system false feedback, misinformation, distraction from the critical task of focusing on outcomes.

The questions, then, are:

- What are the outcomes of concern? What do we value enough to measure? What kind of feedback is required? Which variables? How measured? And how frequently measured? And which covariates are needed to make fair comparisons? (i.e. what predicts the outcomes of concern?).

- How should feedback be provided? What level of aggregation should be used? What degree of confidentiality must be provided at every level of the system? (i.e. who gets to know what?) What kind of feedback is understood with or without additional training?

- Are there process variables which relate to the outcomes of concern? i.e. are there 'alterable variables', things people might choose to do which might make a difference and should therefore be monitored? Can these be measured without raising false hopes of easy answers or risking widespread misinterpretation of correlation as causation?

Thus may we improve the flow of valid information into the system and integrate the old-style search for simplicity with the newly developing mental models of complex systems. We can set up monitoring systems which have a role in exposing both the complexity of the system and its simplicity.

Note

1. The A-Level Information System, the ALIS project, has been based on collaboration between researchers (previously at Newcastle University and now at Durham) and schools and colleges, supported in many instances by local education authorities and training and enterprise councils. Data are collected relating to:

- pupils' achievement in examinations at age 16 (General Certificate of Secondary Education (GCSE)) and at age 18 (A levels);
- pupils' attitudes to each subject studied for the examinations at age 18;
- pupils' attitudes to their school or college and the facilities and resources provided;
- pupils' aspirations for further education;
- pupils' participation in extramural activities (as a 'quality of life' indicator);
- demographic factors;
- process data in the form of classroom teaching and learning activities, and school organizational factors.

The data are specially collected, by representatives of the university directly from pupils, schools and colleges. Reports are prepared for each A-level subject department and fed back promptly to each department.

REFERENCES

Bennett, N. (1978) 'Surveyed from a shaky base', *The Times Educational Supplement*.

Campbell, D. T. and Stanley, J. C. (1966) *Experimental and Quasi-Experimental Designs for Research*. Chicago: Rand McNally.

Davies, P. C. W. (1987) *The Cosmic Blueprint*. London: Heinemann.

Elashoff, J. D. and Snow, R. E. (1971) *Pygmalion Reconsidered*. New York: Wadsworth.

Fitz-Gibbon, C. T. (1984) *Report to Schools: Confidential Measurement-Based, Self-Evaluation*. Newcastle upon Tyne: School of Education.

Fitz-Gibbon, C. T. (1988) 'Recalculating the standard', *The Times Educational Supplement*, **15**, 26 August.

Fitz-Gibbon, C. T. (1991) *Evaluation of school perfomance in public examinations: a report for the Scottish Office Education Department*. Newcastle upon Tyne: Curriculum, Evaluation and Management Centre.

Fitz-Gibbon, C. T. (1994) *Ofsted, Schmofsted*. Newcastle upon Tyne: Curriculum, Evaluation and Management Centre.

Glass, G. V. (1979) 'Policy for the unpredictable (uncertainty research and policy)', *Educational Researcher*, **8** (9), 12–14.

Goldenberg, C. (1992) 'The limits of expectations: a case for case knowledge about teacher expectancy effects', *American Educational Research Journal*, **229** (3), 517–44.

Gray, J. and Hannon, V. (1986) 'HMI interpretation of schools' examination results', *Journal of Educational Policy*, **1** (1), 23–33.

Ibrahim, A. bin (1992) *The A-Level Examination: Qualitative and Quantitative Data in the context of a Performance Monitoring System*. Ph.D. Thesis, University of Newcastle upon Tyne.

Kelly, A. (1976) 'A study of the comparability of external examinations in different subjects', *Research in Education*, (16), 50–63.

Lazar, I. and Darlington, R. (1982) *Monographs of the Society for Research in Child Development: Lasting Effects of Early Education*. Chicago: University of Chicago Press.

Ottobre, F. M. and Turnbull, W. W. (1987) *The International Test for Developed Abilities: A report on the feasibility study*. Princeton, NJ: Report for the International Association for Educational Assessment.

Parsons, H. M. (1974) 'What happened at Hawthorne', *Science* (183), 922–32.

Raudenbush, S. (1984) 'Magnitude of teacher expectancy effects on pupil IQ as a function of the credibility of the expectancy induction: a synthesis of findings from 18 experiments', *Journal of Educational Psychology*, **76** (1), 85–97.

Tymms, P. B. (1994) *Theories, Models and Simulation: School Effectiveness at an Impasse*. Paper presented at the ESRC Seminar Series (see Chapter 6).

Waldrop, M. M. (1992) *Complexity: The Emerging Science at the Edge of Order and Chaos*. London: Viking.

Willms, J. D. (1992) *Monitoring School Performance: A Guide for Educators*. Lewes: Falmer Press.

Part 2

Some Recent Evidence from the Field

Chapter 5

Possibilities and Problems of Small-Scale Studies to Unpack the Findings of Large-Scale Studies of School Effectiveness

Sally Brown, Sheila Riddell and Jill Duffield

INTRODUCTION

The purpose of this chapter is to explore the question of whether traditional forms of school effectiveness research should and can be complemented by a different kind of research (illustrated with reference to a study funded by the Economic and Social Research Council) if it is to play a major and efficient part in bringing about school improvement. This complementary approach is much more detailed (case-study work) than is commonly found in school effectiveness studies, but unlike school improvement initiatives it does not set out to intervene. Its aim is to understand what is going on in schools, especially from the perspectives of the participants themselves and it draws on ethnographic and phenomenological approaches.

There are three facets to the argument for the complementary approach. The first arises from the 'gap' between the outcomes of school effectiveness studies and the limited (and *ad hoc*) use that is made of these outcomes by school improvers. Secondly, there are findings from the research that identify crucial aspects of effective schooling that cannot be given appropriate attention by the 'tweaking' of traditional large-scale school effectiveness methods. And thirdly, there are common and powerful arguments identifying the 'missing link' between effectiveness and improvement with the need for theories (including those of 'change') in an area which has not been characterized by a strong theoretical element. 'Change' covers, of course, both upturns and downturns in the affairs of schools.

THE GAP BETWEEN SCHOOL EFFECTIVENESS AND SCHOOL IMPROVEMENT STUDIES

A cliché of today is the expression of surprise that there have been only tenuous links between, on the one hand, large-scale school effectiveness research and, on the other hand, the extensive movements for school improvement. If it is assumed that ultimately the credibility and value of school effectiveness studies must be judged by the contribution they make to the improvement of education, and that school improvers in their pursuit of change for the better have to take advantage of any potentially relevant knowledge that is available, then the frailty of the links between the two traditions assumes importance. Integration of two paradigms with quite different methodological and philosophical underpinning, however, faces a variety of barriers (Reynolds *et al.*, 1993; Gray *et al.*, 1993).

School effectiveness research has largely been inclined to a quantitative, correlational survey approach, for the most part within a positivist tradition: 'a search for ways – both adequate and reliable – to measure the quality of the school' (Mortimore, 1991a). It has concentrated on descriptions of differences between schools and of effective schools using criteria of student achievements. Indeed, it has been criticized (not always with justification) for its choice of criterion measures which are regarded as narrow, focusing heavily on tests of basic skills and examination grades and neglecting what might broadly be called the social and affective outcomes that often are given high priority in schools' thinking about what they are trying to do. This has formed part of the debate, central to school effectiveness studies, about how effectiveness is conceptualized, in what sense schools are to be deemed more or less effective and how specific features of schools relate to chosen measures of effectiveness. Whatever the criteria used for effectiveness, however, a connection with the dynamic of how schools work is necessary if a causal link is to be established that enables us to understand how schools are to achieve effectiveness and avoid deterioration.

School improvers have had different priorities. Their primary concern has been to identify and implement strategies and processes that lead to improvement in schooling and to the maintenance of such improvement. Their stance has been one of *development* (including a large measure of self-evaluation for schools). Qualitative data have been their mainstay, and a heavy emphasis has been placed on *process* measures rather than achievement outcomes; more recently, however, outcome measures as evidence of improvement have become more central (e.g. Hargreaves and Hopkins, 1991; Louis and Miles, 1991; Fullan and Hargreaves, 1992). The focus has not been on *general* explanations of why things work the way they do but rather on understanding the *specific* processes of change that lead to greater success in the particular schools in which they work; any generalizations developed along the way are a bonus.

There is no lack of enthusiasm for a coming together of effectiveness and improvement research. In the UK the Economic and Social Research Council has funded a seminar series to address this question and participants have identified an 'intellectually and practically unhealthy separation between the effectiveness and improvement communities' (Reynolds, 1993) and regretted 'the reticence to join forces' (Stoll, 1993). Certainly, in principle, school effectiveness researchers are keen that their findings should be implemented into educational practice, have made considerable efforts (in the UK at least) to bring those findings to the attention of policy-makers and seek to extricate causal relationships from the wider population of their correlational findings so they can offer generalizations of substance to those who endeavour to improve schools. There are, however, as Gray *et al.* (1993) point out, considerable difficulties and conflicting pressures in moving from research which sets out to identify and characterize the effective school (the 'one in which pupils progress further than might be expected from consideration of its intake', Mortimore, 1991b) to action where the primary aim is to improve schools (which may include those currently regarded as very ineffective). Differences in the paradigms are not simply matters of academic interest, they influence the information at one's disposal and the use that can be made of it.

> The research design that is required to study school improvement from a school effectiveness perspective is quite difficult and time-consuming to construct and implement ... [It bears] out the old adage that the data one has tends to structure the way one sees the problems, and the way one sees the problems tends to structure the data one attempts to collect (Gray *et al.*, 1993, p. 3).

Suggestions (e.g. Stoll, 1993) about ways in which the two traditions could establish more effective collaboration include:

1. For school improvers:
   (i) the testing of hypotheses established in school effectiveness research about factors influencing effectiveness;
   (ii) attention in planning to variables (e.g. characteristics of groups of students) that school effectiveness research has shown are related to differential effects.
2. For school effectiveness researchers:
   (i) the development of instruments to assess schools on a wider range of effectiveness criteria reflecting schools' own priorities;
   (ii) the focus of attention to be not just on the most effective schools but also other categories such as ineffective schools that are improving;
   (iii) the identification of variables that relate to schools' culture.

In practice, a smooth integration is difficult to achieve. Major school improvement programmes, like the Effective Schools' Project in the Halton Board of Education in Ontario, Canada are founded on a belief that staff involvement and commitment on a wide scale in the school is essential. Once ownership and the responsibility for decision-making is genuinely in the hands of teachers, the handing down of an agenda from 'on-high', based on outsiders' findings of school effectiveness (and not addressing the *process* of change), is unlikely to be enthusiastically received. Such an agenda could be used, of course, as one of several sets of data to stimulate discussion, and we are not suggesting that school effectiveness findings can have no influence; but to realize the full potential of that influence there needs to be a bridge of greater substance and more detailed understanding between the broad findings and the crux of school improvement, i.e. what actually goes on in classrooms, how this affects different groups within the student population and the factors which impinge on these activities. Even if it is accepted that there are powerful arguments for drawing school improvers' attention to the findings of key correlates with school effectiveness, there is also substantial scepticism about the plausible assumption that in order to improve less effective schools must do more of, or have more of, the features which seem to characterize more effective schools. In circumstances where most school effectiveness literature (with the possible exception of Teddlie and Stringfield, 1993) has concentrated on identification of the characteristics of more effective schools, there are convincing arguments for attention to be given to the study of less effective schools, and more particularly to categories which bring together the two traditions such as ineffective schools that are improving or effective schools that are deteriorating (Gray *et al.*, 1993; Stoll, 1993). We have to ask:

> Are different strategies required for low-achieving schools to raise their scores than for high-achieving schools that are beginning to decline? Once a school is deemed academically effective what is needed to maintain its success? And do different improvement strategies affect sub-populations in a school? (Purkey and Smith, 1983, p. 447).

IN-DEPTH STUDIES TO EXTEND UNDERSTANDING OF BROAD FINDINGS

If school effectiveness research is to be extended by in-depth case studies of individual schools, the cases have to be selected on the basis of their effectiveness characteristics, e.g. as the most or least effective 'outlier' schools and/or as institutions that are improving or declining in effectiveness. However the choice is made, the matter of stability is important; an unstable pattern of effectiveness among schools could be seen as either an asset or a problem, depending on the research question to be addressed.

Scheerens (1992) concluded that effectiveness appears to be a fairly permanent school characteristic and Gray *et al.* (1993) added to this that ineffectiveness must be a fairly permanent school characteristic as well. From their brief review, Gray and his colleagues came to the following summary statement: 'All the British studies on the compulsory stages of secondary schooling report reasonable to high levels of stability from year-to-year' (p. 9). That is, of course, bad news for British school improvers who have to have faith that the factors contributing to effectiveness are *not* permanent, are within the power of the school to control and can be changed to effect improvement. This belief is shared by many others, including school effectiveness researchers.

Other findings, especially those from current work in London, have suggested less stability in schools' effects from year to year. While such findings may be explained by local conditions or other idiosyncratic factors, it is clearly important to heed the warnings of Nuttall *et al.* (1989) and to treat with caution measures that are made in just a single year or with a single cohort of students. As time goes on it seems likely that long-time series studies will refine our knowledge of stability and so provide more precise information and, for school improvers at least, create more optimism. What they will not do is contribute in a substantial way to our understanding of what is going on inside schools (especially in classrooms) that results in the observed stability or the improvement/deterioration. Nor will they tell us anything about how the actors (especially teachers) construe what is going on, and that is the kind of detailed knowledge we need if we are to theorize about how change for the better can be accomplished.

In our view, to attain such understanding it would be necessary that such studies display three important characteristics. First, the task for the researchers is to develop understanding but not to carry the additional load of having to instigate change. This work is distinguished, therefore, from school improvement. The school improver's main responsibility is to change things (somehow, anyhow) and while understanding is also essential, it is not the only goal.

Secondly, an important finding from work by Tymms and Fitz-Gibbon at Newcastle University (e.g. Fitz-Gibbon, 1991) and other recent large-scale work is that a substantial proportion of the variation in effectiveness among schools is due to variation among classrooms or departments within schools (Creemers, 1992; Scheerens, 1992). This implies that case-study work should concentrate on classrooms as much as on schools. Furthermore, studies in Scotland (Raudenbush, 1989; Willms and Raudenbush, 1989), the Netherlands (Luyten, 1994) and Newcastle (Fitz-Gibbon, 1991), together with preliminary findings in London (Thomas *et al.*, 1994), support the conclusion that effectiveness measures for particular subject areas are less stable than those for overall school performance.

Thirdly, in so far as the direction of effort towards classrooms acknowledges that the crux of the effectiveness of schools is ultimately to do with the quality of teaching and the ways in which students respond, priority has to be given to extending knowledge of the kind that school improvers have to take account of if they are to help bring about change in classrooms. Elsewhere (Brown and McIntyre, 1993, pp. 15–16) it has been argued that because in any innovation it is necessary to start from where teachers are, the emphasis has to be an exploration of how teachers construe their own teaching, their students and what they are trying to achieve. Observations of classrooms have to be guided by the ways in which the classroom actors make sense of what is going on – an approach which some refer to as empirical phenomenology (Cooper, 1993) and which is different from the survey/evaluative and developmental/action–research stances of the school effectiveness and improvement traditions. It is not enough, for example, to say that qualitative methods will be used to complement the quantitative measures in school effectiveness work. We are aware of several current school effectiveness research teams who are extending their work to include the collection of qualitative data in a subset of their samples of schools and classrooms. The framework within which these data are collected, however, is for the most part that of the *researchers'* constructs and is based on earlier findings of school effectiveness studies. Such findings reflect earlier researchers' hunches about the variables that might be important; they tell us nothing about how the actors in the school or classroom make sense of their educational world. If it is explanations of effectiveness and strategies for improvement that are sought, then we have to attend to the variables that are most salient for the actors and that involves much more open-ended approaches than many of the semi-structured interviews that are used to extend the quantitative paradigm.

An introduction of this kind of case-study work in classrooms and schools might have the added benefit of being able to unpack some of the intriguing questions from thin or inconsistent school effectiveness findings about whether the effects are consistent across gender, ethnic background and different levels of achievement. It could also explore the nature of leadership of the school (and department?), which appears to be important in some countries but not others.

A CONTRIBUTION TO THEORY

Criticisms of the theoretical underpinning of school effectiveness work are not uncommon. Angus (1993), for example, refers to 'a pragmatic and largely unreflective concern with identifying correlations between various school-level factors and narrowly defined (and measured) student outcomes' (p. 333). He goes on to identify:

> a growing concern within the field about the general absence of analysis or theoretical development. When theory is mentioned at all, it is generally in terms of a positivist notion of incremental, empirical theory building which, consistent with the functionalist perspective of school effectiveness work, is directed at discovering 'what works' (p. 335).

Cheap jibes at positivists should not be allowed to overshadow an important general point about the weakness of the theoretical base of the field. David Reynolds (1993), in looking at the need for the development of an international perspective, has argued that

> variation in 'what works' is likely to generate a need for more sensitive theoretical explanations than those at present on offer. Indeed, the present-day situation within school effectiveness displays an absence of theoretical explanations of even a middle-range variety, except for the clearly behaviourist approaches that influenced Rutter *et al.* (1979) and Mortimore *et al.* (1988), or the symbolic interactionist perspective that influenced the work of Reynolds and colleagues working from within a more sociological paradigm (e.g. Reynolds *et al.*, 1987) (p. 4).

Some attention has been given to modelling school effectiveness (e.g. apart from statistical modelling, see Edmonds, 1979; Scheerens, 1992; Teddlie and Stringfield, 1993), and school improvers display 'a preference for frameworks, processes and guidelines' (Stoll, 1993). There is, nevertheless, little theory emanating from this large mass of work which directly and effectively addresses the questions of how and why things work the way they do in schools, what alternatives there are for action for change and the implications of choosing among those alternatives.

Hargreaves (1993) has argued that 'models and theories of change are an essential link between school effectiveness and school improvement'. He examines the concept of 'school cultures' as a contribution to better theory and understanding of the processes involved, explores functions and typologies of such cultures and illustrates the ways in which his models might contribute to the development of theory in the fields of school effectiveness and school improvement. At least for the former field, and probably also links between the two, small-scale, in-depth, non-interventionist studies would be essential to test out the kinds of hypotheses he offers.

It could be argued that the lack of a sophisticated theoretical base for school effectiveness work is the result of researchers, encouraged by policy-makers, regarding the investigation of 'how things are on the ground' as a necessary prerequisite for the formulation of theory which subsequently would be tested. That looks like an argument for theory that is grounded in practice, but the actual approach taken by researchers appears to be rather different. As an example, let us look at the International School Effectiveness Programme (ISERP). The outline (undated) of that programme takes up the arguments for an international perspective (Reynolds *et al.*, 1994, p. 185) which cite opportunities for generating and testing theories by looking 'at the ways in which school and classroom factors travel cross culturally to a very varied degree'. In an initial pilot study of 'outlier' schools in several countries, ISERP makes use of 'a plethora of models, ranging from Stringfield's QAIT model of elementary school effects, to Creemer's model of school and classroom processes ... and to Scheeren's model of school and instructional processes' (ISERP, undated, p. 10).

The *testing* of these models, ISERP argues, is possible only at the instructional level; at school and school/class interface levels, model *generation* will characterize the theoretical activity. In reporting preliminary findings (Annual Conference of the British Educational Research Association, Oxford, September 1994), Creemers indicated that at the instructional level in mathematics quite different patterns of effects of teachers' approaches to their teaching were apparent in different countries. In our view, that is unsurprising and the problem lies with the kind of theory that is being tested. That theory is not grounded in practice, it is grounded in researchers' (and often policy-makers') ideas about what factors are most important in determining effectiveness. That set of factors has been refined by a series of large-scale studies and discussions among researchers from different countries about the centrality of different variables. There is no evidence, however, that these are the most salient variables for those who are in the schools and classrooms and have responsibility for making the schools effective. It is *their* implicit theories, however misguided they may seem to researcher or policy-maker, that will provide the basis for understanding why things turn out the way they do. The dramatically different educational cultures in different countries make it very unlikely that a common theoretical framework grounded in researchers' thinking (mostly from western Europe and North America) can validly be put to the test. Even within one country, there may be profound cultural differences among schools or classrooms that limit the applicability of generalized school effectiveness theories to strategies for improvement.

DESIGNING A SMALL-SCALE, IN-DEPTH RESEARCH PROJECT

The arguments we have put forward for the importance of complementing school effectiveness research by small-scale studies are premised on the assumption that school effectiveness work will have a lasting and positive impact on education only if it is allied to an understanding of what goes on in more and less effective schools, especially in classrooms. Furthermore, the impact will be dependent on how the presentation of the findings takes account of the ways in which those in schools, especially the classroom teachers, already construe what they do. At the very least, the criterion measures of effectiveness have to relate to some of the main thrusts of what teachers are trying to achieve with their students, the targets for action towards improvement have to relate to what is in the teachers' power to influence and there has to be some constructive incentive for change rather than just castigation of schools for being ineffective with official requirements to produce school development plans (as David Hargreaves, 1990, put it 'if you strip a man naked in public, his first reaction is not usually to pull up his socks').

It is inevitable that there will have to be a great many small-scale studies to establish any sort of understanding of what goes on in schools which are identi- fied as 'more' and 'less' effective. The context of this work will be important. The research to which we will refer in this chapter is being undertaken in Scotland where the Scottish Office Education Department (SOED), in collaboration with representatives of the directors of the regional education authorities, is reported (Munro, 1994) as having broadly endorsed the development of a value-added approach to academic achievement measures of effectiveness. It also appears to have argued that other measures of success, such as the enhancement of pupils' social and personal skills, should have their place in judgements about schools. That is, of course, currently just an aspiration for the system, but the Scottish Office has commissioned (but not from us) a £440,000 research project to support and complement its decision-making in this area. This kind of activity is in welcome contrast to an earlier emphasis on raw examination results as the appro- priate effectiveness measures and it signals an acceptance that schools have to be given the opportunity to demonstrate how well they are doing, given the abilities and backgrounds of their pupils.

Our research, started in 1993 and funded by ESRC, was carried out in one regional education authority. Because of the powerful relationship of social class with examination performance, four case-study schools within the authority were selected on the basis of the socio-economic status (SES) of the populations they serve as well as of their effectiveness assessed by progress measures controlling for prior attainment at the level of the individual pupil. All these measures emerge from school effectiveness studies carried out by Lindsay Paterson, Andrew McPherson and their colleagues at the Centre for Educational Sociology (CES) at the University of Edinburgh; we are most grateful for their help.

The four schools were characterized as

A   high SES, high effectiveness
B   high SES, low effectiveness
C   low SES, high effectiveness
D   low SES, low effectiveness

SES information on the schools was the most recent available for pupils in their fourth year of secondary school (S4, age 16) from the region in which the schools are situated (1987/88). It was based on data about work (separately for mothers and fathers), parental education and household structure. The parents of pupils in the two schools identified as 'low SES' have relatively low participation in paid work, their jobs are of relatively low status and they left school at a relatively early age. In contrast, in the two 'high SES' schools parents have relatively high work participation, are in high status jobs and substantially more stayed on longer at school. The household structure indicator of lone parenthood is less clear-cut; the highest incidence is perhaps unexpectedly in one of the two 'high SES' schools.

The statistical regression analysis of attainment in the schools is based on data from S4 in session 1990/91. Attainment on entry to the secondary school is estimated by the performance on the Edinburgh Reading Test (ERT) at the end of primary school. Estimates of attainment at S4 have been carried out for eight measures: overall Scottish Certificate of Education Ordinary or Standard Grade awards at levels 1 to 3, and the average grade of award within each of seven curricular modes defined by the Scottish Consultative Committee on the Curriculum (science, English, mathematics, languages, social studies, aesthetic arts and technology). In comparison with the region as a whole, one each of the 'high SES' and 'low SES' schools had (i) at least three modes on which statistically significant figures suggested the average pupil would have higher attainment if he or she attended that school and (ii) no modes with statistically significant negative figures. The other two schools had no significant positive figures and at least three significantly negative ones. It is worth adding that the modes in which the statistically positive or negative figures were obtained were not identical for each school. Ideally, we would have wished the distinctions between schools to have been in English, mathematics and science but that proved impossible to achieve.

It is accepted that the characterization of schools as displaying high/low effectiveness is inevitably somewhat crude, and the limitations of value-added measures as indicators for league tables and use by parents are becoming more apparent (Paterson, 1993; Young, 1994). Statistical error in the measures results in the bunching of schools with only a few standing out at the top and bottom as extreme cases. While the results on individual departments may be useful for schools themselves, parents may well have difficulty in making sense of them and general judgements about the relative effectiveness of different schools that are based on these progress measures of achievement have to be treated with caution. In selecting our case-study schools we also had to assume stability of relative effectiveness levels over the past few years; that may or may not be a valid assumption. Our choice of schools was further constrained by the SES requirements; we could not automatically select the extremes of the effectiveness measures. The SES profiles of schools are likely to remain fairly stable, but the relevant data were collected six years ago.

AREAS OF UNCERTAINTY

Notwithstanding these caveats, by the criteria of most school effectiveness work, this sample of four schools is not fundamentally flawed and has achieved the contrasts sought in SES, in value-added measures and in the promise of a variety of school cultures. We do not expect, in our context at least, to be able in the near future to categorize schools more subtly (as, for example, ineffective schools that are improving) by simply looking to the findings of large-scale surveys. It would be a mistake, however, to expect to be able to develop neat typologies of school cultures and to uncover simple causal relationships between processes and outcomes. In-depth research in individual schools is less likely to fall into traps of inferring causal relationship from correlations than is quantitative survey work (because of the emphasis on gaining access to the actors' understandings of their experience); however, there are still dangers of placing too much weight on some respondents' accounts when different individuals make sense of complex environments like schools in quite different ways.

There are obvious ethical problems associated with a focus on 'less effective' schools. The schools in this sample were all aware of the findings from the CES study, but we did not openly state that two had been chosen as 'less effective'; this is a source of unease for us. In practice, as we have shown, it was not easy to identify schools in the neat way expressed in our design. Although levels of effectiveness may well be a relatively stable characteristic from one year to the next for schools, we were aware that in this population of schools there has been a 'regression towards the mean' over the past decade. This was not a chance or statistical phenomenon. The region, in pursuing what it saw as social justice goals, redrew school catchment areas in the early 1980s in response to the first phase of the CES research. The aim was to provide as even a social mix as practicable although a few pockets of marked deprivation (such as the locations of our low SES schools) remained. Furthermore, national educational policy changes, that have emphasized competition and the publication of raw examination results, have revealed the lowly 'league position' of both the low SES case-study schools. This acted as a strong and uncomfortable spur not only to redouble their efforts but also to modify their goals in the direction of greater academic emphasis; this occurred in spite of pessimism, on the part of both management and teachers, that their school's relative status on raw achievement measures could be significantly raised given the large numbers of their pupils from disadvantaged backgrounds.

A rather important point, likely to influence schools' reactions to information about their effectiveness, is that despite a shift of emphasis from raw score results to value-added measures, the 'norm-referenced' character of league tables of school effectiveness remains; comparisons with the performance of other schools is what counts. An absolute improvement on the part of an individual school is unlikely to be recognized unless it is sufficiently greater than the improvement of other schools for it to overtake them in the league. Thus schools which have performed poorly in public examinations in the past, but have now achieved what they may regard as a substantial improvement, may find themselves faring little better in their public profile simply because the performance across the country (in Scotland at least) is generally improving. The kinds of arguments, which were common from the 1960s, about the importance of recognizing what had been achieved by even the lowest achieving pupils (i.e. the case for criterion-referenced rather than norm-referenced assessment), are now applicable to school effectiveness measures.

Within the four schools we have a particular focus: on low achievers as the pupils most 'at risk' in education. School effectiveness research has not looked in detail at how they cope with the experience of schooling. In the case of our four case-study schools there was no evidence from the CES analysis that any of them had different effects for pupils of different attainments at the end of primary, or for boys in comparison with girls. Our research is not about confirming that finding but about unpacking the pupils' and teachers' experience in these supposedly differentially effective contexts. However, the expectation must be that what counts as a 'low achiever' will vary from school to school, and that the differences will be most pronounced where the SES gap is greatest. In addition, support for low achievers may look different in schools in different circumstances; schools in low SES areas with prospects of high unemployment, for example, may be faced with quite different patterns of motivation among pupils from those in affluent areas.

COLLECTING DATA

The study focuses on the progress of, and support for, below average achieving pupils aged 12 to 14. It places substantial importance on how *teachers* construe this 'progress' and 'support', and so addresses the concern that many school effectiveness researchers have about how to get a grasp of the models that are in the minds of those *inside* the system that is being judged by *outsiders* as effective or not. It looks at the *processes* of the support provided for lower achievers at both classroom and school level, and follows the progress of 32 target pupils in English, mathematics and science classes over two years.

Data are collected in a variety of ways including analysis of policy documentation, interviews with school managers and teachers, interviews with pupils and test (or other assessment) results. A distinctive aspect of our methods, however, lies in the conjunction of classroom observation and immediate post-lesson interviews with teachers about the events of the lesson. The analysis of the post-lesson interviews is a major source of information about what counts as low achievement, what, in the teachers' eyes, constitutes 'progress' for low achieving pupils and how they make sense of the 'support' they provide for such pupils. This is, in some ways, a process-product approach; but unlike the traditional studies of that genre, it does not assume in advance what is to count as the product nor assert which process variables are to be addressed – it is responsive to the teachers' constructs and it relates these to actual events observed with real students. The methods used are consistent with a phenomenological approach (Brown and McIntyre, 1993).

In relation to school effectiveness research, interest centres on the following kinds of questions.

(i)   To what extent do the constructs of progress subscribed to by those in schools, and especially inside the classroom, reflect the usual criterion measures for school effectiveness? (Does the importance attached to, for example, lower achievers' self-confidence, increased sociability or concentration have to be taken account of by effectiveness research which generally emphasizes basic skills or examination achievements?)

(ii) Are there distinctive differences in patterns of support for, and the progress of, low achievers between the more and less effective case-study schools with high and low SES enrolments? (Can the differentiation between schools on overarching measures be discerned at the school/classroom level? Is there evidence of differential effects of schools on students with different levels of achievement and boys/girls?)

103

(iii)   How do the most salient features of 'support' in the classrooms and schools relate to those characteristics of schools which have been found to correlate with effectiveness in large-scale survey work?

One aspect of the classroom observation focused on particular low achievers as 'target pupils'. The initial identification of these low achievers was not entirely straightforward. We used a combination (somewhat uneasy) of teachers' ratings (which are stage-related) and standardized reading test scores (which are age-related). Our aim was first to select two pupils (one boy, one girl) from each of two classes in the four schools to provide 16 target pupils of *well below average* achievement. The criteria for their selection were that (i) teachers in all three subjects (English, mathematics and science) rated them in this low category, and (ii) their Edinburgh Reading Test (ERT) score on entry to secondary school was in the range 70 to 84. Two boys and five girls among the 16 pupils did not achieve all three low ratings in (i); one boy and two girls had ERT scores above 84. It was particularly difficult to identify girls with a uniformly low achievement profile in the high SES schools. The second group of 16 target pupils were *just below average*; the intention was that they would be (i) rated this way by teachers of the three subjects (ii) have ERT scores in the range 85 to 97. All the boys achieved (i) or below, though two were slightly above 97 on ERT. The girls, however, showed very considerable variation (some above and some below the criterion) across subjects in teachers' ratings, with three above 97 on ERT.

At the time of writing the analysis of the data is by no means complete. However, we do have a sense of the kinds of findings emerging from the study and so the nature of the task that faces us in addressing questions (i) to (iii) above. It is to those preliminary findings we now turn.

PRELIMINARY FINDINGS

Teachers' Classroom Constructs

By focusing on lower than average achievers we have signalled a concern with a population which in school effectiveness circles would be those with below average scores on examinations or formal (often standardized) tests. By identifying target pupils through a combination of test scores and teachers' ratings, we introduced the influence of *teachers'* constructs of the low achiever which we expected to be more complex than a straightforward score (though such scores influence, no doubt, teachers' judgements about pupils). We have not been disappointed. Within teachers' ratings there is a complex set of dimensions on which they base their judgements. From our early analysis it seems that the ways in which the teachers construed differences among pupils, and so low achievers, appear to depend both on perceptions of *enduring characteristics* and *behaviour on the day* (when discussing a given lesson). It appears that these can be categorized and the categories probably include ability, attainment, behaviour (e.g. quiet, disruptive), physical state (tired, hearing impaired), relationships with others (peers, teacher), preferences (grumbles, enjoyments), and approach to work (motivation, independence). The rich complexity of these constructs contrasts with the bluntness of the variables in large-scale work. Not unexpectedly we find a similar multi-dimensional picture when we look at teachers' constructs of support.

The classroom support that teachers see themselves (and are observed by us) as offering the pupils has dimensions that are likely to be unsurprising to anyone studying the repertoires of teaching – informing, directing, explaining, questioning, encouraging, giving feedback, ensuring safety, demonstrating, disciplining, helping, monitoring/observing, eliciting pupils' ideas. From a researcher's perspective we are also looking at how, and how much, the schools use formal learning support in the classroom, setting by ability, differentiated materials and whole-class/group/pair/individual organization of classroom activities. At a more detailed level we are interested in the patterns of teachers' talk, support to individuals or groups, organizing activity and use of different types of pupil task. We shall be looking to see how, in the case studies, emphases on these different kinds of classroom activities relate to the SES and value-added effectiveness as well as other features of the schools such as development planning, general management styles and those factors which school effectiveness studies have identified as important.

In looking at how the teachers think about *students' progress*, six distinctive aspects have emerged so far.

1. Affective: confidence, sociability, responsibility.
2. Procedural/organizational: task completion, catching up with other pupils, learning the teachers' procedures.
3. Tangible product: production of homework, drawing, written work.
4. Cognitive 1: grasp or develop an idea or concept.
5. Cognitive 2: processes (can do, techniques, strategy).
6. Cognitive 3: thinking beyond the lesson or task (e.g. 'thinking mathematically').

As we further analyse these data, on the ways in which teachers construe both children's progress and the support they provide for them, we will be making comparisons

(i)   among subject areas within and between schools;
(ii)   between schools with differing SES and measured effectiveness;
(iii) with the conceptualizations of progress and support used by large-scale school effectiveness studies.

Because we are also interested in the differential effectiveness of schools for different pupils, we focus on the variations among teachers, subjects and schools in how they construe pupils' characteristics.

In a rough and ready way this study could be summarized as a two-strand enquiry. One aim is to explore the extent to which teachers and schools on the one hand, and school effectiveness studies on the other, are similar in the ways they make sense of the education of lower-than-average achievers. The second aim is to see whether we can develop a greater understanding of the apparent differential effectiveness of schools. The first of these aims implies a demanding task, given the preliminary findings above, in which very detailed material has to be analysed and compared with the inevitably broadbrush variables of survey research. This detail, however, makes for even greater difficulties in overtaking the second aim of attempting to explain effectiveness.

The Cultures of More and Less Effective Schools

If we turn to some of the early findings of the research at school as well as classroom level, there are some interesting points to be made in looking at various aspects of the individual schools which relate to their cultures. Perhaps somewhat alarmingly, the most apparent distinction between the two more effective schools (high and low SES) and the two less effective schools is their *history*, and the high level of awareness of that history, as senior secondary (grammar) and junior secondary (secondary modern) schools respectively prior to comprehensivization in the 1960s. Many of the parents of the pupils now in the schools will have had their own secondary education in the decade following the major move towards comprehensive schooling. Their own experiences and views may well have been influenced by the expectations and prejudices which at that time focused on the earlier status of the newly formed comprehensive institutions. Despite the fact that the significance of former school status is well documented in the literature, we are surprised at the extent to which the history, in the minds of some people at least, is thought to affect current decision-making and parental choice.

Some of the other broad features of the schools' culture, as seen through the eyes of their senior management and other teachers, show contrasts between the schools which reflect their differences in SES. It is more difficult, however, to identify contrasts (apart from their histories) that distinguish between the measured high and low effectiveness institutions (we have been careful, of course, to try to avoid prejudging the effectiveness of any activity within schools, especially in the so-called 'less effective' pair). Our strategy is to work with the four schools as separate case studies, but to keep looking across the studies for similarities and differences. At this stage we can offer some preliminary rough and ready portraits of each school and attempt to build in a comparative commentary.

High SES, High Effectiveness (School A)

As in the other schools, staff in School A were concerned about academic, personal and social development goals. Somewhat surprisingly, given that this school has the highest examination results, academic achievement was regarded as by no means the only, nor necessarily the most important, aspect of the school's work; the other schools, in contrast, were giving academic goals increasing pride of place. School A is a large, well-established, high achieving former senior secondary school which was built in the 19th century in a university town. It is secure, therefore, in the privilege it is able to confer on its pupils and the variety of experiences it can offer them so they can fulfil their academic potential. Given its high levels of performance over most of its pupil population, it has the space to turn its attention to personal growth and the development of confidence among its pupils to enable them to cope with whatever they have to face in life.

Teaching time and homework hours are greater than those in the other three schools. The comparisons are particularly marked with the low SES schools where pupils have the equivalent of eight school days less of teaching time per year and about two-thirds the hours of homework set by School A. Like the other schools, School A feels itself under pressure from the 5 to 14 Programme (Scotland's National Curriculum) with the requirement for greater differentiation in the early years of secondary. There is, therefore, a continuing acceptance of setting within subjects (especially mathematics) at this stage. However, this is of some concern in School A, as it is in School B the other high SES school, because it is seen as requiring predictive judgements that may be unrealistic and involve premature labelling of pupils. These views contrast with those in the low SES schools which see considerable advantages in setting.

The content of the curriculum in this school was generally similar to that in the others. However, one interesting divergence was shared with School C, the other high effectiveness (but low SES) school: the opportunity of Latin or a second modern foreign language was offered to some pupils at the end of the first year in the school. This appeared to be a vestige of the senior secondary tradition which was still apparent in the more academic curriculum offered to higher achieving pupils. No such offer was available in the former junior secondaries which comprised our ineffective schools (B and D).

A striking feature of senior management in all the schools was their view that parents had a profound influence on the school's culture. School A, like the other high SES school, was aware that most of its parents appreciated academic success and other spheres of the school's activities, were demanding and conscious of their children's rights, would be prepared to exert pressure elsewhere (e.g. with the regional authority) and expected the very best for their children. As such they were extremely supportive but could take up a great deal of staff time in the school and might even interfere with its smooth running. The influence of these middle-class parents was evident in the support for lower achieving pupils in both the high SES schools. Dyslexia (or specific learning difficulties) had a salience in parents' thinking about their children's learning difficulties that had no place in the low SES schools. School A, with the most extensive learning support staff of the four schools, had one half-post above normal allocation which was designated to provide support for pupils with specific learning difficulties.

The general comparative pattern of learning support deserves some comment. School A is by far the largest of the four schools and so has the largest allocation of learning support staff, since allocations are related to the size of school roll. It also appears to have a substantially lower proportion of pupils with learning difficulties. As a result of these circumstances and the extra half-time post, learning support staff are more likely to be available for cooperative teaching. The contrast with the two low SES schools is particularly marked. Their much higher proportions of pupils with learning difficulties make more stringent demands on learning support and it appears to us that cooperative teaching, with mainstream and learning support teachers collaborating in the classroom, is spread much more thinly than in School A. Our work has been in only a minority of classrooms, however, and conclusions about higher levels of learning support in high SES mainstream classrooms have to remain tentative. It was clear that School A's current strategy was to employ a large measure of cooperative teaching, but a view was expressed that primary schools should be offering more learning support so that the resources at secondary could be focused on those with the greatest needs through, for example, individualized tuition.

The pupil culture in School A reflected its high SES status and had clear similarities with School B. Positive attitudes to school, especially in the early years, enthusiasms and appreciation of the efforts made by the staff were apparent. The programme of extra-curricular activities in School A was very extensive and, unlike many schools in Scotland, revived immediately after the long period of teachers' industrial action in 1986. Even for second-year pupils (14-year-olds), a council was established by the deputy headteacher and consulted on organizational matters, and several third-year pupils acted as prefects, assisting in various ways with the running of the school. Problems, such as they were, seemed to arise mainly from parental pressure and high expectations, although pupils from working-class families might sometimes feel alienated. Low achievers appeared just as committed as high achievers and the interactions between the school and families had the effect of positive reinforcement of shared values.

An important focus of the research was schools' responses to educational changes such as the introduction of development planning, the publication of league tables, marketing of the school and parental choice of school. These are regarded by the government as central to the thrust for improvement in the effectiveness of schools. School A, together with the other high SES school and the other high effectiveness (low SES) school, although not antagonistic to development planning, was conscious of the constraints which might be put on schools' own wider creative ideas by the emphasis on priorities determined externally by the region or SOED. The style of leadership cultivated by the headteacher, inherited from his predecessor, was described as 'listening', 'consensual' and 'discussion-based'. The reaction to league tables of raw results was, as in the other high SES school, relaxed – high SES ensures good examination results. Value-added measures were also regarded with satisfaction as evidence to counter any suggestion that this privileged school was less successful with lower achieving pupils. None of the other schools said anything in favour of value-added measures. The issue of parental choice had scant significance for School A; its geographical position makes it relatively inaccessible from other areas and there are no other secondary schools in the same town to provide competition. Although the school is one of those piloting the region's scheme for devolved school management of resources, there was no sense in which this was construed as some great leap forward with possibilities for increased resources. Indeed, the decision to take part seemed to relate more to the prospect of an enhanced independence rather than to money.

School A has the self-confidence and familiarity with high levels of performance that enable it to reflect on the wider goals of education and to focus a substantial part of its energies on lower achieving pupils. It does not have to strive as hard as other schools to improve the academic achievements of a large proportion of its pupils; they and their parents are already well motivated, accustomed to longer working hours and ambitious. The absence of local competition from other schools adds to the 'space' available to the staff to think about the quality of education rather than the marketing of their wares. Its history and the nature of its local community, of course, bestow real advantages on this school. Innovations like development planning and marketing of the school seem irrelevant in explaining its effectiveness.

High SES, Low Effectiveness (School B)

As we have seen, the high SES status of this school suggested similarities with School A in such matters as parental influence on the school's culture, some aspects of support for low achievers, pupils' attitudes to school, opinions about development planning and reactions to raw results league tables. It also displayed similar attitudes to the other high SES school in its reservations on the value of setting. Indeed, of the four schools it appeared the most committed to mixed-ability teaching and individualized learning and least likely to be observed using whole-class teaching. It was only the incompatibility of this school's preferred practices with the differentiated Standard Grade (Scottish Certificate of Education) mathematics course at Credit level that resulted in some reorganization within mixed-ability classes at the end of the second year to introduce some differential grouping. In almost all these respects it displayed differences from the two low SES schools (C and D), but it was similar to those schools in its increasing emphasis on academic achievement (even at the expense of social and personal goals). It was also closer to Schools C and D than to A in teaching time available and homework hours. Like the other low effectiveness (low SES) school, before comprehensivization its history was as a junior secondary, although it opened as a purpose-built comprehensive.

School B had been involved in the region's pilot phase of school development planning, and was further advanced in this activity than the other three. Many committees relating to this had been set up within the school, although some teachers suggested there was sometimes a reluctance on the part of the headteacher to act on staff views and that the committee structure was overelaborate. Another distinctive feature of School B was its particularly active marketing strategy in direct competition with other schools in the locality. Cultivation of the school's public image, an agenda driven by media concerns, operating the school as a business with the parents as customers, ensuring that school events were reported in local papers and planning to place leaflets advertising the school in banks and building societies were all part of the strategy. Gratification was apparent when preference over other schools, including the private sector, was displayed by parents. Considerable comfort was drawn from the school's relatively good showing on raw results league tables and sympathy was expressed for other local schools where such results looked like 'a disaster'. School B's relatively poor performance in value-added terms, however, seemed to generate little concern; the assumption seems to have been made that negative value-added measures are unlikely to be understood or criticized by that general public. In contrast, high raw results seemed to be attracting more middle-class parents which, in turn, boosted those raw results. The school was quite clear that to sustain this it should not advertise itself as being good with low achievers, though it is pleased to be regarded as a caring institution.

This high SES but low effectiveness school, therefore, is the most market orientated of our case-study institutions. Its SES associates it in many respects with School A, but it is less assured of its academic standing and so puts very great emphasis on academic goals in the light of what it sees as parents' demands. It could be described as the school which more than our other case studies has responded to the government's directives for educational innovations. That and its history as a junior secondary are the most obvious contrasts with the two more effective schools (A and C). Whether its market-orientated approach will pay off in improved value-added measures of effectiveness in the future remains to be seen.

Low SES, High Effectiveness (School C)

In common with the other high effectiveness school, School C is a former senior secondary school though in its establishment as a comprehensive it incorporated a nearby junior secondary with a progressive ethos. The school consciously nurtures its roots in the community by, for example, helping parents to organize a successful school reunion leading to the foundation of a Friends of [School C] Association. Although the school occupies an open site, it is surrounded by local authority housing and the marks of the collapse of heavy industry, and the buildings have many of the disadvantages of early post-Second World War construction. Like the two less effective schools, increasing emphasis was being placed on academic achievement, not least because an HMI report had stressed the need for this (whether HMI had access to the relatively high value-added measures we cannot say). Although there was a view in the school that academic awards were a crucial 'passport' for pupils to take on and that this must be the priority, the headteacher showed considerable concern for a greater focus on personal and social development and on dealing with problems like bullying.

Like the other low SES (low effectiveness) school, School C was conscious of the preponderance of low achieving pupils in mixed-ability classes who 'had a dragging' effect on the rest. Setting in mathematics was welcomed as providing opportunities for those who had the potential to achieve academic goals. In these circumstances, the need to target learning support on those with the greatest need was regarded as more important than the thin spread of learning support across mixed-ability classes. In both low SES schools parents were less demanding, less supportive, less likely to attend parents' evenings, more inclined to leave decisions to the school and more likely to have values different from the school (e.g. with regard to physical violence) than in the high SES schools. Similar contrasts were apparent in the pupil cultures. The low SES schools' populations had significant numbers of disaffected, academically unmotivated pupils. School C placed considerable emphasis on trying to convince these young people that academic success was in their grasp, rewarding good behaviour, attendance and punctuality, and exploring ways of involving pupils in their own assessments to encourage more constructive thinking and activity. The headteacher bemoaned the demise of extra-curricular activities, particularly school sport, which had not been revived after the 1986 dispute over teachers' pay and conditions. The activities were seen as important in helping pupils develop self-discipline and a commitment to the school; their disappearance had had a negative effect on pupil morale. Such circumstances were also indicative of low teacher morale and the headteacher was well aware of the frustrations associated with working in an institution like School

C. In the light of this, he endeavoured to support all teacher-led initiatives, even if they were costly, and urged the staff to seek support from their colleagues.

In considering school development planning the school was concerned, like the high SES schools, that the process was a mechanism for exerting too much external control and stifling a more creative and collegial system that was already operating in the school. Like the other low SES school, there was also anxiety about the unmanageable amount of paperwork and about the damaging effect of raw results league tables. School C saw such tables as essentially destructive with no constructive explanations of why things were the way they were or of action that might be taken to improve things. Despite the school's good showing on value-added measures, these were more or less discounted as incomprehensible to parents and likely to add to the confusion. Nor was there great rejoicing at the extra 200 pupils admitted as a result of parents' placement requests. This addition made little difference to the school's academic profile, and enlarged the school population in ways that have ensured even greater practical problems, especially of space and stress on teachers. Devolved school management was seen as providing opportunities to target extra resources on lower achieving pupils, especially those with learning difficulties, but there was an awareness that this might damage the school's public image in the current climate that puts so much emphasis on performance of the more able. The fear of the re-emergence of 'fast-track' and 'sink' schools haunts the low SES institutions and makes them wary of promoting too enthusiastically their work with lower achieving pupils.

School C's value-added measures identify it as a successful school that is working in difficult circumstances. Its senior secondary history is to its advantage and it may have benefited from an initial upheaval 20 years ago as it was incorporating a progressive junior secondary school. The major task of establishing shared understanding from two different traditions may, in the longer term, have established what seems to be a reflective and creative tradition of collegial management and opportunities for staff to identify and develop their own priorities, opting into developments of their choice. Part of this tradition has included particular concerns for low achievers who form a substantial proportion of pupils. More recently, the tradition seems to be at some risk from central planning developments, concentration on the publication of performance measures and increases in the pupil population brought about by parental choice. As in the other high effectiveness (high SES) school, therefore, we have little evidence that these innovations are likely to have increased the school's effectiveness. Paradoxically, because that effectiveness may depend on the school's creative response to its role in a difficult environment, the innovations may have had a negative influence.

Low SES, Low Effectiveness (School D)

School D, the smallest of the four, serves a socially disadvantaged area of villages/small towns with high unemployment and increasing crime and family breakdown. Its raw examination results are very low indeed. Despite admirable policies to fulfil the comprehensive school ideal, and a new, purpose-built and lavish building, the school has difficulties in attracting pupils. It has replaced a number of former junior secondaries and that replacement did not please all of the villages which lost their local schools.

As we have seen, it has many similarities with the other low SES school. It has a preponderance of low achieving pupils, somewhat alienated characteristics among the parent population, low motivation among many pupils, concern that a move away from mixed-ability teaching towards setting and individual tuition is probably necessary to support both those with academic potential and those with the greatest problems, a belief that insufficient account was taken of social deprivation factors in the regional allocations of learning support staff and a concern that it should not present itself as a school for the less able.

This school currently places very heavy emphasis on academic goals. This is not necessarily of the school's own choosing, given its circumstances, but it is seen as the only performance measure that 'counts'. Within this, however, School D is committed to general improvement in its performance rather than what it sees as currently unattainable targets of excellence. It is frustrated that in a norm-referenced system (whether based on raw results or value-added measures) improvement on the school's own base-line measure of achievement seems to count for little. Creative developments, such as the removal of barriers between a special needs unit attached to the school and the learning support department in order to provide opportunities for special unit pupils to integrate into mainstream classrooms and curricula (a beneficial spin-off from this allowed children in mainstream access to specialist teachers), receive little recognition in a climate that lays so much stress on achievements that are relevant, for the most part, to the more able. Pipe bands and successful dramatic productions are probably of major importance in the achievements of a school of this kind, but the effectiveness measures that are in vogue are destined to ignore these and concentrate on those that rub the nose of School D in the bottom of the heap of failure. It feels crucified by the local press and frustrated that some parents and associated primary schools continue to prefer to send their children to a neighbouring and former senior secondary (but less well-appointed) school. The morale of enthusiastic young teachers recruited when the school opened is seen by some as having been sapped both by its poor academic performance and by the low expectations of older teachers who spent much of their earlier working lives in junior secondary environments. It is difficult to see how the recent government innovations could be regarded as a constructive way of improving this school's effectiveness.

DISCUSSION OF THE FINDINGS

Because the empirical study reported here is not yet complete we cannot draw conclusions about the value of this kind of approach as a bridge between school effectiveness research and work on school improvement. What we can say is that the complexity and multi-dimensionality of the ways in which those in schools and classrooms think about pupils' progress, the support to be provided for that progress and individual differences among pupils, presents an apparently rather different framework from that of much school effectiveness work. The latter, with its emphasis on management structures and practices, at school and classroom level, and on formal measures such as certificate awards and truancy rates, has a very 'bare bones' appearance in comparison with the richness of the portraits that are painted by those inside the schools. Whether these 'bare bones' have been sufficiently well chosen by researchers and policy-makers to provide a 'skeleton' that is an appropriate base on which the teachers' constructs can be fleshed out remains to be seen. We expect to have more to say about that when we have looked at differences between subject areas and differences between schools. If the skeleton is not consistent with the ways in which the actors in schools and classrooms think about their work, then it is unlikely that school effectiveness research in its present form will have anything of use to offer those on whom the responsibility for school improvement rests. This is not to say that ways of thinking cannot be changed, but the push for reform has to start where people are, not where others might wish them to be. Many of the attempts at curriculum innovation in the 1960s and 1970s taught us the lessons of placing too much reliance on outsiders' ideas when insiders control the action.

Inevitably a study like ours has a somewhat uneasy association across different paradigms. In a case-study approach we should be looking in depth and individually at each school to develop a unique understanding of the case; we should not be treating them as a 'small sample'. However, a major aim of the research is to look across pairs of schools that are more (or less) effective, but operate in very different social circumstances. We expect to identify, therefore, some naturalistic generalizations or hypotheses to be tested in relation to effectiveness and social class.

Any aspiration to identify a straightforward common set of factors to account for the differences in value-added measures between the pairs of more and less effective schools seems destined to disappointment. At this stage we have only two factors which appear to be associated with higher effectiveness (Schools A and C). The first of these relates to the history of the institution as a senior (grammar) rather than junior secondary (secondary modern) school before comprehensivization. No doubt that history influences the way parents, and perhaps pupils, still regard the school and what they expect of it. Furthermore, and more surprisingly, it seems also to affect the ways in which at least some staff think about it. This 'senior secondary effect', however, is mediated by social class. In School A the very high commitment of the middle-class parents is channelled directly and indirectly through the school, to influence the regional authorities to provide, for example, additional specialized learning support or to improve transport arrangements. The pattern in School C is for parents to express their support by choosing it for their children over other local schools and engaging in activities like fund-raising. But the school is conscious that it has continually to encourage parental support and involvement. Indeed, even when they do become involved parents still do not expect to participate in the educational decision-making; that they regard as the province of the professionals in the school.

The second factor is less clear-cut and must be tentative at this stage. It seems to relate to the efforts made by the more effective schools to incorporate pupils into aspects of the running of the school and to establish a collegial atmosphere among the teachers. The two schools have, of course, very different social environments and this affects the ways in which this factor is manifest. Thus School C (low SES) concentrates on tangible rewards for pupils; School A (high SES), in contrast, can rely on existing high levels of motivation for involvement among pupils. School C has to put energy into cultivating teacher morale and be ready to use its resources to respond to teachers' ideas in order to cultivate a collegial atmosphere in what is basically a very difficult environment. School A is also concerned to cultivate a collegial atmosphere but is in the position of being able to *assume* a relatively high morale among staff. In both schools, however, there appears to be evidence consistent with the hypothesis that ownership (a word that seems to survive derision heaped upon it) of their activities on the part of teachers and pupils is an important ingredient of effectiveness, in a way that proactive decision-making by the headteacher and strength of line management is not. We did not find significant evidence of similar beliefs and practices in the less effective schools. Neither of the two factors identified here seem to be particularly salient for most school effectiveness studies, although Reynolds (1991) in summarizing work carried out over a decade in Welsh schools has pointed to high levels of pupil involvement, as prefects or class monitors, as features associated with being an effective school.

Perhaps more important than this, however, are the striking contrasts between schools of different SES. The fact that these differences are so much more marked than those associated with differences in effectiveness, suggests that any notion that there is a common set of management reforms, that would be expected to enable schools of all SES levels to become more effective, must be misguided (this is not to deny, of course, that there may be *some* innovations that are of value to all schools).

The most obvious contrast between the high and low SES pairs of schools is their achievement profiles. While for the great majority of pupils in the high SES schools the goals of good certificate examination results seem entirely appropriate, in the low SES schools there is a substantial proportion of pupils for whom other goals would seem to have higher priority and who might well be seen as impeding the progress of the higher achievers. Although in all schools it could be argued that there is a continuum of achievement, in practice the high SES schools are able to take for granted the motivation of the great majority of the pupils and their parents towards awards for academic achievement; the minority for whom this is not the case (or have other reasons for differing from the majority) can then be given special attention. Because learning support staffing is based on the size of school rolls, and middle-class parents can make effective representations for special provision (e.g. for those deemed to be dyslexic), the high SES schools are able to provide effective help for those with learning difficulties. The task for the low SES schools appears to be quite different. Here there is a tendency to see two populations of pupils: those for whom the pursuit of certificate awards is a priority and those for whom other kinds of goals are seen as having much greater urgency. Because the proportions of pupils with learning difficulties are substantial, and parents are less articulate in their demands for specific resources, learning support tends to be spread much more thinly than in the high SES schools. It seems very likely that the most effective structures and strategies for improving the effectiveness of schools in relation to low achievers would vary quite markedly among schools serving different SES populations.

Complementing the contrast of achievement profile in schools of different SES is one of motivation. A very great deal of effort in low SES schools has to be devoted to improving the morale of teachers, the attitudes of pupils towards learning and the level of involvement of parents in their children's education. High SES schools can to a far greater extent take these matters for granted and can expect an annual boost from the publication of raw certificate results which everyone understands; such results offer little comfort for the low SES schools. High SES schools may, of course, have problems such as excessive demands from parents, but these are *different* problems. While the low SES schools may put a priority on, say, the elimination of bullying and the persuasion of parents that physical violence cannot be condoned as 'standing up for yourself', the high SES schools may be more concerned about 'unreasonable' requests from parents for greater shares of resources for their children.

A third contrast relates to the marketing of schools. For both those serving low SES communities, this is a source of anxiety. A major responsibility which they must accept is to provide support for low achievers, yet they are clear that in the current culture of achievement they cannot advertise themselves as specializing in education for those with learning difficulties. Furthermore, the marketing game is very much one of competition on the basis of raw examination results, and low SES schools have little chance of winning. The school with high value-added effectiveness would welcome recognition of that measure, but it is convinced that the complexity of such information will not be grasped by many parents. In any case, it has no wish to increase the school population which is already of a size that produces considerable stresses and strains. For the high SES school with high effectiveness marketing appears irrelevant. For the other high SES school, with low effectiveness, it is a major thrust of policy. It could be seen as a satisfactory strategy, based as it is on good raw examination results and leading to more parents choosing to send their children to the school. But this diverts attention from the less favourable value-added measures which, not surprisingly, are ignored in the marketing; this school, like the low SES schools, assumes that parents will be unaware of, or fail to understand, such measures.

CONCLUSION

This study sets out to investigate to what extent school effectiveness research, in its familiar forms, could play a major role in bringing about school improvement. It started from the assumption, based on past experience, that in presenting findings from school effectiveness studies account has to be taken of the ways in which teachers and schools already make sense of their educational endeavours. In so far as school effectiveness surveys construe the world in ways that are different from those of the people with responsibility for bringing about the improvements, the probability of change (of the kind desired by the proponents of school effectiveness) is slight.

Our empirical findings and examination of school effectiveness studies support six broad propositional points.

1. The ways in which teachers conceptualize pupils' progress and the kind of classroom support that is needed to promote that progress, are much more complex and rich than the conceptions of progress and support implicit on school effectiveness research. The latter operationalizes progress very largely in terms of achievement and easily measurable non-cognitive criteria; support variables are for

the most part management structures and practices, or broad-brush judgements about, for example, teaching methods. As our research proceeds, we expect to say more about whether the relatively crude and management-orientated variables of school effectiveness research can engage with teachers' frameworks of constructs and, indeed, whether there is enough in common among teachers (let alone among countries) to be able to see such engagement as a possibility. We are not suggesting, or course, that the discourse of school effectiveness is unintelligible to teachers. In inservice staff development or at conferences they can patently hold their own in debate; but their thinking about their own teaching and their pupils' learning appears not to have a predominantly management/achievement orientation. (Evidence from other Scottish research, Brown and Swann, 1994, suggests a similar split between teachers' external public dialogues about the 5–14 Programme, Scotland's National Curriculum, using the language and concepts of that programme and their internalized ways of thinking about their classroom teaching.)

2. The well-meaning efforts of school effectiveness studies to incorporate qualitative data collection to complement the quantitative are unlikely significantly to bridge the gap between school effectiveness and school improvement. Their basic problem is that they are still dependent on researchers' frameworks (theoretical or political) and not on the practitioners' implicit theories about what they are trying to do. Until the latter are taken into account the chances of real understanding of why things turn out the way they do (effective, not effective, improving, deteriorating) are negligible. It might be possible, of course, to change the ways practitioners think to bring them more in line with researchers, but to do that a start would have to be made from where the practitioners are now. As long as the qualitative approach or paradigm is essentially the same as the quantitative (but with less precise data, of course) and based on earlier research of the same kind, it is unlikely to advance our understanding.

3. Identification of the characteristics of the most effective schools has been the meat of school effectiveness research. The variables that are explored, however, arise from researchers' and policy-makers' ideas about 'what will work' and, as we have said, emphasize management features. Our research has looked at how four case-study schools view their own distinctive management structures and practices. A striking finding has been the paucity of commonalities between, on the one hand, the more effective and, on the other hand, the less effective pairs of schools. The two characteristics which distinguish the more effective schools are their histories as senior secondaries (grammar schools), and the

opportunities they give to staff and pupils to make decisions influencing their lives in school. However, much more marked are the differences between pairs of schools identified as high and low SES. That implies that strategies for improvement are likely to be highly dependent on the social class of the school population.

4. Among the most salient differences among the schools are the differences in achievement profile between the high and low SES pupil populations. In the high SES schools the majority of pupils are well motivated and able to achieve substantial academic awards at Standard Grade. The learning support staff can focus their attention, therefore, on the minority with learning difficulties. Other research (Willms, 1986; Paterson, 1992) suggests that this minority, even if their own social background is disadvantaged, can benefit from the higher cultural resources of socially advantaged peers. The low SES schools have much more substantial proportions of children with learning difficulties, but similar levels of learning support staff to the high SES schools. (Some authorities make extra staffing allowances for social deprivation, but these do not match the differences in requirements.) Furthermore, as well as the support being more thinly spread, the schools have to deal with large numbers of young people whose self-esteem does not relate to academic achievement and motivation to learn is low. It is on matters of this kind that teachers see efforts for improvement as having to focus. Telling them that effective schools are associated with strong and competent leadership, particular patterns of punishment and reward systems, management structures, committed staff with high expectations and standards, and so on is likely to be greeted with 'that's all very well but somewhat distant from what faces me as a teacher'. Even within the framework of the characteristics that school effectiveness researchers emphasize, the questions of those in low SES schools may well be asking how on earth teachers' morale and high expectations are to be sustained in very difficult and unrewarding circumstances.

5. There is no evidence that management innovations, like school development planning and the competitive marketing of schools, are improving school effectiveness. School development planning seems to be somewhat sidelined, though there is some feeling that it constrains schools' own creative planning. The context in which it is most clearly implemented is the school with the only significant involvement in marketing itself; this is one of the less effective schools.

6. Publication of raw results is seen as a benefit only by the high SES schools, particularly the less effective one. For the latter, the raw results have contributed to the increase in the numbers of parents choosing the school for their children, but they have also allowed

117

the school to discount the value-added findings. Value-added measures, supported by critics of the government and many academics as potentially beneficial to schools serving disadvantaged populations, are seen as irrelevant by the low SES schools; none regard them as having meaning for parents. The norm-referenced nature of both kinds of performance measure do nothing for the incentive to improve.

Clearly the bridging of the gap between school effectiveness research and school improvement has some way to go. The necessary conditions for the former to be able to fulfil a formative role for school improvement as well as its judgemental summative role are by no means self-evident.

REFERENCES

Angus, L. (1993) 'The sociology of school effectiveness', *British Journal of Sociology of Education*, **14** (3), 333–45.

Brown, S. and McIntyre, D. (1993) *Making Sense of Teaching*. Buckingham: Open University Press.

Brown, S. and Swann, J. (1994) *Teachers' Classroom Thinking: The Impact of 5–14?* Paper presented to the annual conference of the Scottish Educational Research Association at St Andrews, 29 September to 1 October 1994.

Cooper, P. (1993) 'Field relations and the problem of authenticity and researching participants perceptions of teaching and learning in classrooms', *British Education Research Journal*, **19** (4), 323–38.

Creemers, B. (1992) 'School effectiveness and effective instruction – the need for a further relationship', in Bashi, J. and Sass, Z. (eds) *School Effectiveness and Improvement*. Jerusalem: Hebrew University Press.

Edmonds, R. R. (1979) 'Effective schools for the urban poor', *Educational Leadership*, **37** (15–18), 20–24.

Fitz-Gibbon, C. T. (1991) 'Multilevel modelling in an indicator system', in Raudenbush, S. W. and Willms, J. D. (eds) *Schools, Classrooms and Pupils: International Studies of Schooling from a Multilevel Perspective*. San Diego: Academic Press.

Fullan, M. and Hargreaves, A. (1992) *What's Worth Fighting For in Your School? Working Together for Improvement*. Buckingham: Open University Press.

Gray, J., Jesson, D., Goldstein, H. and Hedger, K. (1995) 'The Statistics of school improvement', in Gray, J. and Wilcox, B. *'Good School, Bad School': Evaluating Performance and Encouraging Improvement*. Buckingham: Open University Press.

Hargreaves, D. (1990) 'Making schools more effective: the challenge to policy practice and research', *Scottish Educational Review*, **22** (1), 5–14.

Hargreaves, D. (1993) *School Effectiveness, School Change and School Improvement: The Relevance of the Concept of Culture*. Paper presented to ESRC Seminar Series on School Effectiveness and School Improvement at Sheffield, October 1993.

Hargreaves, D. and Hopkins, D. (1991) *The Empowered School: The Management and Practice of Development Planning*. London: Cassell.

ISERP (undated) *The International School Effectiveness Research Programme: An Outline*, distributed at the ISERP symposium, organized by Reynolds, D. at the annual Conference of the British Educational Research Association at Oxford, September 1994.

Louis, K. S. and Miles, M. B. (1991) *Improving the Urban High School: What Works and Why*. London: Cassell.

Luyten, H. (1994) *Stability of School Effects in Secondary Education: The Impact of Variance Across Subjects and Years*. Paper presented at the annual meeting of the American Educational Research Association at New Orleans, 4–8 April.

Mortimore, P. (1991a) 'School effectiveness research: which way at the crossroads?', *School Effectiveness and School Improvement*, **2** (3), 213–29.

Mortimore, P. (1991b) 'The nature and findings of research on school effectiveness in the primary sector', in Riddell, S. and Brown, S. (eds) *School Effectiveness Research: Its Messages for School Improvement*. Edinburgh: HMSO.

Mortimore, P., Sammons, P., Ecob, R. and Stoll, L. (1988) *School Matters: The Junior Years*. Wells: Open Books.

Munro, N. (1994) 'SOED ready to refine "raw" tables of results', *The Times Educational Supplement Scotland*, 2 September, p. 3.

Nuttall, D., Goldstein, H., Prosser, R. and Rasbash, J. (1989) 'Differential school effectiveness', *International Journal of Educational Research*, special issue *Developments in School Effectiveness Research*, **13** (7), 769–76.

Paterson, L. (1992) 'Socio-economic status and educational attainment: a multi-dimensional and multi-level study', *Evaluation and Research in Education*, 97–121.

Paterson, L. (1993) 'A commentary on methods currently being used in Scotland to evaluate schools statistically', in Paterson, L. (ed.) *Measuring Schools: The Rights and Wrongs of Practice in Scotland*. Edinburgh: Centre for Educational Sociology, pp. 3–27.

Purkey, S. C. and Smith, M. S. (1983) 'Effective schools: a review', *Elementary School Journal*, **83** (4), 427–52.

Raudenbush, S. W. (1989) 'The analysis of longitudinal, multilevel data', *International Journal of Educational Research*, special issue *Developments in School Effectiveness Research*, **13** (7), 712–40.

Reynolds, D. (1991) 'School effectiveness in secondary schools: research and its policy implications', in Riddell, S. and Brown, S. (eds) *School Effectiveness: Its Messages for School Improvement*. Edinburgh: HMSO, ch. 3, 21–33.

Reynolds, D. (1993) *School Effectiveness: The International Perspective*. Paper presented to ESRC Seminar Series on School Effectiveness and School Improvement at Sheffield.

Reynolds, D., Sullivan, M. and Murgatroyd, S. J. (1987) *The Comprehensive Experiment*. Lewes: Falmer Press.

Reynolds, D., Hopkins, D. and Stoll, L. (1993) 'Linking school effectiveness and school improvement', *School Effectiveness and School Improvement*, **4** (1), 37–58.

Reynolds, D., Creemers, B., Bird, J. and Farrell, S. (1994) 'School effectiveness: the need for an international perspective', in Reynolds, D., Creemers, B., Stringfield, S. and Teddlie, C. (eds) *Advances in School Effectiveness Research and Practice*. Oxford: Pergamon, pp. 183–201.

Rutter, M., Maughan, B., Mortimore, P. and Ouston, J. (1979) *Fifteen Thousand Hours: Secondary Schools and Their Effects on Children*. London: Open Books.

Scheerens, J. (1992) *Effective Schooling: Research, Theory and Practice*. London: Cassell.

Stoll, L. (1993) *Linking School Effectiveness and School Improvement: Issues and Possibilities*. Paper presented to the ESRC Seminar Series on School Effectiveness and School Improvement at Sheffield, October.

Teddlie, C. and Stringfield, S. (1993) *Schools Make a Difference: Lessons Learned from a Ten-Year Study of School Effects*. New York: Teachers College Press.

Thomas, S., Sammons, P. and Mortimore, P. (1994) *Stability and Consistency in Secondary Schools' Effects on Students' GCSE Outcomes*. Paper presented to the annual conference of the British Educational Research Association at Oxford, 9 September.

Willms, J. D. (1986) 'Social-class segregation and its relationship to pupils' examination results in Scotland', *American Sociological Review*, **51**, 224–41.

Willms, J. D. and Raudenbush, S. W. (1989) 'A longitudinal hierarchical linear model for estimating school effects and their stability', *Journal of Educational Measurement*, **26** (3), 201–32.

Young, S. (1994) 'Fears over "fairer" league tables', *The Times Educational Supplement*, 22 July, p. 3.

Chapter 6

Theories, Models and Simulations: School Effectiveness at an Impasse

Peter Tymms

INTRODUCTION

Many quantitative educational researchers must have felt a sense of frustration the first time they sat down to analyse school effectiveness data. They will probably have found that the 'best' data available were examination data together with some prior cognitive measure and that they were able to explain about half the variance of the criterion at the pupil level. Such relationships become part of our expectations after working in the field for some time, but to anyone meeting it anew and coming from a natural sciences background it seems as though the game has just started. Surely other variables can be found to make inroads into the 'unexplained' area, or maybe the initial measures were of poor quality. Accordingly, many hours must have been spent on 'fishing expeditions', or data refinement, or data collection, to make good a feeling of dissatisfaction with only being able to account for about half of the differences in outcomes of pupils in our schools.

The finding is, however, remarkably robust, but more surprising is the repeated failure to find stable explanatory variables at the class, department or school level which really seem to make substantial headway. A couple of examples will suffice to make the point. Several headteachers had expressed concern about the involvement of their pupils in part-time work during A-level courses and, since questions relating to this were routinely put to students in the A-Level Information System (ALIS) (Fitz-Gibbon, 1991; 1992), it was possible to construct multilevel models using high-quality data collected by university-trained data collectors. The models, however, showed little evidence to confirm the heads' worries (Tymms and Fitz-Gibbon, 1992). Well fine – another hypothesis bites the dust. How about another one – that the type of institution college, school etc. is of importance and that if only we could sort this out we would have a way forward to improve our schools? But again, careful analysis indicated only slight advantages here and disadvantages there (Tymms, 1992), and, the analysis of another year's data, using very similar procedures, produced slight evidence of variation but this time with a different pattern (Audit Commission, 1993, pp. 32–3).

Further examples of disappointingly weak findings from the school effectiveness literature could readily be added and it should be noted that significant findings are more likely to see the light of day in a journal if statistically significance reaches the arbitrary 5 per cent level than if non-significant findings are available (Easterbrook *et al.*, 1991).

School effectiveness researchers have made considerable progress, but the majority of this has been in the methodological field. Substantive progress has been notable by its absence. The answer to the essential question 'How can we improve our schools?' is little clearer now than it was a decade ago. As Fitz-Gibbon has noted (Fitz-Gibbon *et al.*, 1989) we are not going to find answers to this question by comparing successful with unsuccessful schools. The problem is really one of change not of static associations. However, where more focused studies have tried to 'explain' improvements in student outcomes the best explanatory variables have only been associated with 29 per cent of the variance (Louis and Miles, 1991).

The arrival of software designed to handle the complex problems of school effectiveness research in the form of multilevel models (Aitkin and Longford, 1986; Goldstein, 1987; Raudenbush and Bryk, 1986) promised much. There was, for example, the possibility that schools would be found that were more effective with their more able pupils, or with girls or the pupils from deprived backgrounds. But although such effects have been detected in very large data sets recent work has largely failed to find such schools (Jesson and Gray, 1991; Tymms, 1993).

There is also the feeling that, in any analysis, one should separate out the school effect as a gross measure of the differential performance of students in different schools, from the school effect as it appears after account has been taken of school level factors such as the general level of funding outside the control of the schools (Type A and B school effects, see Willms and Raudenbush, 1989; see also Hutchinson, 1993). But little progress has been made in finding different rank orders of schools whilst considering such subtleties.

There are other school effectiveness questions which one might expect to be able to tackle with the kind of data now becoming available, but which we have not even started to consider, since progress has not been sufficient at the more basic level. We have, for example, no evidence of threshold effects in the sense that a pupil, department or school may not attain a certain level unless certain basic conditions pertain.

We have not been able to demonstrate stable interactions in school effectiveness research, although findings do appear in the literature periodically. Teddlie and Stringfield (1993, p. 38) reported differences between the expectations of heads in low, middle and high SES schools. But this has not, so far as the author is aware, been replicated. As noted earlier evidence has been found for variable slopes but these may or may not be stable findings. At the pupil level the distinguished American psychologist Lee J. Cronbach stated disappointingly: 'At one time a conclusion describes a situation very well, at a later time it accounts for rather little variance, and ultimately it is valid only as history' (Cronbach, 1975, pp. 122–3).

There are, of course, several potentially good explanations for our present difficulties. Many of the data sets, especially in the early days of school effectiveness research, have been rather too small, either in terms of numbers of pupils or numbers of schools, although this is steadily being rectified. There is also the problem of poor quality (unreliable and/or biased) data sets in some cases and the lack, in many instances, of much other than cognitive outcomes to work with. Furthermore, there is a general lack of good-quality longitudinal data sets although there are notable exceptions to this. But even for those which do exist, the data are never collected more frequently than once a year. (The growing volume of qualitative data is much more detailed but is necessarily specific and not in a form which permits overviews or seamless matching across schools.)

But perhaps the greatest flaw in school effectiveness research is the almost total lack of experimental data. As Fitz-Gibbon (1985) notes: 'The use of meta-analysis techniques to synthesize findings from multiple replications allows these small experiments to contribute to the accumulation of knowledge in the social sciences in the way that innumerable small experiments have contributed to knowledge in the physical sciences.'

This difficulty hardly needs to be expanded since all researchers are aware of the fallacy of correlation being taken to indicate causation. And yet, our best funded research employing state-of-the-art statistical methods and the latest theories rests exclusively on associations. Such procedures would never have provided firm evidence for early years interventions (Lazar and Darlington, 1982) or for small class sizes (Finn and Achilles, 1990). We will simply never know the impact of actions without trying them out in a controlled fashion.

Many will argue that it is difficult to set up the kinds of experiments needed to deal with school effectiveness questions, but, once monitoring systems are up-and-running, it really becomes quite straightforward to integrate school improvement programmes with monitoring and to test out important hypotheses (Fitz Gibbon 1990; Tymms 1995).

In continuing to rely on survey-type data and in trying to fit associations into causal linear models we constrain our progress in yet another way. The general linear model, as presently employed, does not permit us to build on previous work. Of course, prior experience allows one to avoid some previously fruitless paths and to focus on previously successful patterns, but, a relationship cannot be held to be true next time round – it must be refound in each new data set or data analysis. This is a fundamental limitation which follows inevitably from the use of correlational techniques and can be illustrated by the dilemma of class size. In constructing a multilevel model a researcher may introduce a term at the class level to gauge the importance of class size and this term will be retained or removed from the model on the basis of its statistical significance. Now, our limited but best evidence is – from random assignment – that smaller classes do better. However, this is often not found in survey-type data. Presumably teachers and/or organizations have compensated for the more difficult circumstances presented by large classes, or perhaps important variables are not available to permit a sufficient good model to be constructed. Many reasons could be formulated, but the problem remains. The dominant methodology restricts our progress. We are not able to build on prior knowledge both because our knowledge is not firm (i.e. it is simply based on associations) and because of the kind of modelling that we employ.

All this has meant that theoretical progress has been disappointing simply because a firm foundation does not exist on which to build.

It is conceivable that better data collected over longer periods of time at more frequent intervals, combined with the random assignment of potentially valuable school improvement packages will start to make sense of schools. But, it is also conceivable that they will not, because the events occurring within schools are chaotic – in the scientific sense of the word. This does not mean that things are random or that there are no patterns or even that they are not subject to entirely determinist laws but it does mean that changes are unpredictable and ultimately cannot be mathematically modelled with precision. It also means that educational innovations, school plans, expert advice and school effectiveness knowledge are bound to be severely restricted in their impact (see, for example, the catalogue of failures in Fullan, 1991).

THE WAY FORWARD

Consider the smoke of a cigarette rising slowly in the air. Initially it follows a smooth pattern snaking its way upwards. Entirely predictable in all its aspects including the form of the curve as it is subject to draughts and cooling. But then, all of a sudden, when a parameter known as Reynolds number has reached the critical point, the smooth flow breaks; whorls and eddies are seen as turbulent flow ensues. Now, general patterns can be discerned – the smoke still goes upwards and draughts still blow the smoke but the detailed movement of the smoke particles becomes unpredictable. Tiny fluctuations in the initial conditions are magnified into major influences on the curls high in the column of smoke. Such situations are said to be chaotic and have been observed in a wide variety of well-documented situations (Crutchfield *et al.*, 1986; Gleick, 1988; Tritton and Egdell, 1993) as well as being modelled mathematically (Pritchard, 1992).

It is important to be clear about what is meant by the term chaotic in this situation. It does not imply that patterns do not appear in the data – turbulent flow has a characteristic appearance and considerable work is accumulating on what are termed 'strange attractors' and 'emergence'. Nor does it indicate indeterminism, but it does mean unpredictability in the long term – within certain parameters.

Amazingly it has become clear that chaos can give rise to complexity and much innovative work in this area has led workers to suggest that 'The world is undeniably complex, but its complexity is of an *organized* variety .... It has emerged from primeval chaos in a sequence of self-organizing processes that have progressively enriched and complexified the evolving universe' (Davies 1992, p. 196). 'The essential feature is that something of value emerges as a result of processing according to some ingenious pre-existing set of rules' (p. 214).

One might ask why it is that researchers have only recently started to take a real interest in chaos and only now have been able to make some progress in the area of complexity. After all, turbulent flow has been known for a very long time and Poincaré discussed the mathematical properties of chaotic situations in the last century. The answer must surely lie in the advent of electronic processing which permits the repeated calculation of parameters in situations where mathematical relationships are hypothesized to act over and over again in well-defined situations. Two examples follow to illustrate the modelling of chaos.

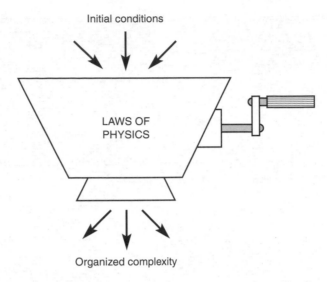

Figure 6.1 *Symbolic representation of the cosmic evolution. The universe starts out in some relatively simple and featureless initial state, which is then 'processed' by the fixed laws of physics to produce an output state which is rich in organized complexity (Davies, 1992, p. 214).*

Consider 300 people whose stands on an issue are sampled and a black or white marker allocated according to their strength of feeling on some issue. These people are arranged in such a way that they only communicated with a neighbour to their left and right. It is as though they were in a circle. Now suppose that after a certain interval during which each person has shared his or her own stand with that of two neighbours, and that the new strength of feeling is an average of the three. Then, according to the level of this position, he or she comes down on the issue in a certain way which is again given a marker. This is then repeated over and over again.

This simple, entirely deterministic process, can, depending on the starting conditions, give rise to an amazing variety of changing patterns of opinion. The process is chaotic in the sense that slight differences in the initial conditions can give rise to very different outcomes at a later stage. The outcomes of one such simulation is shown in Figure 6.2 below which is organized so that people are represented in a series of columns – 300 in all – and their views change as time moves down the page. As can be seen there is some structure to the way that things evolve with areas of stability as well as instability. A survey would find a considerable amount of variation with some clustering of attitudes, whereas in-depth studies would find pockets of surprising stability and others of rapid change.

The patterns of appearance and disappearance, and of stability followed by change, which appear in such systems are to be found in a world of revolutions and evolution. There are grand examples to be found in history and smaller examples known only to individuals. One extreme example of rapid change following a long period of stability within education was recounted by Dockrell at the American Educational Research Association in 1991. In it he described the almost

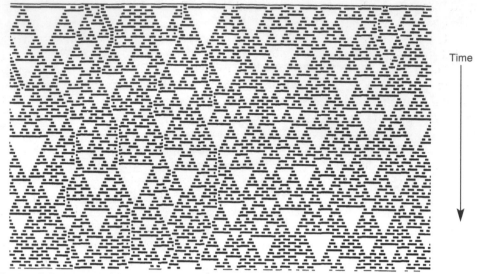

Time

Figure 6.2 *The program capable of generating such forms can be found in Pritchard (1992, p. 30)*

miraculous dropping of physical chastisement from Scottish schools in an extraordinarily short period considering the extent to which it had become part of the Scottish scene. 'The report had immediate impact. The two largest LEAs banned corporal punishment in their schools immediately.'

Dockrell interprets the switch in terms of the impact of research and he details the nature of the switch which he characterizes as the most massive impact of education research on policy in his entire career. But, it is interesting to note that similar things were happening in other parts of the world without the associated research, albeit at slightly different times, and in slightly different circumstances.

The point is that the same kinds of patterns found in the affairs of people appear to emerge from programs which start with a set of random points and in which there is a simple rule repeatedly applied. This leads to the intriguing possibility of more realistic simulations of situations found in life.

IS IT POSSIBLE TO GENERATE SCHOOL EFFECTIVENESS DATA ARTIFICIALLY?

Several writers (Preece, 1990) have suggested that learning can be conceptualized in terms of processes, which can be given mathematical form, and which do not necessarily lead to a world which can be represented by the general linear model. Similar ideas are employed in what follows in an attempt to simulate school effectiveness data.

Data from the ALIS project for biology in 1992 were used to abstract 30 departments with 30 pupils in each department. These artificially round numbers were achieved by randomly sampling from large departments and joining together some smaller departments in geographically similar areas. For each pupil, data were available for the best predictor of A-level biology (the average GCSE grade), gender and the A-level grade achieved. These data are referred to as the actual data.

The A-level grades were coded 10, 8, 6 etc. to represent grades A, B, C, etc. and GCSE grades were coded 7, 6, 5, etc. Boys were coded 0 and girls 1.

The average GCSE grades were then used to simulate the pupils' learning during the A-level course. During each lesson a pupil's learning was assumed to increase in proportion to his or her learning in the previous lesson and in relation to his or her learning ability, which was assumed to be related to the average GCSE grade. It was also assumed that he or she would forget a little – with more learning being lost if there was more to be lost. It was further assumed that the amount of learning for an individual would depend on the amount of learning for the class on average. The simulation was a refined version of the simplest example commonly used to demonstrate chaotic behaviour (Pritchard, 1992, p. 32; Gleick, 1988).

One hundred lessons were then allowed to 'run' in the simulation and the learning made during each lesson was added to the progress towards A-level biology, which was assumed to start at a level proportional to the average GCSE score. It was further assumed that those with a higher average GCSE score would retain more of their learning in the long run.

The final stage was to convert the results of the pupils' progress after 100 lessons into seven grades giving each grade the same proportion of exam entrants found in the 1992 data. The results of this exercise are referred to as the simulated data.

A parallel series of statistical analyses, relating the outcome measure to the inputs, were then carried out – one on the actual data and the other on the simulated data. The analyses started with scatterplots:

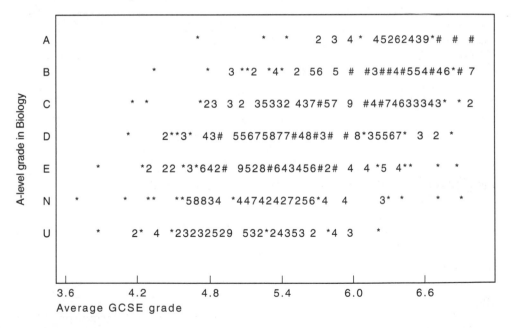

Figure 6.3a *Actual data*

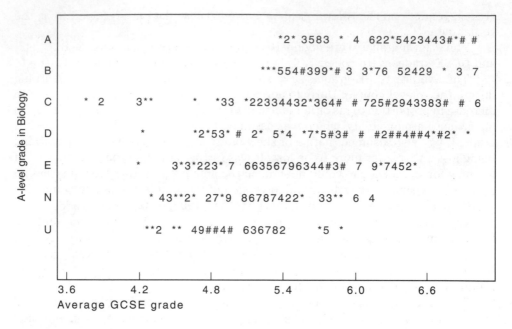

Figure 6.3b *Simulated data*

The scatterplots showed considerable similarities and multilevel models were constructed for both sets of data. Details of the 'null' model appears below:

Table 6.1 *Null model*

Pupil level	Actual data	Simulated data
Random constant	11.79 (0.57)	12.04 (0.58)
Fixed constant	4.35 (0.18)	4.22 (0.22)
Departmental level		
Random cons/cons	0.58 (0.25)	1.03 (0.37)

Table 6.2 *Fixed slopes model*

Pupil level	Actual data	Simulated data
Random constant	6.96 (0.33)	7.91 (0.38)
Fixed constant	−14.82 (0.78)	−13.64 (0.83)
Average GCSE	3.36 (0.14)	3.12 (0.15)
Gender	−0.43 (0.19)	−0.33 (0.20)
Departmental level		
Random cons/cons	0.40 (0.16)	0.68 (0.24)

As expected the null models indicate that the average A grade in both sets of data were very similar (4.35 compared to 4.22). The variances at the pupil level were also comparable (11.8 compared to 12.0). The variances across the 30 departments, on the other hand, whilst of similar magnitude did not show such striking similarity with the actual data showing about half the variation which appeared in the simulated data (0.58 compared to 1.03).

In the next stage the A-level grades in biology were modelled as functions of the average GCSE grades and gender.

The pupil level variance dropped considerably in both sets of data (by 41 per cent for the actual data and by 34 per cent in the simulated data). A similar fall was also noted for the departmental level variance (31 per cent for the actual data and 34 per cent for the simulated data).

Additional similarities are the coefficients associated with the average GCSE score (3.36 compared with 3.12) and the errors associated with those coefficients (0.14 and 0.15). But, the most surprising similarity is the indication that girls made less progress between GCSE and A-level biology – by 0.43 in the actual data and by 0.33 in the simulated data. This appeared despite the superior average GCSE scores of the girls (girls=5.89; boys=5.60; effect size =0.43 p <0.001), which was, of course, the same for both data sets.

A further refinement of the model would be to add the average class score for the average GCSE to level two. In neither of the data sets was this addition statistically significant and the analysis moved on to consider variable slopes.

Now the similarity between the two data sets starts to break down. The errors in the random part at the second level of the actual data model showed no variation in the relationships between average GCSE and biology A grade across departments. In the simulated data there were variable slopes. Nevertheless, both models indicate a tendency for more shallow slopes to be associated with greater intercepts.

In comparing the simulated data with the actual data it has become apparent that there were considerable similarities between the two sets of data. Not only were the relationships between input and outcome variables very similar but the error structures were also parallel. In fact, traditional analysis, using ordinary least squares regression techniques, would not readily have spotted the main difference between the two sets of data – variations in slopes across departments.

Table 6.3 *Variable slopes (using centred average GCSE scores)*

Pupil level	Actual data	Simulated data
Random		
constant	6.85 (0.33)	6.64 (0.32)
Fixed		
constant	4.59 (0.19)	4.47 (0.21)
Average GCSE	3.38 (0.16)	3.26 (0.34)
Gender	−0.4 (0.19)	−0.31 (0.19)
Departmental level		
Random		
cons/cons	9.75 (7.12)	87.52 (27.0)
avGCSE/cons	−1.54 (1.19)	−15.98 (5.0)
avGCSE/avGCSE	0.25 (0.20)	2.93 (0.90)

The implications of the simulation and data analyses are taken up later but it should be recorded that in addition to the simulation described above several other versions were run. If very slight changes were made to the simulation equation then the details of the output varied but the same broad patterns remained. However, when changes to the constants in the equation were made dramatic differences were noted. With some values no chaotic behaviour appeared whilst with others the 'school effects' are so large as to make the situation appear quite unrelated to the findings of educational researchers. Indeed, under some conditions, schools either scored high or they scored low and as the iterations proceeded schools would stay in one camp for a long time and then, quite abruptly switch positions. Under other conditions gender effects appeared, sometimes with girls doing better and sometimes with boys.

Clearly the simulations were complex and sensitive to initial conditions as well as to the constants used in the equations. Under the conditions used for the simulation the outcomes behaved in a manner reminiscent of exam outcomes in school effectiveness research but in others, where the outcomes flipped in the unit of analysis, the pattern appeared to be more like attitude changes in small groups.

DISCUSSION

It is not suggested that the simulations described above provide anything like a complete representation of schools or that the basic assumptions of the model are the best that could be formulated to describe schools and classrooms, but it does demonstrate that the kind of data structure found in school effectiveness research can emerge from a set of very simple rules and reasonable starting values.

Further work would enable more realistic simulations to be set up which may be able to test some of the theoretical perspectives of research into school differences. Such models would hopefully be able to generate predictions from sets of assumptions and represent some of the extraordinary complexity in our schools. In the meantime the simulation described above should go some way to indicate that it is at least possible that our schools are chaotic and complex, in the scientific sense, and that the natural occurring phenomenon of emergence can explain some of what we see in school effectiveness data.

IMPLICATIONS

Suggestions that chaos and complexity may be found in social science data are open to the allegation that what is being said is only supported by analogy and that is clearly so. But, as Davies (1992) points out, the closer that an analogy fits, the more it starts to have the force of an important argument. Our belief that other human beings have minds is a belief stemming from an analogy with our own mind!

The amazing success of computer simulations of complexity seen in the context of the limitations of conventional science in many areas provides very powerful reasons at least to look carefully at what is being written and created. It may be that this approach could lead to a dead end but it promises much and one way to start is to consider the implications of taking this approach and try to suggest a way forward.

Implications from the Simulations

In thinking of the world as chaotic and as capable of being simulated, rather than as being explicable by the general linear model, a number of new lines of research and new ways of thinking open up.

Attempts to 'explain' much more of the school or pupil level variance, than is presently explained in school effectiveness studies, are doomed. If there really are chaotic processes at work within individual brains, in individual lives, in classrooms and in schools it will simply not be possible to construct multilevel models or comprehensive theories which explain the vast majority of the variation in outcomes in terms of input and process variables. Chaotic situations, whilst being subject to deterministic laws, are unpredictable beyond a certain point. We need to move beyond the limits of predictability to study the nature of the evolving complexity within our schools. One way forward would be to study the extent to which *particular knowledge* can improve the proportion of variance explained.

Since the idea behind chaos in education is that small changes can magnify into large effects it should be possible for case studies and/or teacher knowledge to provide convincing explanations of specific outliers. It may well be that specific events, or combinations of events, can be identified to account for groups or individuals having certain outcomes. This particular knowledge should be able to 'explain' some of the, as yet unexplained, variance. Such insights may not be valuable as generalizations but the integration of particular and generalized information should help to understand the nature of the data. Naturally, there is the need to guard against the human tendency to overlay explanations on things once they have been seen and any research in this area would need to guard against this. One way would be to ask trained 'blind' observers for estimates of the success of teachers, departments or schools before the results of any assessment were seen. These explanations could be quantified and used to define the limitations of generalized explanations and to extend our understanding of the limits of our ability to explain the success and failure of educational systems in general terms.

A further line of research starts by viewing classrooms as places where relationships and attitudes ebb and flow, where groups form and disband and where these processes influence attitudes to learning. One can only hope to investigate this by detailed almost continuous data collection. It might be possible to do this for a whole school or a class using repeated sampling of the type employed in studying animal behaviour. Qualitative researchers have been doing this detailed work for some time but the need to link these processes to a more global view requires that quantitative data be collected. (The world is too complicated for words.)

Under some conditions the pattern of events might be clearly rhythmic and predictable and in others more complex but still predictable. But there are surely some classes where prediction is not on. Nevertheless, it may still be possible to find 'strange attractors' in amongst the action. Plots of the time taken for one phase against the time for the next phase, or the value of one parameter against another – so-called 'phase diagrams' – have proved to be remarkably revealing in such chaotic situations as stock market (see Pritchard, 1992) and even the bubbling of gas from a pipe (Tritton and Egdell, 1993). Such phase diagrams have helped researchers to study chaotic simulations and the well-known Maldebrot set, which has been called the 'most complex object known to man' is an example of a phase diagram. This approach would not seek to construct rigorous quantitative explanation of how classroom variables interact to produce outcomes, rather it would seek to find patterns of behaviour which form and disband within a classroom setting and which ultimately relate to learning. The 'emergence' of disruptive and enhancing situations would be particularly interesting.

Of course there has been a considerable amount of classroom study, and of group interaction and it is interesting to note a similarity between computer simulations and such studies. It has generally been found that simulation models, starting with their initial conditions, take some time to settle down into the rhythm of a strange attractor, or for the emergence of some structure to take over. Analogously, we know that newly formed groups often have a period during which adjustment takes place (forming, storming, etc., Tuckman and Jensen, 1977). So, there may be some mileage in looking at educational courses from a quantitative perspective which tries not just to look at input, process and output measures, but also at attainment measures a short time into the course. These measures might be expected to be much closer to the final outcome than any prior measures. For example, end of first-term exams during A-level courses might be much more closely related to A-level grades than GCSE grades and may be nearly as good as 'mock' exams as predictors of A-level results. (Personal experience as an A-level teacher supports this hypothesis.)

The hypothesis is that the dynamics of a particular situation have important implications for outcomes and that patterns of behaviour, which define the dynamics, become established quite early on during a two-year course.

Turning now to a more global view of the educational scene, it has been said that systems evolve towards the 'edge of chaos'. 'Instead, all these complex systems have acquired the ability to bring order and chaos into a special kind of balance. This balance point – often called the edge of chaos – is where components of a system never quite lock into place, and yet never quite dissolve into turbulence either' (Waldrop, 1992, p. 12).

If the educational world fits this description then its behaviour should demonstrate the power law which indicates that the average frequencies of upheavals of a particular size is inversely proportional to the intensity of the upheaval raised to some power (see Lewin, 1992). In wanting to collect data on this to start to test the hypothesis that the educational world is chaotic the problem is to get a measure of the size of upheavals and their frequency. Perhaps with the advent of newspapers' records on CD-ROM it will be possible to make estimates of the frequency and size of the impact education is making simply by the proportion of column inches devoted to educational matters.

But whatever the possibilities are for future research, the more direct implication of a chaotic view is that it is very dangerous to ascribe any meaning to a single statistic either for the purposes of research or for accountability or school improvement purposes. In a sense this idea has been (Willms and Raudenbush, 1989), and is being (Gray et al., 1993) investigated under the heading of stability and it is already clear that apparently 'significant' results are not nearly as stable as a single year's data implies. Simulation models would suggest that even if it were possible to arrange for exactly the same class to have exactly the same teacher for two years in the same classroom living through the same two years that the outcomes would not be the same.

Furthermore, because chaotic situations have unpredictable outcomes, attempts to find blueprints for success at the school, pupil, LEA or country level are futile. As pointed out by Tymms (1991) and Fitz-Gibbon (1996) a viewpoint which accepts that chaos and complexity are relevant to educational situations leads to the conclusion that there is a need to monitor and the monitoring must be used to inform action. That viewpoint on the one hand suggests a way in which the educational system can be improved and at the same time provides a testable hypothesis.

The corollary of that view is that the ability to respond to feedback and to absorb new data must surely be an attribute of successful behaviour in chaotic situations. If this is so then it may be possible to demonstrate that the effective teacher is the teacher who can 'read' a class better than others. This means that such a teacher would be able to spot nuances of behaviours which indicated the need for action. Such a teacher might also be expected to be able to see very quickly if a particular teaching point is not being taken on board by a class. Conversely the inexperienced or ineffective teacher might be expected not to be so perceptive. This view of effective units in chaotic situations can be extended to whole schools and their behaviour where effective schools, if they exist, might be expected to gather and deal with data about their functioning on a regular basis and to act on that data. The study by Louis and Miles (1991) is relevant here in that the most successful variable in explaining changes in student outcomes was 'implementation management' and 'coping behaviour'.

The study of school effectiveness has made great strides since its start in the late 1960s but it has reached an impasse. We have, despite enormous efforts worldwide, failed to develop a firm knowledge base and testable theories. More importantly, we do not have clear, defensible advice on how to improve schools. This chapter has argued that this is partly because controlled interventions have not been part of the researchers' methodology and partly because the educational world is chaotic and complex. This view suggests several ways forward which would not only extend our understanding of schools and classrooms but also suggests testable hypotheses about improving their performance.

REFERENCES

Aitkin, M. and Longford, N. (1986) 'Statistical modelling issues in school effectiveness studies', *Journal of the Royal Statistical Society, Series A*, **149** (1), 1–43.

Audit Commission (1993) *Unfinished Business: Full-time Educational Courses for 16–19 Year Olds*. London: HMSO.

Cronbach, L. J. (1975) 'Beyond the two disciplines of scientific psychology', *American Psychologist*, **30**, 116–27.

Crutchfield, J. P. F., Packard, N. H. and Shaw, R. S. (1986) 'Chaos', *Scientific American*, **255**, (6).

Davies, P. (1992) *The Mind of God*. New York: Touchstone.

Dockrell, W. B. (1991) *Making a Difference: The Contribution of Research to Policy and Practice*. Paper presented at American Educational Research Association, Chicago.

Easterbrook, P. J., Berlin, J. A., Gopalan, R. and Mathews, D. R. (1991) 'Publication bias in clinical research', *Lancet*, **333**, 867–72.

Finn, J. D. and Achilles, C. M. (1990) 'Answers and questions about class size: a statewide experiment', *American Educational Research Journal*, **27** (3), 557–77.

Fitz-Gibbon, C. T. (1985) 'The implications of meta-analysis for educational research', *British Educational Research Journal*, **11** (1), 45–9.

Fitz-Gibbon, C. T. (1990) 'Learning from unwelcome data', in Hopkins, D. (ed.) *TVEI at the Change of Life*. Clevedon, Avon: Multilingual Matters, pp. 92–101.

Fitz-Gibbon, C. T. (1991) 'Multilevel modelling in an indicator system', in Raudenbush, S. W. and Willms, J. D. (eds) *Pupils, Classroom and Schools: International Studies from a Multilevel Perspective*. London and New York: Academic Press.

Fitz-Gibbon, C. T. (1992) 'The design of indicator systems', *Research Papers in Education*, **7** (3), 66–78.

Fitz-Gibbon, C. T. (1996) *Monitoring Education: Indicators, Quality and Effectiveness*. London: Cassell.

Fitz-Gibbon, C. T., Tymms, P. B. and Hazelwood, R. D. (1989) 'Performance indicators and information systems', in Reynolds, D. (ed.) *School Effectiveness and Improvement: Proceedings of the First International Congress*, London, 1988. Cardiff and Groningen: Cardiff and Ruon, pp. 141–52.

Fullan, M. G. (1991) *The New Meaning of Educational Change*. London: Cassell.

Gleick, J. (1988) *Chaos: Making a New Science*. London: Heinemann.

Goldstein, H. (1987) *Multilevel Models in Educational and Social Research*. London: Griffin.

Gray, J., Jesson, D., Goldstein, H. and Hedger, K. (1993) 'The statistics of school improvement', in Gray, J. and Wilcox, B. *'Good School, Bad School': Evaluating Performance and Encouraging Improvement*. Buckingham: Open University Press.

Hutchinson, D. (1993) 'School effectiveness studies using administrative data', *Educational Research*, **35** (1), 27–47.

Jesson, D. and Gray, J. (1991) 'Slants on slopes: using multilevel models to investigate differential school effectiveness and its impact on pupils' examination results', *School Effectiveness and School Improvement*, **2** (3), 230–47.

Lazar, I. and Darlington, R. (1982) *Monographs of the Society for Research in Child Development: Lasting Effects of Early Education*. Chicago: University of Chicago Press.

Lewin, L. (1993) *Complexity: Life at the Edge of Chaos*. London: Dent.

Louis, K. S. and Miles, M. B. (1991) 'Managing reform: lessons from urban high schools', *School Effectiveness and School Improvement*, **2** (2), 75–96.

Preece, P. F. W. (1990) 'Imitatio physicae', *British Educational Research Journal*, **16** (3), 297–304.

Pritchard, J. (1992) *The Chaos Cookbook: A Practical Programming Guide with type-in-and-go Listings*. Oxford: Butterworth–Heinemann.

Raudenbush, S. W. and Bryk, A. S. (1986) 'A hierarchical model for studying school effects', *Sociology of Education*, **59** (Jan), 1–17.

Teddlie, C. and Stringfield, S. (1993) *Schools Make a Difference: Lessons learned from a 10-year study of School Effects*. New York and London: Teachers College Press.

Tritton, D. J. and Egdell, C. (1993) 'Chaotic bubbling', *Physics of Fluids and Fluid Dynamics*, **5** (2), 503–5.

Tuckman, B. W. and Jensen, M. A. (1977) 'Stage of small group development revisted', *Group and Organisational Studies*, **2** (4), 419–27.

Tymms, P. B. (1991) 'Can indicator systems improve the effectiveness of science and mathematics education?' *Evaluation and Research in Education*, **4** (2), 61–73.

Tymms, P. B. (1992) 'The relative success of post-16 institutions in England (including assisted places schools)', *British Educational Research Journal*, **18** (2), 175–92.

Tymms, P. B. (1993) 'Accountability: can it be fair?', *Oxford Review of Education*, **19** (3), 291–9.

Tymms, P. B. (1995) 'Influencing educational practice through performance indicators', *School Effectiveness and School Improvement*, **6** (2), 123–45.

Tymms, P. B. and Fitz-Gibbon, C. T. (1992) 'The relationship of part-time employment and A-Level results', *Educational Research*, **34** (3), 193–9.

Waldrop, M. M. (1992) *Complexity: The Emerging Science at the Edge of Order and Chaos*. London: Viking.

Willms, J. D. and Raudenbush, S. W. (1989) 'A longitudinal hierarchical linear model for estimating school effects and their stability', *Journal of Educational Measurements*, **26** (3), 209–32.

Chapter 7

School Autonomy and School Improvement

Tony Bush

INTRODUCTION

During the 1980s and 1990s there has been a shift towards greater self-management for educational institutions in many countries, particularly in the English-speaking world. This trend is evident in a variety of forms in Australia, Canada, New Zealand, the UK and parts of the USA. Caldwell and Spinks (1988; 1992) argue that self-management is now so widespread that it merits classification as a 'megatrend'. They define self-management as follows:

> A self-managing school is a school in a system of education where there has been significant and consistent decentralization to the school level of authority to make decisions related to the allocation of resources ... The school remains accountable to a central authority for the manner in which resources are allocated (Caldwell and Spinks 1992, p. 4).

The widespread introduction of systems of self-managing schools is motivated by the desire to raise standards. The underlying philosophy is that by devolving control over finance and real resources to school boards and principals they will be empowered to deploy those resources in support of school objectives, and to evaluate the effectiveness of those policies. Keeping decisions 'close to the action' allows funding to be aligned with school needs instead of the priorities of local and national governments. This is a normative model, in that it represents the opinions of its protagonists about the most appropriate way to develop schools. In England and Wales, self-management is underpinned by 'new right' concepts of consumer choice in education and the values of an enterprise culture. Stuart Sexton of the right-wing pressure group, the Institute of Economic Affairs, argued for self-management before the 1988 Education Reform Act:

> If the system itself were changed to one of self-governing, self-managing, budget centres, which were obliged for their very survival to respond to the 'market', then there would be an in-built mechanism to raise standards (Sexton, 1987, pp. 8–9).

In this chapter, we seek to establish whether this normative model is also operational, by examining the evidence for and against the view that school autonomy leads to school improvement.

DEFINING SCHOOL IMPROVEMENT

According to Glatter (1988), the International School Improvement Project (ISIP) adopted the following definition of school improvement: 'A systematic, sustained effort aimed at change in learning and other related internal conditions in one or more schools, with the ultimate aim of accomplishing educational goals more effectively' (Miles and Ekholm, 1985, quoted in Glatter 1988, p. 125).

Blum and Butler (1989) identify three elements of effective leadership for school improvement:

- Set a long-term mission or vision

  'School leaders must set an overall direction for the improvement of the school within relevant national and local policies ... [they] need the process and social skills to carry people with them in support of the mission and vision' (p. 19).

- Balance goals and maintain quality

  'Closely associated with the vision is the identification of short-term, manageable goals which are in line with the overall direction of the school. School leaders ... must keep in balance the time and energy demands of innovations with the requirements for maintaining existing activities at a high level' (p. 19).

- Manage the context

  'Externally, school leaders need to establish effective working relationships with the various groups who have a stake in the school. This implies an interactive approach wherein the school seeks to influence the various segments of its environment and is open to influence by them' (p. 20).

The implication of this body of research is that school improvement depends primarily on the quality of the *internal* leadership of the school. Establishing a vision for the school and setting specific goals are not activities that can be carried out on behalf of schools by external agencies. Broad educational aims do arise from the educational system but they need to be tailored to the needs of individual schools by their heads, staff and governing boards. Managing the context requires interaction between these individuals and groups and those external bodies with a legitimate interest in its activities. However, it is internal leaders who have the main responsibility for ensuring good relationships with these stakeholders.

When the goals of a school have been established, specific policies are required to translate them into action. These strategies provide a link between school aims and the operational, or day-to-day, activities of staff and students. In a school committed to school improvement, some of these policies are directed towards enhanced performance. Gray *et al.* (1995) give examples of departmental and school strategies to secure school improvement:

- Departmental

  reviewing and setting fresh targets;

  careful monitoring of pupils' progress;

regular feedback to pupils on their development.

- School

  increase the total number of exams entered;

  monitor differences in departments;

  changes in the time allocated to different subjects;

  identification of particular pupils and groups of pupils for additional support.

All these policies are within the control of the school. Their effective implementation depends, in part, on deploying resources in support of the strategies. This process is facilitated by locating control of finance and real resources at school level. The ability to shift, or move, resources from one activity to another is an important element in the process of improvement and a central component of self-management in the UK and elsewhere.

Change and Implementation

School improvement inevitably requires certain adjustments to existing policies and practice. Fullan (1982; 1992) emphasizes the problematic nature of the implementation of change. New policies at the school level do not necessarily mean changes in classroom activity. As Becher (1989) emphasizes, there may be an 'implementation gap' between the enunciation of policy initiatives and real changes in practice. Fullan (1992) sets out six key aspects of an effective implementation process.

- *'Vision-building* ... permeates the organization with values, purpose and integrity for both the what and how of improvement .... While virtually everyone agrees that vision is crucial, the practice of vision-building is not well understood' (p. 121).

- *Evolutionary planning*. The most successful schools adapt their plans as they proceed to improve the fit between the change and conditions in the school to take advantage of unexpected developments and opportunities.

- Initiative-taking and *empowerment*. Following Louis and Miles (1990), Fullan stresses the importance of 'power sharing' amongst teachers, administrators, and sometimes parents and students as a means of achieving change. 'Working together has the potential of raising morale and enthusiasm, opening the door to experimentation and increased sense of efficacy' (p. 122).

- Staff development during implementation is vital to successful change. 'Research on implementation has demonstrated beyond a shadow of a doubt that these processes of sustained *interaction and staff development* are crucial' (p. 123).

- *'Monitoring* the process of change is just as important as measuring outcomes .... Monitoring the results and the process of change is especially important at the school level' (pp. 123–4).

- *Restructuring*. 'Time for individual and team planning, joint teaching arrangements, staff development policies, new roles such as mentors and coaches, and school improvement procedures are examples of structural change ... conducive to improvement' (p. 124).

These characteristics of successful change are largely within the control of the school and its leaders. The focus on vision-building and planning echo Blum and Butler's (1989) emphasis on these strategies. The stress on empowerment is a recurring theme in the literature on school improvement as we shall see later in this chapter. Staff development policy is increasingly located at the school level, certainly in England and Wales. Monitoring and restructuring are also strategies available to leaders within schools.

School Effectiveness

The school effectiveness literature shows that there are substantial differences in pupil outcomes that cannot be explained by socio-economic or intake variables but are attributable to the characteristics of schools as organizations (Reynolds, 1992). The conclusion to be drawn from this body of research (Reynolds, 1976; Rutter *et al.*, 1979; Mortimore *et al.*, 1986) is that the schools themselves do make a significant difference. 'Studies which have collected a very wide range of data concerning the intakes into different schools have still found large differences in the outcomes of the schools, even when allowance has been made for differences in intakes' (Reynolds, 1992, p. 3).

Mortimore *et al.* (1986) conducted longitudinal research in 50 junior schools within the former Inner London Education Authority (ILEA). They found that the organizational character of the schools was a significant variable in determining the progress of children and claim that: 'It is the factors *within* the control of the head and teachers that are crucial. These are the factors that can be changed and improved' (p. 34).

The researchers identified 12 such factors that all contribute to school effectiveness:

- purposeful leadership by the headteacher;
- the involvement of the deputy head;
- the involvement of teachers;
- consistency amongst teachers;
- structured sessions;
- intellectually challenging teaching;
- work-centred environment;
- limited focus within sessions;
- maximum communication between teachers and pupils;
- record-keeping;
- parental involvement;
- positive climate.

The researchers conclude that effectiveness depends on the behaviour and strategies of headteachers and staff:

> While these twelve factors do not constitute a 'recipe' for effective
> junior schooling, they can provide a framework within which the
> various partners in the life of the school – headteacher and staff,
> parents and pupils, and governors – can operate. Each of these
> partners has the capacity to foster the success of the school. When
> each participant plays a positive role, the result is an effective school
> (Mortimore *et al.*, 1986, p. 38).

The focus on internal groups and individuals, including the governing body, supports the contention that a significant measure of institutional control is important to enable schools to maximize their effectiveness. It also leads to the hypothesis that improvement can be fostered by enhancing school autonomy.

DOES ENHANCING AUTONOMY LEAD TO SCHOOL IMPROVEMENT?

International Evidence

The international trend towards greater autonomy for educational establishments is predicated on the assumption that it will lead to school improvement. 'The case for self-management is being argued on the basis of findings from studies of school effectiveness … a form of self-management provides the best framework wherein these characteristics [of effective schools] may be fostered in all schools' (Caldwell and Spinks, 1988, p. 8).

Caldwell and Spinks quote Finn's (1984) view that transforming the findings of effective schools research into improved educational practice is being hampered by the tension between school-level autonomy and system-wide uniformity. They argue that:

> It is simply more efficient and effective in the late twentieth century
> to restructure systems of education so that central bureaucracies are
> relatively small and schools are empowered to manage their own
> affairs within a centrally determined framework of direction and
> support. Two arguments have usually been offered, one is concerned
> with responsiveness, the other with priorities for resource allocation
> in times of economic restraint or budgetary crisis (p. 14).

They add that self-management empowers people inside schools. 'Certain groups of people in the school community now have the opportunity to influence the course of events in the life of the school to a greater extent than in the past' (p. 18). This implies that improvement is dependent on dispersed management *within* the school as well as devolution of power to the institutional level.

Beare *et al.* (1992), following Miles (1987), argue that a large measure of school autonomy is a pre-condition for successful implementation of change. At minimum, autonomy should extend to a measure of control over staffing and other resources. They endorse Purkey and Smith's (1985) view that school-site management *and* collaborative decision-making are essential components of the framework for successful change:

> The staff of each school is given a considerable amount of
> responsibility and authority in determining the exact means by which
> they address the problem of increasing academic performance. This
> includes giving staffs more authority over curricular decisions and
> allocation of building resources (p. 358).

If this view is accepted, autonomy is a necessary but not a sufficient condition for
school improvement. It has to be accompanied by devolution of power to teachers if higher standards are to be achieved. This emphasis on the need for internal
change makes the link between autonomy and improvement problematic as we
shall see later in this chapter.

The British Experience

Since 1988, the British government's policy has been to increase the extent to
which schools and colleges are able to determine their own priorities, albeit within
a framework of central regulation, including the imposition of the National
Curriculum. The introduction of local management of schools (LMS), grant maintained (GM) schools and incorporated colleges are all part of the drive towards
self-determination. These radical developments have been accompanied by much
government rhetoric, notably in the 1992 White Paper:

> The objective has been both to put governing bodies and head
> teachers under the greater pressure of public accountability for
> better standards and to increase their freedom to respond to that
> pressure. The autonomy acquired under local management of schools
> and, in ever greater numbers, as GM schools, offers schools enhanced
> powers to achieve better performance in their schools to match their
> increased accountability for that performance. Together with the
> senior staff of schools, governing bodies have reacted very positively
> to their new autonomy, using their greater flexibility to deploy
> resources, including the selection and use of staff, to better effect
> (DES, 1992a, p. 18).

The advocates of LMS and GM status believe that giving control of policy and
resources to governing bodies and headteachers provides both the motivation and
the wherewithal to raise standards. The aim of the LMS policy is to locate the main
decision-making powers with those *internal* groups and individuals best placed
to assess the impact of decisions on their pupils and students, as Coopers and
Lybrand (1988) suggest:

> The underlying philosophy of financial delegation to schools stems
> from the application of the principles of good management. Good
> management requires the identification of management units for
> which objectives can be set and resources allocated; the unit is then
> required to manage itself within those resources in a way which
> seeks to achieve the objectives; the performance of the unit is
> monitored and the unit is held to account for its performance and for
> its use of funds (para. 1.5).

Schools are the 'management units' referred to by Coopers and Lybrand. Governing bodies and headteachers are expected to link their financial planning to their educational polices. Direct control of budgets is expected to enable schools to become more effective in allocating resources to support their aims. Monitoring occurs largely through the quadrennial programme of school inspections foreshadowed by the 1992 Education Act and implemented by the Office for Standards in Education (OFSTED).

Coopers and Lybrand (1988) go on to claim several advantages for LMS:

> There can be major gains from delegation. It will increase the
> accountability of schools for providing value for money; it will give
> schools the flexibility to respond directly and promptly to the needs
> of the school and its pupils in a way which will increase the
> effectiveness and quality of the services provided. Schools will have
> more incentive to seek efficiency and economy in their use of
> resources since they will be able to apply the benefits of their good
> management to further improvements in their services (para. 1.8).

The basic philosophy is that it is more appropriate for school governors and staff to determine priorities, and to deploy resources in line with those priorities, than it is to have the local education authority (LEA) allocate resources on the basis of its LEA-wide policies. The LEA process was based on the perceived needs of the system as a whole and could not match the individual requirements of schools in the way that governors and heads can do.

The implementation of LMS created initial difficulties because there were both 'winners' and 'losers' as school budgets reflected the greater degree of objectivity required by the government. 'Losing' schools were often those with above-average salary costs, due to a significant proportion of older and experienced staff. The government's insistence that schools be charged the actual cost of staff, rather than an 'average' cost, meant that certain schools had limited opportunity to benefit from delegated budgets. Marren and Levacic's (1992) research shows that there were substantial variations in budgets arising from the shift to LMS. Their case-study schools ranged from a gain of 8.06 per cent to a loss of 12.30 per cent. Despite this variation, all schools welcomed the budgetary freedom arising from LMS.

Grant Maintained Schools

The provision for GM schools is arguably the most radical of the fundamental changes introduced by the Conservative government's many Education Acts. GM status might be regarded as a 'pure' form of LMS. Schools may opt out of LEA control and thus gain access to more resources than LMS schools which have money withheld to fund the LEA's central services. The GM policy has enjoyed a measure of success with some 1,100 opted-out schools by 1996, although this figure is below government expectations. Opting out has been supported by much rhetoric extolling its benefits:

> GM schools are self-governing schools. That autonomy is at the heart
> of the GM school idea, and at the heart of the government's
> education policies. The common experience of GM schools is that

their status significantly enhances the work of the school. The real sense of ownership they enjoy has proved highly motivating (DES, 1992b, p. 19).

If school improvement depends, in part, on the degree of control exerted by school staff and governors, it leads to the hypothesis that increasing institutional control should facilitate improvement. This is implied by HMI in a brief comment on standards in GM schools:

> Standards of work in grant-maintained schools were rather higher than those in the maintained sector as a whole and many of the schools had been able to improve the quality and extent of their accommodation, equipment, book stock and other learning resources through the use of capital grants and a redeployment of the recurrent grant now within their control (DES, 1992b, p. 21).

A subsequent report by OFSTED is more equivocal about relative standards:

> Overall standards in grant maintained schools were slightly higher; in 3 per cent more of the lessons the standards were judged to be satisfactory or better ... the differences [were not] large enough to be statistically significant .... The quality of teaching could not be said with any confidence to be either better or worse in grant maintained than in LEA maintained schools (1993, p. 10).

Analysis of the 1992 GCSE results at the first 93 GM secondary schools shows a higher level of achievement in GM schools than in the rest of the maintained sector (see Table 7.1). Even if all 30 selective schools are omitted from the sample, GM schools appear to be more successful on this indicator: 41.3 per cent of pupils in non-selective GM schools achieved five or more A–C grades compared with the national average of 38.1 per cent (Bush *et al.*, 1993, p. 212).

These figures should be interpreted with care. Most of the early GM schools were in Conservative-controlled areas in the suburbs and rural areas where good results could be expected. There is also some evidence of 'selective' admissions policies although these would have little or no effect on the 1992 GCSE cohort. The first 100 GM schools also enjoyed certain financial advantages and were able to increase their real resources which should have benefited teaching and learning.

In addition, the 1992 figures give a static picture of achievement on this indicator. In order to establish a link between autonomy and school improvement it would be necessary to examine year-on-year change. Gray *et al.* (1993) suggest that at least three years should be assessed to establish a trend.

Table 7.1 *GCSE Pass Rates of GM Schools in 1992*[1]

Type of school	Number of schools	Percentage of pupils with 5 A–C passes
Selective	30	89.7
Non-selective	63	41.3
All	93	56.9

[1] First 93 GM secondary schools

Many governors and staff of GM schools believe that autonomy contributes to higher standards through the process of empowerment referred to by Caldwell and Spinks (1992). Eighty per cent of the participants in the author's GM research state that independence from the LEA is one of the main benefits of opting out. The following comments illustrate this point:

- 'Freedom, financial freedom and a feeling that we are in control of our own destiny' (teacher union representative)
- 'Freedom to determine our own priorities. Freedom from bureaucracy. Making decisions for our own school at a local level rather than the whole area' (chair of governors)
- 'The main advantage is the sense of autonomy; that you can make decisions without constant referral to a remote body that has little sympathy to your needs' (headteacher)
  (Bush *et al.* 1993, pp. 200–201).

Thompson (1992, p. 140) also refers to increased morale and says that the change to GM status can 'empower both teachers and governors'.

The GM evidence points to a link between autonomy and improvement but it is by no means conclusive. There are several contradictory factors that may weaken the case and suggest a more problematic relationship between autonomy and improvement.

SCHOOL AUTONOMY VERSUS SCHOOL IMPROVEMENT?

The work of several researchers in both the school improvement and effectiveness traditions shows that factors within the control of the school are crucial to its effectiveness (Mortimore *et al.*, 1986; Gray *et al.*, 1993). The hypothesis is that increasing that control should facilitate greater effectiveness leading to school improvement. However, the putative link between autonomy and improvement is unclear. It may be difficult to establish that improvement is due to the 'autonomy effect' and even harder to establish *how* autonomy leads to improvement.

Several more fundamental arguments have been advanced to suggest that autonomy may hinder school improvement or that the external or internal climate may prevent the achievement of the potential benefits.

Centralization and Decentralization

The potential for autonomous schools to deliver improvement is limited by the imposition of a programme of reform that is simultaneously centralist and decentralist. Schools are encouraged to compete for pupils but within a curriculum or 'product' that is largely prescribed by the government. Local autonomy is circumscribed by the implementation of a national agenda for change. School governors and staff may not determine the content of the curriculum, only how it shall be taught. 'The weaknesses of the traditional "top-down" approach to educational change are almost daily being exposed in our newspapers, and there is a growing recognition that neither centralization nor decentralization works' (Hopkins *et al.*, 1994, p. 2).

According to Hopkins *et al.* (1994, p. 16), LMS is 'a superficial initiative'. The tension between centralization and decentralization makes it very difficult for schools to implement innovations that make a real difference to the quality of schooling and pupil achievement. They accept the argument that the school should be the centre of change but stress that they have individual needs: 'This means that external reforms need to be sensitive to the situation in individual schools, rather than assuming that all schools are the same' (p. 69).

Contrived Collegiality

The case for a causal link between autonomy and improvement rests in part on the assumption that delegation of authority to schools will be matched by new internal processes that empower staff and others with a legitimate interest in the school. The notion of teacher 'ownership' of innovation is thought to be essential if change is to permeate classroom practice. Joyce (1991) describes collegiality as one of the five 'doors' that open the passageway to school improvement. He argues that developing cohesive professional relations within schools is essential to achieve real change. This claim is supported by several British writers (Campbell, 1985; Wallace, 1989) who stress the value of collegial approaches to school management.

There are two main difficulties about the assumption that collegiality is required to 'unlock' the potential for autonomy to generate school improvement. First, there is some evidence that GM status, for example, has not been accompanied by internal devolution of power. Heads and senior management teams have tended to retain control of decision-making rather than developing a distributed system which empowers teachers (Bush *et al.*, 1993; Thompson, 1992).

A more fundamental critique of collegiality is offered by Hargreaves (1994) who argues that it is being espoused by official groups in order to secure the implementation of national policies. He claims that genuine collegiality is spontaneous, voluntary, unpredictable, informal and geared to development. 'Contrived collegiality', in contrast, has the following contradictory features:

- 'administratively regulated rather than spontaneous;
- compulsory rather than discretionary;
- geared to the implementation of the mandates of government or the headteacher;
- fixed in time and place;
- designed to have predictable outcomes' (pp. 195–6).

Within the post-Education Reform Act context in England and Wales, this analysis is persuasive. These dimensions of 'collegiality' support his analysis:

- collegiality receives official support (Campbell, 1985);
- the National Curriculum largely prescribes content and assessment;
- the concept of 'directed time' enables heads to require participation in the decision-making process.

These elements do not necessarily eliminate the informal and spontaneous aspects of collegiality but they do support the view that participation may be mainly about implementation of externally imposed change rather than an open exploration of potential new policies to generate school improvement. It is a limited form of collegiality that focuses on how the National Curriculum may be delivered effectively rather than starting with the needs of the pupils and developing a curriculum to meet those needs.

School and Community Values

Underpinning the debate about whether and how autonomy promotes school improvement is the wider normative issue of what is the most appropriate division of powers between schools and representatives of the communities they serve. In the UK context, should the dominant values in the education system be those of the local authorities or those of individual schools? LEAs stress the needs of the educational system as a whole while the schools tend to emphasize their own unique qualities and requirements. The 1988 Education Reform Act supports the position of the schools, loosening their links with the LEAs and offering them the opportunity to seek autonomy through GM status.

While much of the school improvement literature stresses that schools should be at the centre of change, links with external groups are also regarded as important in the search for beneficial change (Blum and Butler, 1989). This includes 'networking' with professional colleagues as well as meeting the perceived needs of their local communities. This recognition leads to what Hopkins *et al.* (1994) describe as 'a multilevel perspective':

> The school is embedded in an educational system that has to work
> collaboratively or symbiotically if the highest degrees of quality are to
> be achieved. This means that the roles of teachers, heads, governors,
> parents, support people (advisers, higher education, consultants,
> etc.) and local authorities should be defined, harnessed and
> committed to the process of school improvement (p. 69).

The early evidence from the GM sector is that teachers are concerned about their potential divorce from the main professional networks, particularly in those areas where few schools have opted out. Of teacher respondents to the author's survey (Bush *et al.*, 1993), 48 per cent refer to 'isolation from LEA schools' as one of the main disadvantages of GM status.

Pryke (1994) reports on the devolution of power to schools in New Zealand, a process analogous to GM status but applying to all schools:

> Schools ... regret the loss of co-ordination and networking between
> schools as they are encouraged to compete for pupils and staff ....
> Has a proper division been made between management of individual
> schools and governance of individual schools within a total system?
> (p. 498).

As Director of Education for Kent, Pryke can be expected to be sceptical about the GM programme but the issue of the most appropriate balance between school and community responsibilities is significant. The OECD (1989) discusses the concern that certain services may be vulnerable in a system of autonomous schools:

> Shifts of responsibility to the school level raise the possibility that some functions, formerly carried out at the centre, will not be effectively performed .... External support for schools, reorientated to meet specific school-defined needs ... must be sustained (p. 2).

The services most likely to be vulnerable are those that schools find difficult to provide for themselves because they require a large scale of operation to be cost-effective. Primary schools, for example, find it difficult to meet the cost of inservice training from a limited staff development budget.

CONCLUSION – DOES AUTONOMY FOSTER SCHOOL IMPROVEMENT?

The international trend towards school autonomy has been accompanied by claims that it will foster beneficial change by allowing those most concerned with the school to determine their objectives, allocate resources in support of those aims and to monitor whether and to what extent they have been achieved. This hypothesis is well supported in government rhetoric and by the management literature but it has received only limited empirical verification. Similarly, the concerns of opponents of decentralization are based on ideology as much as evidence.

A programme of research is required to establish whether and how increasing school autonomy leads to improvement. Because the shift to self-management is widespread and based on the assumption that it will enhance pupil outcomes, the need for research is both important and urgent. The research agenda needs to address the following issues:

- Is it possible to establish a link between school improvement and autonomy?
- Can the 'autonomy effect' be isolated from other factors influencing pupil and school achievement?
- What are the components of the 'autonomy effect' and to what extent are they independent of other school variables?
- In the UK context, is LMS sufficient to ensure school improvement or is the more radical step of GM status needed to deliver all the benefits of autonomy?
- Is dispersed leadership an essential component of school improvement or does the 'autonomy effect' operate even if there is no change in internal management processes?
- What is the appropriate balance between autonomy and centralization?

The debate about self-managing schools has been largely normative, informed by ideology and vested interest. The research agenda proposed here should lead to the generation of additional evidence to support the limited data available from previous enquiries. A programme of research would help to establish whether the massive policy changes of the 1980s and 1990s produce the outcomes they were intended to achieve.

ACKNOWLEDGEMENT

The author is grateful for the help of his University of Leicester colleagues Marianne Coleman, Derek Glover and John O'Neill who offered valuable comments on a draft of this text.

REFERENCES

Beare, H., Caldwell, B. and Millikan, R. (1992) 'A model for managing an excellent school', in Bennett, N., Crawford, M. and Riches, C. (eds) *Managing Change in Education*. London: Paul Chapman.

Becher, T. (1989) 'The national curriculum and the implementation gap', in Preedy, M. (ed.) *Approaches to Curriculum Management*. Milton Keynes: Open University Press.

Blum, R. E. and Butler, J. A. (1989) 'The role of school leaders in school improvement', in Blum, R. E. and Butler, J. A. (eds) *School Leader Development for School Improvement*. Leuven: Acco.

Bush, T., Coleman, M. and Glover, D. (1993) *Managing Autonomous Schools: The Grant Maintained Experience*. London: Paul Chapman.

Caldwell, B. and Spinks, J. (1988) *The Self-Managing School*. London: Falmer Press.

Caldwell, B. and Spinks, J. (1992) *Leading the Self-Managing School*. London: Falmer Press.

Campbell, R. J. (1985) *Developing the Primary Curriculum*. London: Holt, Rinehart and Winston.

Coopers and Lybrand (1988) *Local Management of Schools*. London: HMSO.

Department of Education and Science (1992a) *Choice and Diversity: A New Framework for Schools* (Cmnd 2021). London: HMSO.

Department of Education and Science (1992b) 'Standards in Education 1990–1991', *The Annual Report of HM Senior Chief Inspector of Schools*, February.

Finn, C. E. (1984) 'Towards strategic independence: nine commandments for enhancing school effectiveness', *Phi Delta Kappan*, February, pp. 518–24.

Fullan, M. (1982) *The Meaning of Educational Change*. Ontario: OISE Press.

Fullan, M. (1992) 'Causes/processes of implementation and continuation', in Bennett, N., Crawford, M. and Riches, C. (eds) *Managing Change in Education*. London: Paul Chapman.

Glatter, R. (1988) 'The management of school improvement, in Glatter, R., Preedy, M., Riches, C. and Masterton, M. (eds) *Understanding School Management*. Milton Keynes: Open University Press.

Gray, J., Jesson, D., Goldstein, H. and Hedger, K. (1995) 'The statistics of school improvement: establishing the agenda', in Gray, J. and Wilcox, B. *'Good School, Bad School': Evaluating Performance and Encouraging Improvement*. Buckingham: Open University Press.

Hargreaves, A. (1994) *Changing Teachers, Changing Times: Teachers' Work and Culture in the Postmodern Age*. London: Cassell.

Hopkins, D., Ainscow, M. and West, M. (1994) *School Improvement in an Era of Change*. London: Cassell.

Joyce, B. (1991) 'The doors to school improvement', *Educational Leadership*, **48** (8), 59–62.

Louis, K. and Miles, M. B. (1990) *Improving the Urban High School: What Works and Why*. New York: Teachers College Press.

Marren, E. and Levacic, R. (1992) 'Implementing local management of schools', in Simpkins, T., Ellison, L. and Garrett, V. (eds) *Implementing Education Reforms: the early lessons*. Harlow: Longman.

Miles, M. B. (1987) 'Practical guidelines for school administrators: how to get there'. Paper read at a symposium of Effective Schools Programs and the Urban High School, Washington DC, Annual Meeting of the American Educational Research Association.

Miles, M. B. and Ekholm, M. (1985) 'What is school improvement', in van Velzen, W. G., Miles, M. B., Ekholm, M., Hameyer, U. and Robin, D. (eds) *Making School Improvement Work*. Leuven: Acco.

Mortimore, P., Sammons, P., Stoll, L., Lewis, D. and Ecob, R. (1986) *The Junior School Project: A Summary of the Main Report*. London: Inner London Education Authority.

OECD (1989) *Decentralization and School Improvement*. Paris: OECD/CERI.

OFSTED (1993) *Grant Maintained Schools 1989–92*. London: HMSO.

Pryke, R. (1994) *Education*, **183** (25), 498.

Purkey, S. C. and Smith, M. S. (1985) 'School reform: the district policy implications of the effective schools literature', *Elementary School Journal*, **85**.

Reynolds, D. (1976) 'The delinquent school', in Woods, P. (ed.) *The Process of Schooling*. London: Routledge & Kegan Paul.

Reynolds, D. (1992) 'School effectiveness and school improvement: an updated review of the British literature', in Reynolds, D. and Cuttance, P. (eds), *School Effectiveness: Research, Policy and Practice*. London: Cassell.

Rutter, M., Maughan, B., Mortimore, P. and Ouston, J. (1979) *Fifteen Thousand Hours: Secondary Schools and their Effects on Children*. London: Open Books.

Sexton, S. (1987) *Our Schools: A Radical Policy*. Warlingham: Institute of Economic Affairs.

Thompson, M. (1992) 'The experience of going grant-maintained: the perceptions of AMMA teacher representatives', *Journal of Teacher Development*, **1** (3), 133–40.

Wallace, M. (1989) 'Towards a collegiate approach to curriculum management in primary and middle schools', in Preedy, M. (ed.) *Approaches to Curriculum Management*. Milton Keynes: Open University Press.

Chapter 8

Turning Around Ineffective Schools: Some Evidence and Some Speculations

David Reynolds

INTRODUCTION

The problems involved in 'turning around' schools which are perceived to be 'failing' in the OFSTED definition or which are ineffective viewed from a school effectiveness perspective are now beginning to engage the three communities of researchers, policy-makers and practitioners much more than hitherto. Part of this represents an understandable reaction to the risk of closure that can now follow on from apparently unsatisfactory inspections and action plans. Additionally, the recent reporting of the characteristics of some of those schools which appear to have improved their functioning over the three years in which academic results have been routinely published has also served to direct attention towards schools in the 'ineffective' category.

From the research community also have come some enhanced concerns about these schools, their problems and their potential importance as generators of knowledge for the effectiveness and improvement knowledge bases (Gray and Wilcox, 1994; Reynolds and Packer, 1992; Reynolds, 1991). What follows in this chapter is an attempt to conceptualize the extent to which ineffective schools have to be understood as 'different' from schools with other levels of effectiveness and to speculate upon the types of improvement strategy which may be appropriate for them. It is based upon two small-scale empirical studies: the hitherto partially reported study from South Wales of a consultancy-based attempt to turn around a historically underperforming secondary school (Reynolds, 1987; Murgatroyd and Reynolds, 1985), and a previously unreported study of the introduction of school effectiveness knowledge into a similar school between 1990 and 1994, the period in post of a new headteacher who was personally and professionally highly committed to the school effectiveness knowledge base and to its utility. It is also based upon the experience of doing inservice work, particularly 'Baker days', in a large number of secondary schools of varying levels of apparent effectiveness over the past ten years, mostly in Wales, and the experience of recently joining the governing body of a primary school which is currently in receipt of OFSTED 'special measures'.

THE POLICY AND INTELLECTUAL CONTEXT OF CONCERNS ABOUT INEFFECTIVE SCHOOLS

In the broader educational context, it is entirely possible that a higher and higher proportion of schools are becoming ineffective in that they fall below a threshold of basic organizational adequacy. This may be as a consequence of the following factors.

1. The retrenchment of local authorities over the past five years may have removed the props and supports that have kept some schools from 'bottoming out', leaving some schools now to find their natural level of ineffectiveness.

2. The enhanced requirements involved in being organizationally competent or effective as a school in the 1990s may have differentiated out a higher proportion of ineffective school regimes who are unable to cope with enhanced responsibilities in areas such as local management, budgeting and development planning.

3. Enhanced levels of stress for all schools and of pressures upon them may have differentiated schools out over a much wider continuum, with the stress producing both more effectiveness and more ineffectiveness depending upon schools' organizational capacity to 'cope'.

4. The effects of naturally occurring educational changes in which individual schools exercise of their powers in such areas as their choice of inservice, their school development planning and their teacher appraisal results in the 'raising of the ceiling' by competent schools who improve the quality of their practice but in the 'lowering of the floor' by the less competent, who abuse or misuse new opportunities and become more ineffective.

5. The effect of market-based educational policies in leading to the removal of children, particularly more able children, from certain apparently low-performing schools with consequent adverse effects upon school ability balance and staff morale. Some schools may be in a spiral of decline, in which ineffectiveness is increased by the consumer reaction to that ineffectiveness.

The intellectual problems faced by those of us who wish to understand these ineffective schools may be severe, however. Our existing knowledge bases may not reflect their contribution representatively because the 'drop-out' schools that refuse to participate in effectiveness research are likely to be weighted towards the ineffective. Within school improvement, it is likely that less effective schools have not played a full part in generating our knowledge base because they are less likely to hire school improvement persons or to be visited by such persons. The other routine involvements between effectiveness/improvement persons and teachers in such areas as higher degrees and in continuing professional development are also likely to be lower within ineffective institutions than in effective ones. Simply, we may not have much knowledge about, or relevant to, these schools because we have little routine research or professional involvement with them.

Additionally, the paradigm within which school effectiveness has been historically situated can be argued to have involved a deficit model of the ineffective school, based upon conceptualizing and studying the effective school and then turning to the ineffective school to see what it is that the ineffective school may lack. This intellectual structure, with the aim of bringing the 'good' things of the effective school to the ineffective school to improve it, is particularly in evidence in the work of the American school effectiveness movement from the very earliest initial links made between school effectiveness and school change by Edmonds (1979).

However, rather than seeing ineffective schools as 'not having success characteristics', it might have been more productive to see them as 'having failure characteristics', and to view them as having factors not necessarily seen in the effective schools. Additionally, the problem of the ineffective school may not be just the lack of the effectiveness correlates and the possession of additional specific factors generating ineffectiveness – it may be that the ineffective schools have *antithetical* characteristics to the effectiveness ones present in other effective schools. As an example, an ineffective school may not evidence simply the absence of 'strong purposeful leadership' – it may possess additionally 'fragmented, confused and inconsistent leadership' (Myers, 1994).

In our purported strategies for the improvement of ineffective schools, we again have intellectual and practical problems. As Gray and Wilcox (1994) note, most school improvement work concerns the study of more general processes of improvement, and even the recent more sophisticated blends of improvement/ effectiveness/evaluation strategies of practitioners like Hopkins *et al*. (1994) are quite clearly based upon experiences in quite atypical school samples. Besides, one is not sure from the existing range of effectiveness and improvement studies which of the effectiveness correlates are the results of effectiveness rather than the cause, and one is also not sure whether the factors that have been identified in the studies of schools that have become effective are the same as the factors that would be necessary to get schools that are 'ineffective' to 'effective' status. This latter issue about the possibly different factors related to improvement rather than to effectiveness is, of course, the subject of the current ESRC-funded study in Gloucestershire and Shropshire secondary schools directed by John Gray, David Hopkins and myself.

The argument here is, then, that we may have been deficient in our exposure to, and understanding of, the ineffective schools within the UK effectiveness-and-improvement research community. Whereas in the USA there have been some attempts to understand and conceptualize the problems of such schools (as in the case of the 'depressed' schools of Louis and Miles (1990) and the 'stuck' schools of Rosenholtz (1989)), we have as yet no sizeable British enterprise. What follows is a preliminary and brief description of work with two 'ineffective' schools in an attempt to begin some British discussion of the ineffective school context.

STUDY ONE: TURNING AROUND AN INEFFECTIVE SCHOOL THROUGH SCHOOL EFFECTIVENESS-BASED CONSULTANCY

This research-and-development activity took place over a three-year period in a comprehensive school taken from a very deprived valley community within Gwent local education authority. The school in the late 1980s featured in the bottom three for 'value-added', based upon simple local education authority analysis of census data and examination results. An approach for help to David Reynolds and Stephen Murgatroyd by the headteacher had followed from the outbreak of a considerable degree of media attention being devoted to the issue of why schools in Wales were underperforming on examination achievement by comparison with those in England. An initial whole-day session with school staff was used to outline the school effectiveness knowledge base, with further opportunities for staff to discuss this in groups and to consider whether they wished to persevere further with effectiveness/improvement-related activities. Positive initial staff reactions, plus the desire of the headteacher and senior management team to improve the school, led to a programme of work that involved:

1. 'Pupil pursuit' work that aimed to establish baseline descriptions of school climate and to encourage teachers to visit each other's classrooms and share professional practice.

2. On-site training activities to transmit effectiveness knowledge and in the diagnosis of organizational dysfunction, utilizing a conventional OD knowledge-based approach.

3. Attending a large number of senior management team meetings to verify what were the needed organizational changes (the team initially had no agenda, no minutes and a completely informal structure).

4. Work with the headteacher to improve his management style, 'where it was possible to see him making impulsive decisions, making no decisions, making considered decisions and then not acting upon them, and making decisions that other people in the school should make (as with the working groups he set up)' (note from our original consultancy report).

5. Work to improve communication and management in the school, where informal networks were used rather than formal ones (e.g. the weekly news consisted of administrative trivia) and where there were no mechanisms for communicating issues 'upwards' or 'sideways' for resolution. There were additionally no clear definitions of managerial roles and no clear responsibilities for middle management.

Our work in the school led us to view its culture as one that was posing severe difficulty for any purported change attempts. Knowledge of the literature on organizational development (Sarason, 1971) and school improvement (Fullan, 1982) had not prepared us for the considerable shock of encountering a culture with the following characteristics and multiple barriers to change. There were:

1. *The fantasies* Change was someone else's job other than the body of line staff within the school (e.g. the job of the senior management team or of the headteacher). Indeed the majority of the staff cried out for 'top-down' change that would tell them what to do, not for ownership of the change themselves.

2. *The cling-ons* The belief that the school staff should carry on doing things in the way that they had done formerly because 'we've always done it this way!'

3. *The belief of safety in numbers* The reluctance of individuals in school to stand out from the prevailing group culture, even though they may have wanted to, because of a desire to 'hide' behind the group.

4. *The fear of failure* The reluctance of the staff to take the risks that successful change involves, fearing that failed change would further damage them.

5. *The externalizing of blame* The ability of the school staff to avoid the implications of evidence like examination achievement showing their ineffectiveness, by projecting their difficulties on to the children, and by explaining their failure as due to deficiencies in home background.

6. *The knowledge deficiency* The absence of any understanding about alternative policies, the nature of the present institution's functioning, about how to change, about how to evaluate change, and about how to relate to each other.

7. *The fear of outsiders* The belief that outside school persons had little to offer the school, which reflected the fear that outsiders may see the school's ineffectiveness. This was hidden behind a 'macho' façade that negated the potential importance of the outsiders as help agents.

8. *Grossly dysfunctional relationships* The presence of numerous personality clashes, feuds, personal agendas and fractured interpersonal relationships within the staff group, which operated to make rational decision-making a very difficult process. The tendency was to take stands on issues based upon 'reactive' decision-making, based upon the characteristics of persons putting forward ideas and proposals rather than upon the intrinsic merits or demerits of the ideas/proposals themselves.

9. *The presenting problems/The 'real' problems* The school's apparent presenting problems on which it had wanted definitive advice (e.g. the problems that had followed from the move to a five-period day from one of eight periods) were masks for the 'real' problems of morale, competence and feelings of failure that the school evidenced. In a situation like this, discussion often appeared 'unreal' and superficial because the school could not reveal the real problems that it wanted help with.

It was clear within the first six months of the process that the introduction of the school effectiveness knowledge into the school was a thoroughly problematic activity. In a staff group that was unused to discussing education, the discussion of 'means' and 'goals' generated much heat, because the staff had not realized until this point that they differed significantly among themselves as to what the role of the school should be within their type of community. Working parties that were set up and subsequently 'hijacked' by different interest groups led to an even greater solidification in the new heterogeneous ideologies on offer and a further significant disintegration of what had been a solidaristic, consensual staff. The various mechanisms of pupil pursuit, involving teachers shadowing their colleagues' interactions with a pupil in the course of a morning or afternoon of normal school, did not produce the outbreak of the 'ownership' of change, of the sharing of effective strategies or of the collegiality that had been hoped for. The involvement with the senior management team, intended to systematize school governance through adequate communication of team decisions and through the introduction of proper minuting and representation in the dealings of the team, led to the undermining of the headteacher's position.

The result of our involvement with the school was a considerable degree of turbulence then in its internal dynamics. Staff turnover, which had been historically of the order of 5 to 6 per cent per year, increased within a year to double that figure, partly as a result of the virtually complete changeover of the senior management team as its members went to other schools. Examination results showed no improvement over three years, nor did examination entry rates, often a more sensitive initial indicator of internal change. Pupil absence rates by contrast actually increased markedly in the first six months of our work in the school when the staff disturbance was at its height, with the attendance rate falling by some 5 per cent compared to the previous year's comparable time period. Although the attendance rate had recovered to its old levels within 18 months and although there was evidence of more enhanced competence, openness and of some embryonic management structures as our three-year period of time in the school ended, no one could say that the ineffective school was in any way 'turned around'.

STUDY TWO: A NEW HEADTEACHER ATTEMPTS TO USE SCHOOL EFFECTIVENESS KNOWLEDGE TO IMPROVE HIS SCHOOL

This study involved a study of a new headteacher over four years as he attempted to change his school through giving a high profile within inservice training to school effectiveness and school improvement insights. He took over the school in January 1990 and remained until the end of 1993, leaving then somewhat symbolically for a headship in a rural area of Botswana! His involvement with the school effectiveness community also included attendance at three International Congress for School Effectiveness and Improvement meetings, presenting papers at two of them on what he was trying to do with his institution. In value-added analyses conducted by the LEA, the school was in the bottom four out of 32 on examination results (using an ability measure at age 11 as a predictor variable).

The effectiveness knowledge input to his staff involved two entire inservice training days, consultancy-based support to his staff as they attempted certain crucial changes (e.g. the integration of children with special needs) and the involvement of some of the senior management team in a Master's course taught at a local university on school effectiveness and school improvement.

155

The headteacher's programme of activities with the school over his four years in post centred upon a number of areas frequently discussed as associated with positive school outcomes:

1. There was intensive work with parents and with the community to improve the image of the school and to improve the levels of participation of parents in the school and their interest in their children's education. (It had been customary to obtain an average attendance of only 20 per cent of parents at the termly 'year meetings' held for each year of the school, and the parental attendance at the annual Prize Day numbered normally perhaps 75, indicating that since over 100 children got prizes or certificates of some kind, many even of these children were not supported by their parents' attendance.) This work involved parental newsletters and intensive work with the local news media highlighting the school's achievements. The school in fact became the one with the highest public visibility out of the approximately 100 secondary schools situated in South Wales.

2. Extensive whole-school policies were implemented to update the school's academic organization involving changed routine assessment procedures, integration of 'remedial' streams (as they had still been entitled in 1989) into mainstream classes, curriculum reform and the attempted generation of the effective schools 'correlates' of high expectations, high academic pressure and frequent use of homework.

3. Policies were followed to encourage 'ownership' of school management and decision-making processes by the staff, by means of improving the communication flow from staff to senior management, by having an 'open door' policy to encourage staff to drop in and talk to the headteacher, and by means of an extensive committee/working party system to involve as many people on the staff as possible in routine determination of policies.

Staff reaction to the school effectiveness knowledge was only moderately favourable, with many seeing it as 'not right for our sort of children' who by contrast needed firm punishment and other quasi-correctional solutions to improve their achievements. The school saw itself as not being any kind of 'problem' and as not needing to change radically – the low levels of school outcomes were externalized on to the catchment area of the school, a late 1950s council estate which had been increasingly used as a dumping ground for perceived problem families by the local authority.

Many of the attributes of the school culture noted in School 1 were also present, in the case of this school combined with a very weary fatalism that was related to the age distribution of the staff, since three-quarters of teachers were over their mid-40s. Staff relationships were more harmonious than in the case of School 1, with the major split being with one group of staff nicknamed 'the old lags' by the rest of the staff, who had strong reciprocated friendship patterns with each other, and very hostile attitudes to outsiders of the group, very negative reactions about the need to change and very negative attitudes and behaviours towards the children and their parents.

School 2 had already been involved in a series of routine administrative solutions to its problems involving a series of 'tightening' of procedures practised in such areas as pupils' punishments, pupil absence, pupils' classroom behaviour, and pupils being out of a classroom during lessons (by contrast to School 1 which had done little tightening in any of these areas). As the time needed for the practice of school development began to increase, a normal corollary of any ownership-related school improvement scheme, many of the administrative procedures became weaker, leading to a widespread feeling that the school was falling apart. The rump of staff noted above (the 'old lags') then used these feelings to discredit the process of school development that the headteacher was trying to implement.

School 2 also evidenced by contrast to School 1 a small number of apparently very competent staff, probably attracted to the school because of its location in the Welsh capital. These staff were in many cases helped with responsibility allowances by the new headteacher, which seemed to lead to further enhancement of their professional competence and personal self-esteem. However, the presence within the same staff group of a rapidly rising 'ceiling' of the professionally competent together with a floor (the 'rump') who celebrated professional incompetence meant that the variation between the school staff in their practices and in their levels of individual and departmental effectiveness was greater at the end of the headteacher's programme of activities than at the start. For pupils in the school, greater heterogeneity of staff behaviour may well have led to perceptions of an apparently more confusing and inconsistent school than had existed hitherto.

The results of the series of programmes over four years were to generate a more weary, more fatalistic and more cynical staff group than at the programme's start, with the mechanisms that had been used to attempt to create ownership leading to exhaustion. There was no major evidence of success, either in improved school processes or in enhanced outcomes, that could have been used to improve morale or to build a coalition of persons to radically transform the school. Public examination results were as follows:

	Entered 1 or more exam	Achieved 1 or more exam pass	Achieved 5 or more A–C exam passes
School 1982/83	61	58	8
School 1990/91	71	63	8
School 1991/92	84	67	11
School 1993/94	90	73	8

The school's rates of entry and of achievement of one or more passes at any grade virtually parallels the overall improvement for all schools in Wales over the decade, and for the years for 1990–94. On the key publicly used indicator of 'five or more' subject passes at grades A–C, the school's position was static for a decade and represented a decline relative to other schools in Wales.

The only other positive change, was an increase of 2 to 3 per cent in the school's mean attendance rate over the four years, bringing it from the high 70s to the low 80s, a change that exceeded the minor change in attendance for all schools in Wales.

HOW DO WE TURN AROUND THE INEFFECTIVE SCHOOL?

We must be clear firstly about which schools are concerned, since clearly nearly all schools are 'ineffective' relative to the top decile of effectiveness, and clearly the bottom half of schools are ineffective relative to the top half of the distribution by effectiveness. What we would argue this chapter relates to is schools which are probably in the bottom 10 or 15 per cent of the distribution by effectiveness, although some schools with higher overall levels of effectiveness may have some features, or some departments, with aspects of the ineffective schools' organization, culture and relational patterns. It goes without saying that effective schools would be most unlikely to have more than a few staff or departments with the sorts of processes noted in our two case studies above.

The precise methods we might utilize to turn around such schools are of course a matter of considerable controversy. Gray and Wilcox (1995) argued that any improvement schemes needed to motivate teachers by capturing their enthusiasm and their commitment to change, and to show teachers that they will gain personally from any successful programme. Ownership of the change attempt by staff, even if only by a small group of staff initially, is also argued as likely to be essential. Brown, Duffield and Riddell (1995) also seek to 'root' school improvement in ineffective schools (and indeed in all schools) in a clear and precise understanding of how teachers make sense of their worlds and construct their professional ideologies of practice. What is offered below is a further, rather different set of possibilities for the improvement or 'turning around' of such schools, posed as questions for the effectiveness and improvement community to consider:

1. Will the ineffective schools have the prior competencies that are clearly required to engage in the round of activities (such as school development planning or involvement in school improvement activity) which may be needed to improve their organizational functioning? If not, how do we develop these competencies?

2. Will the schools be able to engage with the 'rational/empirical' paradigm if they possess a culture of 'non-rationality' or 'competing rationalities'? How do we change this culture?

3. Will the schools be able to act as an organization in the sense of adopting any cohesive organizational approach if there are numerous cliques, a substantial heterogeneity of practice and a fragmented rather than interlinked staff group? How do we deal with the relational problems in these schools?

4. Will school improvement and/or school development activities that focus on change to the formal organizational level of the school be successful in engaging the commitment of staff members who have been historically mostly uninvolved with the school level and whose focal concerns are not 'organizational' but more 'teaching and curriculum'? Is teacher effectiveness research appropriate for these schools, rather than school effectiveness research?

5. Will the schools engage with activities which have been brought to them from 'outsiders' in the worlds of higher education, school effectiveness research and school improvement practice? Is the solution to their problems to rather encourage they themselves to work on their own within-school variation, where there are likely to be some departments relatively more effective than others (Fitz-Gibbon, 1992) and potentially some departments absolutely effective when measured in the context of departments in all schools?

6. Will school improvement and school development activities generate a greater variation in teacher behaviours if applied to ineffective schools, as the gap between moving 'leading edges' and static 'trailing edges' increases? Given the evidence that shows effective schools as reducing the range of teacher behaviour and ideology (Teddlie and Stringfield, 1993), how do we prevent the range of behaviours increasing in ineffective schools over the improvement time?

7. The process of improving ineffective schools is likely, given their problems, to involve intervention in the formal organization, the culture and the relational area. How do we operate on these three areas together?

8. School improvement and development can be historically described as attempting to 'improve the good' or to 'accentuate the positive' in school settings. In ineffective schools would it be more effective to attempt to 'eliminate the negative', which would impact greatly both on the range of student achievement scores and also on the mean (the thesis here is that improvement in a small number of 'low effectiveness' staff may generate a substantial effect upon mean school performance)?

9. Should we consider different outcomes as being the important goals for the development of ineffective schools? Change in ineffective schools is likely to take a much longer time than in schools of other levels of effectiveness. Given the general agreement that it is likely to take two to four years to substantially improve examination performance in an 'ordinary' school, in an ineffective school it might be unwise to expect major outcome change in academic areas in under four to five years (the recent OFSTED list of rapidly improving schools one

would be inclined to take as evidence for year-on-year variation in performance rather than for rapid improvement). Given the importance of the attainment of success criteria in building and sustaining improvement, is there a case for improvement in ineffective schools being targeted more at easily alterable outcomes like the attendance rate (where change in a minor number of individuals can have grossly disproportionate effects) rather than at academic outcomes, or is there a case for targeting at more intermediate level outcomes (pupil attitudes for example) in ineffective schools?

10. Change in ineffective schools may need intervention of a quasi-therapeutic nature to make any change possible. Situations of 'presenting' and of 'real' problems, of a lack of openness, of dysfunctional relationships and of various pathological cultural states may not be changeable without the techniques historically utilized to change individuals and other institutions exhibiting such problems. What are these skills and how do we acquire them?

11. Change in ineffective schools may be best attempted by bringing the outside knowledge that such schools 'need' to the schools in the form of a school 'insider' rather than in the form of the threatening 'outsider'. Simply throwing ideas about school effectiveness, school improvement and school change at the ineffective school is likely to be even more problematic in the ineffective school than in the cases of others of higher effectiveness levels. The ideas need to be attached preferably to a person, as in the process of academic diffusion, rather than simply being allowed to root or not through cultural diffusion. Using school personnel as school change agents – as Trojan horses – and transmitting to them the range of skills and knowledge that ineffective schools need, as in the Cardiff Programme of Institutional Change (Reynolds et al., 1989), may be the best way of improving practice.

12. If getting reinforcement of a positive kind is problematic for teachers in ineffective schools because of a situation of staff hostility to organizational development, should we see the most useful reinforcement for change as coming from the pupils? If so, is it imperative to distance school improvement in ineffective schools from attitudinally based change models of school improvement and utilize only behaviourally orientated programmes, whereby the change in individual teacher behaviours is reinforced by the reaction of pupils, which in turn leads to attitude changes by staff?

13. Is focusing upon the discussion of school goals early on in the process of school development (e.g. Hargreaves and Hopkins,

1991) appropriate for ineffective schools where 'goals debates' may reveal and promote dissensus? Is a 'means' orientation (i.e. the concentration upon organizational features with goals implicit) a more suitable way of school development and of building staff competence, with the aim of engaging with issues of 'mission', 'goals' and the like later in the process of improvement? Is indeed a technological or technique-based approach (for example, using coaching sessions at lunchtimes to develop candidates who may possibly improve to score a grade C at GCSE) more likely to succeed in ineffective schools than the other, broader approaches (for example, a policy to improve negative teacher expectations)? Is the most important thing in the ineffective school for staff to do something and then later think about what the broader picture may be?

CONCLUSIONS

This chapter has used the experience of direct involvement in two attempts to turn around ineffective schools and the experience of more general inservice work with such schools to argue for the potential context specificity of the improvement programmes and their characteristics that should be utilized with these schools.

It is argued that what the schools may need is directive skilling, means-orientated activities, and potentially quasi-therapeutic programmes to give the schools knowledge and skills which they currently do not possess. At heart, the 'problem' of the ineffective school simply throws into sharp relief the more general dilemma of how we reconcile the need for teachers and their institutions to develop from their present state with the need to ensure they own that process of development, in order to generate the likelihood of the process of development continuing. How we conceptualize the problem of knowledge transmission and knowledge generation for ineffective schools is likely to have wider importance for the improvement community more generally.

REFERENCES

Brown, S., Duffield, J. and Riddell, S. (1995) 'School Effectiveness Research: The Policymakers' Tool for School Improvement?', *EERA Bulletin,* **1** (1), 6–15.

Edmonds, R. (1979) 'Effective schools for the urban poor', *Educational Leadership*, **37**, (15–18), 20–24.

Fitz-Gibbon, C. (1992) 'School effects at A level', in Reynolds, D. and Cuttance, P. (eds) *School Effectiveness*. London: Cassell.

Fullan, M. (1991) *The New Meaning of Educational Change*. New York: Teachers College Press.

Gray, J. and Wilcox, B. (1995) *'Good School, Bad School': Evaluating Performance and Encouraging Improvement*. Buckingham: Open University Press.

Hargreaves, D. H. and Hopkins, D. (1991) *The Empowered School*. London: Cassell.

Hopkins, D., Ainscow, M. and West, M. (1994) *School Improvement in an Era of Change*. London: Cassell.

Louis, K. S. and Miles, M. (1992) *Improving the Urban High School*. London: Cassell.

Murgatroyd, S. J. and Reynolds, D. (1985) 'The creative consultant', *School Organisation*, **4** (3), 321–35.

Myers, K. (1994) 'Why schools in difficulty may find the research on school effectiveness and school improvement inappropriate for their needs'. Unpublished paper.

Reynolds, D. (1987) 'The consultant sociologist', in Woods, P. and Pollard, A. (eds) *Sociology and Teaching*. London: Croom Helm.

Reynolds, D. (1991) 'Changing ineffective schools', in Ainscow, M. (ed.) *Effective Schools For All*. London: Fulton.

Reynolds, D. *et al.* (1989) 'The Cardiff Programme: an effective school improvement programme based on school effectiveness research', *International Journal of Educational Research*, **13** (7), 800–814.

Reynolds, D. and Packer, A. (1992) 'School effectiveness and improvement in the 1990s', in Reynolds, D. and Cuttance, P. (eds) *School Effectiveness*. London: Cassell.

Rosenholtz, S. (1989) *Teacher's Workplace: The Social Organization of Schools*. New York: Longman.

Sarason, S. (1971) *The Culture of the School and the Problem of Change*. Boston: Alleyn & Bacon.

Teddlie, C. and Stringfield, S. (1993) *Schools Make a Difference*. New York: Teachers College Press.

Conclusions

Facing up to the Challenge of Securing Improvement

Chapter 9

The Challenges of School Improvement: Preparing for the Long Haul

John Gray, David Jesson and David Reynolds

INTRODUCTION

During the 1980s up to half the school districts in the USA claimed to have been involved in implementing improvement programmes based on the findings of research on school effectiveness. These were districts and institutions which had been impressed by the evidence that 'schools made a difference' and, in many cases, by the particular work of Edmonds (1979) who proposed a so-called 'five-factor' theory of school effectiveness. A series of improvement efforts followed on.

Britain in the 1990s has been marked by the growth of similar programmes. In Scotland the Scottish Office Education Department has launched a major programme into *Improving School Effectiveness* involving some 60 schools in change efforts (MacBeath and Mortimore, 1994; Tibbitt *et al.*, 1994). Meanwhile, in England, a recent survey undertaken for the Office for Standards in Education (OFSTED) has revealed evidence of even more widespread activity, identifying in the process some 60 projects, frequently involving numbers of schools (Barber, 1994). The survey was confined to 'urban education' so there will undoubtedly have been more across the country as a whole. There have also been signs of growing interest in Wales and Northern Ireland.

What have been the main areas of schooling these various initiatives have targeted for 'improvement'? The OFSTED study provides some clear indications (see Table 9.1). Not surprisingly, improving 'pupil attainment' was the area most frequently mentioned (by 85 per cent of all projects). 'Raising expectations' and 'pupils' self-esteem' featured prominently (mentioned respectively by 72 per cent and 67 per cent of the projects). It is also clear from the table, however, that many of the projects had multiple aims – between them the 60 projects listed an average of just under six areas each in which they sought 'improvement'.

Table 9.1 *Main areas focused on by 60 English improvement projects*

Area intended for improvement	Projects targeting this area (%)
Pupil attainment	85
Pupil/teacher expectations	72
Pupil self-esteem	67
Parental involvement	60
Pupil/teacher morale	53
Curriculum change	50
Pupil behaviour	42
Staying on rates post-16	37
Truancy	33
Discipline	22
Bullying	18
Racial awareness/tolerance	18
Other areas	43

Note: Based on reports from 60 projects. Projects could identify more than one area as 'intended for improvement'.
Source: Barber (1994, Table 8).

PROSPECTS FOR SUCCESS?

Given so much activity what are the prospects for successful improvement? It is early days to say much about the British efforts although there are already some pointers. Some North American evidence collected by Louis and Miles (1992) is, however, especially instructive at this juncture. They followed up a sample of over 200 schools which had adopted so-called 'effective school' practices about three years later to find out more about what had happened.

Louis and Miles used interviews with school principals (headteachers) to gather evidence about 'improvements' that had taken place as a result of the change initiatives. It is hard to see how they could, in the circumstances, have used any other approach but one needs to bear this in mind when judging the principals' responses. Having signed up for change it would be an unusual educator who reported *no* worthwhile developments.

The various outcomes were tallied under three main headings by Louis and Miles. In terms of outcomes for *teachers*, around four out of ten principals claimed that 'staff morale', 'staff communication about education' and 'staff commitment to student achievement' had 'greatly improved'. (We focus on this answer category as indicating the likelihood of at least some change.) There were broadly similar claims in relation to such *organizational outcomes* as the school's 'image', the extent of 'inter-departmental collaboration' and 'student–faculty relations'. Indeed, in only two areas was the amount of progress claimed less impressive: the proportions reporting 'greatly improved' teaching methods and 'teachers' mastery of new skills' were both around a quarter (see Louis and Miles, 1992, pp. 322–3, tables not shown).

The patterns of outcomes reported for *students* were more variable, depending on which areas were looked at. In Table 9.2 we have ranked the outcomes from those where least 'improvement' was claimed upwards.

Table 9.2 *Reported outcomes/effects of 'effective schools' programmes on participating students in North America*

Area of outcomes	Principals reporting 'greatly improved' (%)
Employment of graduates	12
Student dropout rate	15
Student achievement	24
Student attendance	38
Student attitudes	43
Student behaviour	49

Note: Principals were asked when interviewed to reply in terms of three answer categories: 'greatly improved', 'somewhat improved', 'no change'. The table is based on 177 responses.
Source: Louis and Miles (1992, Table C6).

In well over four out of ten cases 'great' improvements were claimed in respect of students' behaviour and attitudes; in the principals' views these would appear to be areas where fairly rapid change was possible. In the area of 'student achievement', however, the claims were more muted. Only about a quarter (24 per cent) claimed that outcomes were 'greatly improved'. Progress on the academic front would appear to be more of a struggle.

How might the picture look on this side of the Atlantic? The OFSTED survey offered respondents the opportunity to indicate which, if any, of nine 'performance indicators' were being used to 'measure the success of the initiative'. Four out of five projects appear to have replied to this question suggesting that in up to one in five cases there were no explicit performance criteria (yet) in place. Of those that replied to the question just over two-thirds (69 per cent) reported that they would be/were using 'test and examination results' whilst just over half (52 per cent) mentioned 'attendance'. Half the projects (50 per cent) also mentioned 'parental involvement' whilst over four out of ten (44 per cent) mentioned 'post-16 staying-on rates' (table not shown). Projects replying to this question reported an average of four performance indicators each although whether they were using several of these because they matched their targets or because they were readily available remains an open question (Barber, 1994, p. 24).

The OFSTED survey asked 'what evidence of success for the project exists so far?' A space was then provided for open-ended responses. Just under one in five (19 per cent) of the 60 projects said that it was 'too early to assess'. Of those projects which were prepared to say something about their 'success' about three out of ten (31 per cent) said they 'had achieved their goals'; three out of ten (29 per cent) reported 'perceptions of improvement'; three out of ten (31 per cent) cited 'evaluation and/or feedback evidence'; and three out of ten (29 per cent) also mentioned 'continued interest and growth' (table not shown; percentages sum to more than 100 as projects could mention more than one criterion). Smaller proportions reported 'evidence for success' based on 'increased interest' and 'increased good practice'. A few projects also mentioned 'increased parental involvement', 'improved attendance', 'media interest' and 'obtaining (further) funding' (Barber, 1994, p. 26).

Such replies seem a bit vague. Indeed, Barber himself described them as 'disappointing' (1994, p. 36). They are not, however, in our experience generally untypical of improvement projects which have tended to ignore 'harder' measures of success, either because they have seen them as inappropriate to their aims and objectives or because they have lacked the opportunities or motivation to collect them. The problem is touched on in Fullan and Hargreaves' widely read account of change and improvement strategies entitled *What's Worth Fighting for in Your School?* (1992). They comment that 'pupil achievement and performance data, widely-defined and interpreted, should also be used as a springboard for action ... effective collaborative schools are actively interested in how well they are doing and seek evaluative data to monitor and improve on progress' (p. 127). The tentativeness with which this recommendation is stated is probably illuminating. The issue is faced more squarely in Stringfield's review of improvement efforts where he concludes, in rather stark terms, that most school improvement efforts have probably had rather little impact on student achievement (Stringfield reported in Hopkins *et al.*, 1994). Such uncompromising assessments prompt further questions about the available evidence.

HARDER EVIDENCE OF SUCCESS?

Researchers of school effectiveness have tended to concentrate their efforts on obtaining estimates of the differences between schools in their *effectiveness*; only relatively recently have they begun to explore the extent of school *improvement* in a more systematic way. Such studies as are available indicate that it would be very easy indeed to overestimate the amount of 'improvement' occurring in the system. As Louis and Miles found, a commitment to improvement may be a necessary condition for change but it is not necessarily a sufficient one. But first we need to distinguish between absolute and relative patterns of improvement.

Over the last few years *more* pupils have been obtaining *more* examination passes; in England, for example since 1990 the average has gone up by over one pass per pupil. The schools which have produced these results may be said, in an absolute sense, to have 'improved'. But have they actually improved their *effectiveness*? In this context 'effectiveness' is a relative concept, relative that is to performance in other schools. When this latter kind of question is posed 'improvements' which occur across all shcools are discounted. Given a particular cohort of pupils, have certain schools developed ways of 'adding more value' than in previous years and 'adding more value' than other schools? If they have, have the improvements been of a one-off nature or have they been sustained?

The meaning of 'improvement', as it might used by school effectiveness researchers, requires careful explication. The first step is to produce estimates of each school's 'effectiveness' in terms of the extent to which it boosted pupils' (GCSE) examination or test performances above the levels that would have been predicted from knowledge of their starting points. The second step is to compute each school's 'effectiveness' in each of the subsequent years. The third step is to identify those schools whose 'effectiveness' has been increasing. The 'improving schools' in this kind of study are those which manage, by one means or another, to increase their 'effectiveness' with the next cohort of pupils in the second year and then to increase it still further in the third year with the cohort after that (and, indeed, with further cohorts in subsequent years). Schools which improve one year and then drop back are not of particular interest in this kind of study.

To date hardly any studies have been in a position to estimate such 'improvements in effectiveness'. The main British example indicates that whilst a sizeable number of schools proved to be more 'effective' in one or other of the years of the study only a handful (three or four of the 35 schools under review) turned out to be *consistently* and *systematically* improving their 'effectiveness' over time (Gray *et al.*, 1995; 1996). One of these schools was already 'more effective' but managed to boost its effectiveness still further over a period of years; this school would have been of interest within the framework of a traditional study of school effectiveness. One of the other schools which improved, however, would previously have been ignored in such study. It started off being 'fairly ineffective' but subsequently improved, first becoming of 'average effectiveness' and then beginning to move towards the position of being 'more effective'. If we are to obtain a greater understanding of how other schools may set about improving themselves, then documenting the experiences of schools like this latter one may be crucial. We should, however, note that there do not seem to have been many of them around. In brief, the 'harder' evidence would seem to suggest that whilst there has been a good deal of change there has been rather less improvement.

THE MAIN MESSAGES OF RESEARCH ON SCHOOL EFFECTIVENESS

What do schools need to do in order to improve? One answer might be to look at the research on factors associated with school effectiveness.

A variety of attempts have been made in recent years to summarize the main messages of this research. Recently Sammons *et al.* (1994) completed a comprehensive review, again for OFSTED. Basing their summaries on some 160 studies they eventually concluded that there were basically 11 'key factors'. These are listed in Table 9.3, although it should, perhaps, be stressed that no attempt has been made to rank them in terms of their importance. Furthermore, the authors were careful to counsel against simple causal attributions. As one of the co-authors of the report has subsequently written: 'these factors should not be seen as a blueprint for effectiveness. They have not been conclusively proved to be essential but, given the consistency of their identification by researchers working in different countries and employing different methods, the probability of their importance is clear' (Mortimore, 1995, p. 10).

To relate 'key factors' concerning school effectiveness to school improvement one must draw on some (largely) implicit causal chains. If, for example, a 'more effective' school possesses 'professional leadership', then it seems reasonable to suppose that a 'less effective' one may lack this element or, alternatively, possess it in some 'less professional' form. The *implicit* improvement strategy is that those involved in and with the school should work on leadership issues.

Let us suppose, for a moment, that they do so. Greater effectiveness should result. However, this eventuality will be modified by two considerations. First, by the extent to which, within the list of 'key factors', matters related to 'professional leadership' are *absolutely central* to a school's effectiveness and could be demonstrated in causal terms; many studies might, of course, lead one to suppose that this was, indeed, the case. And second, on the strength of the underlying

Table 9.3 *Eleven factors associated with effectiveness identified in the OFSTED review*

1.	Professional leadership	Firm and purposeful
		A participative approach
		The leading professional
2.	Shared vision and goals	Unity of purpose
		Consistency of practice
		Collegiality and collaboration
3.	A learning environment	An orderly atmosphere
		An attractive working environment
4.	Concentration on teaching and learning	Maximization of learning time
		Academic emphasis
		Focus on achievement
5.	Purposeful teaching	Efficient organization
		Clarity of purpose
		Structured lessons
		Adaptive practice
6.	High expectations	High expectations all round
		Communicating expectations
		Providing intellectual challenge
7.	Positive reinforcement	Clear and fair discipline
		Feedback
8.	Monitoring progress	Monitoring pupil performance
		Evaluating school performance
9.	Pupil rights and responsibilities	Raising pupil self-esteem
		Positions of responsibility
		Control of work
10.	Home–school partnership	Parental involvment
11.	A learning organization	School-based staff development

Source: Sammons et al. (1994, Table 1)

correlations; many of the relationships identified in such research are, at best, *tendencies* rather than certainties. There is, however, a more fundamental problem. 'More effective' schools may be more likely to have more 'professional leadership' than their 'less effective' counterparts – but not invariably so. Furthermore, some of the 'ineffective but improving' schools are likely to have had 'professional leadership' as well. Leadership, in other words, may be correlated with both effectiveness *and*, to some extent, ineffectiveness at the same time but for different reasons. As most reviewers (including those mentioned here) are careful to stress the identification of so-called 'key factors' is just a starting point for further enquiry and action.

Returning again to Table 9.3, it seems reasonable to suppose that a 'more effective' school might be one which 'concentrated (more) on teaching and learning'. The implication is that somehow a 'less effective' school concentrates less on these matters and should, if it wants to improve, increase its concentration on them. Such a strategy would certainly seem worthwhile and appropriate. However, whilst to outsiders such observations may seem self-evident, their meaning and implications for those inside a school may require a good deal more exploration and commitment in order to understand what is at stake and how to proceed. How exactly, they might ask, does a school like ours 'concentrate' more? And on exactly what? They might be short on 'learning time' but, without good comparative evidence that went beyond, for example, the sheer length of the teaching day or week, it would be hard for them to know.

In short, as most reviewers (including those mentioned here) have been careful to point out the identification of so-called 'key factors' is just a starting point for further enquiry and action. There are inherent difficulties in moving directly from statements about the correlates/causes of 'effectiveness' to the formulation of strategies for improvement.

THE MAIN MESSAGES OF RESEARCH ON SCHOOL IMPROVEMENT

The dominant concern in school improvement programmes is to get the action going. But, again, where should one start? At one point in their study Louis and Miles (1992) offer the advice that leaders should 'do – and then plan'. Anything, in other words, that gets something off the ground and creates a sense of 'movement' is worth contemplating. The need actively to manage it, they would argue, comes later.

Research on school improvement has probably generated as many lists of factors which 'seem to work' as research on school effectiveness. The advice Fullan and Hargreaves (1992) offer is a typical and prominent example. Interestingly, just as in most of the work on school effectiveness, the focus is squarely on the nature, responsibilities and style of leadership available to a school. Successful school leaders, they argue, concentrate on certain kinds of improvement strategies. They spend time, for example, understanding the culture of the school; they invest in their staff, valuing what teachers do and promoting their professional growth; they are prepared to extend what they value to take on other people's agendas; they express what it is they value, both through words and actions; they promote collaborative working practices amongst their colleagues; in drawing up lists of what should be on the school's change agenda their preference is to make menus for change rather than to impose mandates; they use bureaucratic means to facilitate, not to constrain; and they make special efforts to link and 'connect' with the wider environment outside the school (Fullan and Hargreaves, 1992, p. 112).

Advice from other researchers runs along similar lines. Reflecting on the factors which characterized the 'moving' (synonymous in this account with improving) schools in their project, Hopkins et al. (1994) identified a number of 'internal conditions for improvement'. These included the school's commitment to staff development and the attention given to the potential benefits of enquiry and reflection; the practical efforts made to involve staff, students and the community in formulating school policies and decisions along with the commitment to collaborative planning that this implies; and the existence of a 'transformational' approach to leadership.

Comparing this list with that in Table 9.3 there would appear, at first glance, to be a sizeable degree of overlap. Leadership styles, management strategies, staff participation, and staff development feature on both lists, albeit with rather different emphases. Nonetheless there seem to be some important differences. 'Transformational leadership', for example, has a radical edge to it that may not be provided by the 'firm and purposeful' leaders identified in the school effectiveness research. And 'school-based staff development' may or may not have the same drive for change in it that is implied by 'attention to the potential benefits of enquiry and reflection'.

In short, there are differences of perspective and of purpose to be mediated, understood and overcome. The differences in emphasis may, of course, be explained by the fact that schools which are already effective are a good deal less likely to need (or for that matter want) leaders who can 'transform' things or to find that they need staff development strategies which focus attention on the school's change agenda. There are, in other words, some more fundamental barriers to linking the knowledge of 'what works' from the two paradigms with their respective commitments to understanding 'effectiveness' and 'improvement'. What has been perceived as a simple matter of integrating two knowledge-bases turns out not to be as simple as first supposed. Whilst there is, doubtless, a fair measure of agreement at the level of values and purposes between researchers of the two persuasions, the ways in which they turn these commitments into practice still differ substantially (see Reynolds *et al.*, 1993 for a fuller discussion of some of these differences). A good deal of ground-clearing will be required before further progress can be made.

FIRST STEPS TOWARDS INTEGRATION

Acknowledging that integration may not be a simple matter is not quite the same as saying that it is complicated. Our view is that there are some intermediate stages and problems which need to be better researched and understood. It is to some of these issues that we now turn.

Both approaches have their different ways of conceptualizing schools' performances. Within the 'effectiveness' paradigm estimates are typically made of each school's performance in terms of some measure of outcome(s). Similarly, within the 'improvement' paradigm, assessments are made of the nature and extent of improvement in one or more areas of its functioning such as its ethos or climate. But what does actually *integrating* the two approaches imply. In Table 9.4 we have sought to bring them together within the context of a single framework.

First, we posit that schools may vary in terms of their 'effectiveness'. For the purposes of this preliminary discussion they are either 'more' or 'less effective' (i.e. just two categories). Second, we posit that they may also vary in terms of their rates of 'improvement'. Since most schools have been 'improving' to some extent over the last few years, for the purposes of the argument we suppose that there are just two categories – 'improving' and 'improving (but more) slowly'. Table 9.4a shows the two dimensions co-existing alongside each other in much the same way as the available research does.

As a next step we need to be more specific about the measures along which we are measuring/estimating 'effectiveness' and 'improvement'. In terms of the former we might say that pupils are to be judged in terms of the academic progress they make (which we shall term Outcome I). When we make this explicit in terms of the framework in Table 9.4b it also begins to give a specific meaning to the notion of 'improvement' which relates to the extent to which schools are *increasing* their effectiveness in terms of boosting pupils' academic progress (Outcome I). School A in this example is 'improving' because it is 'increasing its effectiveness' in terms of Outcome I: School D is 'less effective and not improving'.

Table 9.4   *Frameworks for integrating effectiveness and improvement*

Table a

Schools may vary in terms of their effectiveness. They may be 'more effective' or 'less effective'.

Schools may vary in terms of their rates of improvement. They may be 'improving rapidly' or 'improving (but more) slowly'.

Table b	*Outcome I*			
	Improving rapidly	*Improving slowly*		
More effective	School A	School B		
Less effective	School C	School D		

Table c	*Outcome I*		*Outcome II*	
	Improving rapidly	*Improving slowly*	*Improving rapidly*	*Improving slowly*
More effective	School A	School B	School A	School B
Less effective	School C	School D	School C	School D

Table d	*Outcome I*		*Outcome II*	
	Improving rapidly	*Improving slowly*	*Improving rapidly*	*Improving slowly*
More effective	School A	School B	School D	School C
Less effective	School C	School D	School B	School A

This is not, however, the only possible meaning of improvement or area in which improvement might have occurred. It might, for example, have been in terms of pupils' attitudes (Outcome II); given earlier information from the OFSTED survey about schools' concerns in relation to improvement, this is quite a likely prospect. In this case schools would need to be judged in terms of their effectiveness in relation to Outcome II alongside Outcome I (and the position described in Table 9.4c would occur).

Table 9.4c is premised on the notion that schools that are 'effective' and 'improving' in respect of one outcome measure are equally 'effective' and 'improving' with respect to others. This is a convenient but not necessarily accurate summary of the empirical evidence which suggests that they vary somewhat. Table 9.4d therefore assumes that the relationship is entirely reversed with School D being the 'more effective/improving' institution with respect to Outcome II.

Whatever the underlying reality it will already be clear that there are (theoretically at least) no fewer than 16 different combinations when Tables 9.4b and 9.4d are brought together. Indeed, if we posit a slightly more extended (but also more familiar) categorization of schools' effectiveness as being 'more effective', of 'average effectiveness' and 'less effective', and think at the same time of schools as 'improving rapidly', 'improving, but more slowly' and perhaps 'standing still', then the equivalent of Table 9.4b will have nine cells and the combination of Tables 9.4b and 9.4d will have no fewer than 81. Furthermore, if we were to take account of within-school variations across subject departments or across different groups of pupils, then the combinations would rise still more dramatically.

There is clearly a danger that the possibilities will quickly outstrip our capacity to understand them. The purpose of this example is to demonstrate that we should be cautious in recommending simple 'treatments' for whole ranges of schools. A much better grasp of each institution's strengths and weaknesses as well as their starting positions will be required. Most importantly, schools themselves will need to know rather more about where they stand and start within the framework.

PATTERNS OF STRENGTH AND WEAKNESS

Knowledge of the positions of individual schools should help us to draw up agendas for their improvement. What is the overall pattern nationally of strengths and weaknesses as regards effectiveness and improvement? What follows are some 'best guesses', informed by research evidence and national surveys such as those conducted by OFSTED inspectors and their predecessors. In terms of 'effectiveness' the widely held view (supported by research) is that only a small number of schools are 'excellent' *across the board*. By the same token only a small number are 'very weak' or 'poor' *all round*. The greater majority of schools have both strengths *and* weaknesses; they are neither plainly 'good' nor plainly 'bad'.

Take, for a moment, the four broad criteria proposed by OFSTED for the identification of so-called 'at risk' or 'failing' schools requiring 'special measures'. In schools of 'average effectiveness' the *achievements of pupils* can be expected to rise above 'low standards' or 'poor examination results and levels of attainment in relation to those of children in comparable schools' by considerable margins. Some departments might be stronger, others weaker but there would be an element of consistency of approach, of expectations and of standards across almost all. In terms of *behaviour* most pupils would 'attend regularly', few would truant and few would be 'regularly disruptive'. As regards *the staff and teaching* some teachers would be highly committed and a few might be serving out their time but, between them, the vast majority would manage to deliver only a relatively small number of 'unsatisfactory' lessons; most would hold appropriate expectations for their pupils' work; and 'abrasive and confrontational relationships with pupils' would not be much in evidence. Finally, in the area of *management*, both the head and senior management team would be fairly sensitive to staff needs; would retain the confidence of teachers, parents and governors; and basically would manage to keep the whole show on the road (OFSTED, 1992).

We estimate that between two-thirds and three-quarters of all schools might be expected, at any one time, to fall into this broad category of schools performing 'about as expected'. Boring as it may be for those who pay attention to newspaper headlines, the considerable majority of schools perform around the levels one would predict from knowledge of their intakes.

Improvement agendas for the majority of schools follow on from these observations. Some prioritizing might be needed: a small number of departments and individual teachers might require emergency support and intervention but, in the majority of cases, improvement on most fronts would be the order of the day.

Researchers of school effectiveness would expect around one in eight schools to be performing at levels which they would characterize as being of 'above average effectiveness'. The proportions might vary from one LEA to another.

Whether all such schools might be characterized as 'excellent' is another matter. Very few institutions, in our experience, achieve a uniformity and consistency of purpose across all (or even most of) their outcomes and activities. 'Excellence' is a term of approbation which is, perhaps, to be anticipated in only a small number of areas. What leads to wider application of the term is the knowledge that to sustain such performances a solid infrastructure is probably required. In terms of improvement the management team are likely to be thinking about which *particular* areas can be supported with a view to developing 'excellence' further. As Lightfoot (1983) put it in her study of six 'good' schools such institutions are likely to be 'conscious of their imperfections' and 'willing to search for their origins and solutions'. There are also likely to be several directions in which the school might move as well as several ways of getting there.

If one in eight schools are to be characterized as being of 'above average effectiveness' then it follows that a roughly similar proportion will be of 'below average effectiveness'. In terms of OFSTED's criteria they will have had problems securing 'satisfactory' levels of achievement from their pupils, will have had discipline and attendance problems, will have suffered from low morale amongst teachers and will have put on a large number of 'unsatisfactory' lessons, as well as experiencing management difficulties of one form or another.

Again we need to be careful about applying glib labels concerning quality here – even the 'worst' school will probably have some seeds of inspiration within it. But whereas the logic of the researchers' position is to identify a fairly sizeable number of schools, the practitioner's instinct has been to go for considerably lower numbers. When first asked how many schools might be 'at risk', for example, former HMCI Anthea Millett replied: 'It is not a simple thing to identify a school at risk and it is not a category we have used before. If we take the experience of last year we could be talking about 100 or 200 schools, both primary and secondary' (*Times Educational Supplement*, 11 September 1992).

On these figures, no more than 1 per cent of schools nationally would have fallen into this category. By the researchers' yardsticks this would seem to be an exceptionally small number but, in the event, practice has borne Millett's estimates out. Over the first 18 months of the OFSTED regime only some 40 schools were, in fact, identified as requiring the drastic kinds of action associated with 'failure' (see *The Times*, 4 April 1995). Interestingly, some LEAs seem to have had more than their 'fair share' of such schools. But truly 'bad' schools, at least as judged by OFSTED inspectors, seem to have been mercifully rare.

INCIDENCE OF THE 'CAPACITY TO IMPROVE'

Most schools, Fullan argues, can take on a degree of change over short periods of time – the real challenge is to sustain it over extended periods. As he suggests: 'the main problem in teaching is not how to get rid of the deadwood but rather how to motivate good teachers throughout their careers' (Fullan, 1992, p. 121). To achieve this kind of 'cultural change requires strong, persistent efforts because much of current practice is embedded in structures and routines and internalized in individuals, including teachers'. Those who seek improvement should, in his view, prepare themselves for the long haul.

Many educators involved in school improvement have been attracted by the vision of Rosenholtz's (1989) 'moving' schools – learning-enriched environments in which teachers themselves have taken on responsibility for initiating and sustaining the improvement process. This willingness to improve is something, she believes and echoing Fullan, that schools build up over time. Louis and Miles (1992), trying to identify the sources of change in their improving schools, took recourse to similar notions. For them the key lay in the schools' 'coping strategies' which they described in the following terms:

> Active problem-coping efforts are extremely central in successful
> implementation. Passive avoidance, procrastination, 'doing business
> as usual' and shuffling people from job to job do not work, if they are
> the only strategies used. They must be accompanied by 'deep' coping
> strategies such as vision-building and sharing, rolling planning,
> substantial restaffing, increasing school control over the environment,
> empowering people and redesigning the school organization (p. 281).

It will be clear from this account that 'coping' is really a bundle of ideas rather than just a single one. It runs deeper than the existence in a school of mechanisms for school development planning or the simple 'determination to get better results' which Scheerens (1992) identifies as the most important factor. In brief, most accounts of *sustained* school improvement are underpinned by (explicit or implicit) notions of what we should like to term the school's 'capacity to improve'. Such a 'capacity' is built up over a period of time; it does not simply emerge overnight with the introduction of new managements. Understanding what such a 'capacity' is, knowing what its essential components are, and finding better ways of building and nurturing them, provide the keys to improvement.

Whilst we are attracted by this idea of the 'capacity to improve' we are also aware of its limitations. The history of research on school effectiveness has been dogged by its fascination with concepts such as 'ethos' and 'culture' which have proved difficult to operationalize, and especially difficult to sort out in terms of causal mechanisms, whilst being simultaneously and popularly hailed as the keys to effectiveness. As Hargreaves has argued: 'school culture may be a cause, an object or an effect of school improvement: indeed all three are possible' (1995, p. 41). Under certain conditions schools may have many of the characteristics *associated* with improvement without producing any strong drive towards greater effectiveness. It would be unfortunate if the 'capacity to improve' turned out to be the school improvement researcher's equivalent.

How many schools nationally already possess the 'capacity to improve'? The honest answer is that we do not know. In what is currently one of the most spectacular omissions in the history of school evaluation, the OFSTED *Handbook* (1993) is largely silent on this issue. A number of potentially pertinent questions are posed. Does the school have a development plan? How much monitoring and evaluation takes place? But these are basically single probes, not part of a co-ordinated framework of questions designed to determine the extent of more fundamental orientations towards change and improvement. We understand that a new section in the manual, offering advice on how to judge the extent of improvement (and the factors contributing to it), may be emerging. Indeed, three recent case studies of individual schools produced by members of OFSTED (1994)

Table 9.5   *The incidence of effectiveness and the capacity to improve*

Estimate of effectiveness	Number of schools per 100 in this category	Guesstimate of incidence of 'capacity to improve'	Number of schools per 100 in this category
Above average	12	High proportion (two-thirds)	8 or 9
Average	76	About a third	24 or 25
Below average	12	Rather few (one-fifth or one-sixth)	2 or 3
TOTALS	100		34 or 37

show signs of movement in this direction. Nonetheless, whatever the reasons for the current state of affairs, the lack of attention to improvement issues for an agency whose corporate strategy is 'improvement through inspection' is still surprising. In posing questions about the incidence of the 'capacity to improve' we are entering the realm of informed speculation. We proceed on the grounds that some view about where things are up to is important. Making an assessment which errs on the side of optimism we would guess that around one-third of schools of 'average effectiveness' might have developed such a capacity. Amongst schools of 'above average effectiveness' the proportions might be as high as two-thirds; in schools of 'below average effectiveness' the proportions might be as low as one-fifth or even one-sixth. In other words, and in our view, the less effective the school, the lower the likelihood of it possessing the 'capacity to improve'.

If we combine these various estimates with our earlier ones about the extent of variations in schools' effectiveness we can come up with something by way of a national picture (see Table 9.5). Our assessment would be that around one-third of schools might possess something approaching the 'capacity to improve'. The prospects for *immediate* improvement across the majority of schools, on this judgement, would appear rather modest.

ENHANCING THE RESEARCH BASE

It will be evident from our account that there are sizeable gaps in our understanding of how to turn knowledge about school effectiveness into enhanced strategies for school improvement. We can, however, identify a number of issues which we believe researchers of both persuasions should be trying to address. Some of these are outlined below. We start with some of the problems facing researchers of school effectiveness.

First, we suspect there have been too many 'snapshots' of effective schools and too few studies which have attempted to explore schools' 'natural histories' over time where time is measured in years rather than months. We need to learn more about how schools *become* more effective alongside portraits of how they remain effective. To address this omission is on our own research agenda but should be recognized as posing formidable methodological and logistical problems.

Second, more time needs to be spent trying to establish whether some 'key factors' are more important than others and, if so, by how much. Numerous studies to date have generated numerous correlates of effectiveness (sometimes as many as 20 or more) without really providing much guidance about which one or two might be good places to start. Scheerens' (1992) meta-review is an obvious exception to this more general observation. He argued that of 16 factors that have been canvassed as important just three stood out across study after study. These were the determination to get better results; the maximization of learning time; and the amount of structured teaching. It would be interesting to find out how schools which have followed this 'slimline' recipe have developed their approaches and whether they made greater improvements than others.

Third, we need to become still clearer about causal directions and chains. Again we do not underestimate the size of the challenge. How teachers' 'high academic expectations' for their pupils and their pupils' 'good results in exams and tests' interact still eludes us.

On the school improvement side there are some equally important problems to be tackled. We have already mentioned the most important in our opening sections. It will continue to be difficult to make worthwhile assessments of the results of school improvement efforts for as long as researchers and practitioners remain reluctant to assess the impact of their activities on pupils. Whilst we understand and share many of their reasons for being reticent about making such links (because, for example, they are interested in developing certain styles of professional practice or are genuinely uncertain about what the outcomes of their activities might be) failure to engage with these issues will continue to frustrate efforts to achieve greater understanding.

Second, we need to get better at learning from so-called 'failures'. In our experience most improvement efforts 'fail' merely in proportion to the rhetoric on which they are launched. More realistic assessments on the part of policy-makers and practitioners regarding what schools operating in constrained circumstances can realistically achieve are required. Such perspectives, of course, have implications for the ways in which initiatives are set up. More experimentally based approaches, in which plausible ideas are 'tested out' against each other, should be the order of the day. The Scottish study *Improving School Effectiveness* has the potential to operate in this way on the wider stage but the same approach needs to be developed within smaller groups of schools as well as on the national front.

Third, there is a need to resist the temptation to load change initiatives down with multiple objectives. We recognize that, at the initial stage of building coalitions for change, some compromises will probably need to be made. However, for every additional objective that a change programme embraces the difficulty of sorting out causal mechanisms is doubly compounded. We are not arguing here for the heavy armoury of statistical analysis to be imported into school improvement studies but simply for a clearer sense to be injected into such studies of what might be influencing what.

There are also some issues which relate almost equally to both paradigms. There are still very few convincing case studies of 'effective' and, especially, 'ineffective' schools or of schools which are 'improving' or merely 'standing still'. The absence of rich case-study-based explanations (and explorations) of change almost certainly reduces the practitioners' points of contact with the research evidence. There is a need to generate accounts which get considerably closer to the fine-grained reality of school processes. There is, as yet, no British equivalent of Louis and Miles' (1992) case studies of improving urban schools although some work being conducted by the National Commission on Education may go some way towards remedying this position (see especially the case study by Rudduck *et al.*, 1995).

Second, the idea that 'what works' does not vary much according to a school's context and circumstances needs to be challenged. Table 9.4 earlier demonstrated just how complex the position might be and this perspective is reinforced by some of the North American work. Several studies show variations *between* schools according to their socio-economic, cultural, ethnic, gender or 'ability' mixes (Hallinger and Murphy, 1986; Wimpelberg *et al.*, 1989; Teddlie and Stringfield, 1993). Some British research also offers evidence of differential effectiveness *within* particular schools (Nuttall *et al.*, 1989); some schools do better with some kinds of pupils as opposed to others. It is, in our view, inappropriate to cling to the view that there is basically 'one right way'.

Third, more studies need to build from the individual classroom upwards. School effectiveness researchers have demonstrated (using the most sophisticated multilevel modelling techniques) that the larger part of the variation to be explored lies at the classroom level (see Creemers, 1992 for a review of some of the evidence). By the same token school improvement researchers have under-lined the importance of capturing teachers' enthusiasms for (and commitments to) the change process. Both groups need to engage still further with the evidence that teachers' concerns are predominantly with the content of their curricula and the nature of their instructional practice rather than with the broader stage of the school. By ignoring the classroom level there is a distinct risk that change efforts will be only tinkering with the 'variables which matter'.

There are, at the same time, some more fundamental problems in working from the classroom upwards. As Brown and McIntyre remind us, most teachers are not only unaccustomed to talking about their own teaching but find it difficult (1993, p. 35). Furthermore, they seem to have considerable difficulties in gener-alizing from their particular experiences. Researchers need to ensure that the realities they attempt to describe come closer to the frameworks and assumptions practitioners bring to bear on their practices. Much current research may be too remote.

Finally we need to sound a note of caution about the limits and possibilities of changing the ways in which researchers work. Although we prefer to think otherwise, changing the ways in which they think and behave is probably a research field in its own right and only marginally less difficult than changing schools and teachers!

THE INEFFECTIVE SCHOOL: A SUITABLE CASE FOR TREATMENT?

The fascination of both the Labour and Conservative parties with the closure of 'failing' schools provides the policy context for much of the current work of researchers on school effectiveness and school improvement. How much do we actually know about improving 'ineffective' schools? Do they, in other words, provide suitable cases for treatment or are those who have rapid demises in mind being more realistic?

The honest answer, based on the available research evidence, is that we do not really know. Researchers, for one good reason or another, have largely ignored such schools – they have been more concerned with 'what (appears to) work' across the board; such schools have resisted working with researchers or been more likely to drop out of their studies; and observing 'improvements in effectiveness', as opposed to simply 'effectiveness' or 'ineffectiveness', takes more time than has usually been available. Policy-makers, meanwhile, have had different reasons for keeping their activities under wraps – partly through fear of compounding already difficult problems; and partly, one suspects, because the options available for change may have involved undertaking actions which would not necessarily command widespread respect throughout the profession without a good deal of talking through.

In both cases the consequences have been largely the same. The *ineffective* school which has *improved* is largely missing from the research to date; and policy-makers have tended to celebrate those occasions on which their interventions have worked, remaining diplomatically silent about those where the outcomes have been more ambiguous. Either way the available evidence is likely to be considerably biased with too much emphasis being given to the pursuit and attainment of 'virtuous' approaches to school improvement – with their attendant emphasis on the particular strengths of specific personalities. Much 'improvement', we suspect, is rather more messy.

Two strands of thought have begun to crystallize amongst researchers about what 'ineffective' schools need to do in order to improve. However, neither is, as yet, particularly well grounded in the specific experiences of 'ineffective' schools which have actually turned the corner and started to improve.

Searching for the common messages across a large number of research studies Gray and Wilcox (1995) concluded that the effects of improvement schemes will be minimal unless ways are found of motivating classroom teachers by capturing their enthusiasms and commitments to change. The biggest challenge, on this argument, is to find ways of showing and convincing individual members of staff that they themselves will benefit from successful initiatives. Change programmes need a specific focus; their objectives need to be 'owned' by those most closely involved; and they demand time and space to allow them to flourish. The role of 'leadership' in such situations is to facilitate the action, providing both support and resources (usually in terms of time). In such situations more than one leadership 'style' is likely to be required.

Reflecting on his experiences of working with two very different but 'ineffective' schools, Reynolds argues in this volume (chapter 8) for a rather different approach. The biggest problem, as he sees it, is that one of the reasons ineffective schools got to be the way they are is that they *cannot* focus or plan joint action. To propose that this is how they should attempt to move forward is therefore dysfunctional. It needs to be acknowledged that they may be either 'non-rational' or combine rather more 'competing rationalities' than might be hoped. In such situations different concerns become priorities. There will be a need: to 'eliminate the negative'; to isolate the rump of teachers sustaining poor practice; and to find better ways for insiders to share insights into what has 'worked for them'. It might even be worth contemplating the introduction of quasi-psychotherapeutic techniques to 'exorcise the ghosts' of ineffective pasts.

THE CLOSURE DEBATE

Against such a background of research and experience the quick closure/quick reopening scenario may seem more attractive. The decision would be made that a school had finally 'failed'; it would be quickly closed down and staff laid off (with suitable arrangements being made for teachers to be redeployed or 'retired early') during the summer term; a new leader would be hired with (some) new staff; the new team would take over the old buildings; and, by the following September, a 'new' school would be up and running (see *Guardian*, 12 April 1995).

Britain is rather short of experience in handling such issues publicly. At first sight they seem more appropriate to 'hire and fire' cultures. Nonetheless, one can anticipate some problems. First, whilst we have individuals with some experience of identifiying schools as requiring 'special measures', only a handful have developed expertise in diagnosing terminal decline and recommending closure. LEAs' experience in this respect is often mixed – they have mostly learnt to be cautious. Second, we currently lack a cadre of educationists willing or able to take on the role of 'company doctors' to the bankrupt cases. However, the willingness of Hammersmith LEA in inner London, whilst stopping short of actual closure, to hire a new headteacher to take over a newly renamed Phoenix High School and to pay a £60,000 salary (a third over the going rate for a 700-pupil school) may represent a significant step towards a new specialism here. Third, it assumes that teachers (even highly experienced ones) can create and re-create an educational institution and environment at short notice. Fourth, and perhaps most importantly, it assumes that pupils can adjust and recommit themselves within equally short periods of time. Fifth, it is premised on the belief that communities will welcome the change. They may – or they may not choose to resist. The acid test for such a policy will come when an 'ineffective' school serving a middle-class catchment is on the line. The central assumption and logic of school effectiveness research is that such schools are, given their intakes, (almost) as prevalent as their inner-city counterparts. This nettle, however, is one policy-makers may prove reluctant to grasp.

We have very few accounts indeed of what has happened after a school has been brought back from the brink by one means or another. Such accounts as we do have often assign a major role to 'high-profile', larger-than-life leaders who secure change by force of will and personality but they also prompt questions. In Lightfoot's (1983) study of George Washington Carver High School on the 'wrong side of the tracks' in Atlanta, for example, it is hard to convince oneself that the changes were largely unproblematic. Commenting on the progress the school had made since Dr Hogans (an ex-American footballer) had taken over, she concluded that 'the school had progressed from terrible to much better' but, in the round, it had merely achieved the 'minimal standards of goodness which (she) envisioned as a first stage of movement towards higher goals'. Some readers of her account have felt she was being somewhat charitable in her assessments – other views could be sustained.

The main problem with the 'closure' route to school improvement (and the levering up of educational standards by this means) transcends the question of whether it works or not. No one is seriously suggesting that it is appropriate for anything other than the most desperate of cases. Phoenix High School in

Hammersmith, for example, has to find a way of coping with a whole series of problems identified by OFSTED inspectors, starting with pupils' aggression towards each other and towards their teachers, teachers' unwillingness to intervene and a sense amongst some teachers that a more positive disciplinary regime is not possible (see *The Times Educational Supplement*, 21 April 1995). It seems doubtful whether more than several handfuls of schools fall into this category. Millett's 1 per cent of all schools, referred to earlier, is probably an upper limit especially if one acknowledges that some of those deemed 'at risk' will be capable of redemption. However, there is another problem. Whilst the extent of 'failure' is seen as rather limited, fairly drastic measures can be contemplated. But is anyone really proposing that the much higher number of schools which researchers define as 'ineffective' be treated in this way? It seem improbable.

In brief, the main purpose of canvassing the 'closure' option is doubtless to galvanize the teaching profession. On its own it would be a truly radical proposal. Added to the list of other 'galvanizing' policies which have been introduced in recent years (more testing, league tables, inspections and so on) it is likely to be absorbed by a profession which has rapidly developed a variety of immunization strategies. Cast against the challenge of raising educational standards across the country its effects are likely to be modest – as anyone who has calculated the 'leverage' of a few extreme cases on the overall average across thousands of schools will confirm. The problem of the 'ineffective' school runs deeper and a broader portfolio of 'remedies' will be required.

PREPARING FOR THE LONG HAUL

Three decades have passed since the Plowden Committee visited some of the most disadvantaged schools in the country. They were evidently appalled by what they saw. 'The first step,' they declared 'must be to raise the schools with low standards to the national average; the second, quite deliberately to make them better (than the national average)' (DES, 1967). In what can now clearly be seen as the precursor of current school improvement efforts they not only recommended new and refurbished buildings but, at the same time, a programme of educational innovation and experimentation to find the best ways forward. Different communities were to be given the opportunity to explore for themselves what might work. Given Plowden's focus, most of the drive for change concentrated on the early years. Secondary schools, in so far as they participated, largely retained a low profile.

By the mid-1980s the push for change had spread to cover the whole gamut of compulsory education. The various committees of enquiry set up by the Inner London Education Authority, for example, made the case for more systematic *improvement* across primary, secondary *and* special schools. Nonetheless, such concerns were still probably a minority interest. What they shared in common with their Plowden predecessors was a faith in the mutability of educational institutions and their capacity to transform themselves (although not by any means exclusively) from within.

In the mid-1990s the improvement agenda has become much more widely shared – *almost* mainstream. A reluctance to commit one's institution to seeking improvement of some sort may result in problems – by simply standing still one runs the risk of falling behind. Even the more optimistic evidence, however, suggests that we are in for a long haul. For an 'ineffective' school to move into the pack will take at least three to four years; for it to move ahead of it at least as long again.

The challenge for school effectiveness and school improvement researchers and practitioners is to discover what it is that would make such dramatic improvements possible. We strongly suspect that suspension of historic disciplinary disagreements and a willingness to merge historically determined disciplinary beliefs are both essential for the effectiveness and improvement communities in the remainder of the 1990s.

REFERENCES

Barber, M. (1994) *Urban Education Initiatives: the National Pattern*. A Report for the Office for Standards in Education, University of Keele.

Brown, S. and McIntyre, D. (1993) *Making Sense of Teaching*. Milton Keynes: Open University Press.

Creemers, B. (1992) 'School effectiveness, effective instruction and school improvement in the Netherlands', in Reynolds, D. and Cuttance, P. (eds) *School Effectiveness: Research, Policy and Practice*. London: Cassell.

DES (1967) *Children and their Primary Schools* (The Plowden Report). London: Advisory Council on Education.

Edmonds, R. (1979) 'Effective schools for the urban poor', *Educational Leadership*, **3**(7), 15–27.

Fullan, M. (1992) *Successful School Improvement*. Milton Keynes: Open University Press.

Fullan, M. and Hargreaves, A. (1992) *What's Worth Fighting for in Your School?* Milton Keynes: Open University Press.

Gray, J. and Wilcox, B. (1995) *'Good School, Bad School': Evaluating Performance and Encouraging Improvement*. Milton Keynes: Open University Press.

Gray, J., Goldstein, H. and Jesson, D. (1996) 'Improvements in effectiveness: five-year trends in school performance', *Research Papers in Education*, **11**(1), 35–51.

Gray, J., Goldstein, H., Jesson, D., Hedger, K. and Rasbash, J. (1995) 'A multilevel analysis of school improvement: changes in schools' performance over time', *School Effectiveness and School Improvement*, **6** (2).

Hallinger, P. and Murphy, J. (1986) 'The social context of effective schools', *American Journal of Education*, **9**(4), 328–55.

Hargreaves, D. H. (1995) 'School culture, school effectiveness and school improvement', *School Effectiveness and School Improvement*, **6** (1), 23–46.

Hopkins, D., Ainscow, M. and West, M. (1994) *School Improvement in an Era of Change*. London: Cassell.

Lightfoot, S. L. (1983) *The Good High School: Portraits of Character and Culture*. New York: Basic Books.

Louis, K. S. and Miles, M. B. (1992) *Improving the Urban High School: What Works and Why*. London: Cassell (British edition).

MacBeath, J. and Mortimore, P. (1994) *Improving School Effectiveness: A Scottish Approach*. Paper presented to the Annual Conference of the British Educational Research Association held at the University of Oxford.

Mortimore, P. (1995) 'Effective schools', Inaugural Directorial Lecture, London Institute of Education.

Nuttall, D., Goldstein, H., Prosser, R. and Rasbash, J. (1989) 'Differential school effectiveness', *International Journal of Educational Research*, **13** (7), 769–76.

OFSTED (1992) *Framework for the Inspection of Schools*. London: Office for Standards in Education.

OFSTED (1993) *Handbook for Inspection*. London: Office for Standards in Education.

OFSTED (1994) *Improving Schools*. London: HMSO.

Reynolds, D. (1994) Inaugural Lecture, University of Newcastle upon Tyne.

Reynolds, D., Hopkins, D. and Stoll, L. (1993) 'Linking school effectiveness knowledge and school improvement practice: towards a synergy', *School Effectiveness and School Improvement*, **4** (1), 37–58.

Rosenholtz, S. (1989) *Teachers' Workplace: The Social Organization of Schools*. New York: Longman.

Rudduck, J., Clarricoates, K. and Norman, R. (1995) 'A school in the market-place', in *Success Against the Odds*. London: Routledge, for National Commission on Education.

Sammons, P., Hillman, J. and Mortimore, P. (1994) *Key Characteristics of Effective Schools: A Review of School Effectiveness Research*. London: Office for Standards in Education.

Scheerens, J. (1992) *Effective Schooling*. London: Cassell.

Teddlie, C. and Stringfield, S. (1993) *Schools Make a Difference: Lessons Learned from a Ten-Year Study of School Effects*. New York: Teachers College Press.

Tibbitt, J., Spencer, E. and Hutchinson, C. (1994) 'Improving school effectiveness: policy and research in Scotland', *Scottish Educational Review*, **26** (2), 151–7.

Wimpelberg, R., Teddlie, C. and Stringfield, S. (1989) 'Sensitivity to context: the past and future of effective schools research', *Educational Administration Quarterley*, **25**, 82–107.

Name Index

Sammons, P. 6, 15–16, 19, 20, 21, 24, 51, 169
Sarason, S. 153
Sass, Z. 55
Scheerens, J. 3, 6, 11, 13, 14, 15, 23, 24, 25, 53, 54, 55, 57, 96, 97, 98, 176, 177–8
Schein, E. 35
Sexton, S. 136
Sime, N. 12
Siskin, L. S. 57
Sizer, T. 46
Slavin, R. 34, 46
Smith, D. J. 7, 18–19, 20–1
Smith, M. S. 53, 54, 140
Snow, R. E. 83
Spinks, J. 57, 136, 140, 144
Stanley, J. C. 87
Stoll, L. 46, 57, 60, 94, 95, 96, 98
Stringfield, S. 13, 44, 53, 54, 55, 56, 96, 98, 122, 159, 168, 179
Summers, A. A. 24
Swann, J. 116

Teddlie, C. 44, 51, 53, 54, 55, 56, 96, 98, 122, 159, 179

Thomas, S. 6, 8, 14, 16, 18, 19, 21, 97
Thompson, M. 144, 145
Tibbitt, J. 165
Tizard, B. 6, 13, 14
Tomlinson, S. 7, 18–19, 20–1
Tritton, D. J. 124, 131
Tuckman, B. W. 132
Turnbull, W. W. 81
Tymms, P. B. 77, 97, 121, 122, 123, 133

van Velzen, W. 51, 52, 61
von Neumann, J. 77

Waldrop, M. M. 76, 132
Wallace, M. 68, 145
West, M. 39
Wilcox, B. 150, 152, 158, 180
Willms, J. D. 7, 12, 14, 17–18, 19, 20, 21, 87, 122, 132
Wimpelberg, R. 179

Yelton, B. T. 7, 13
Young, S. 101

Subject Index

A-Level Information System (ALIS)
7–8, 81–2, 84–8, 121, 126–30
absolute difference, school
effectiveness and 23
academic outcomes 6–11, 23–4, 55,
82, 106, 112
affective outcomes of education 10–11,
24
age of pupils, school effectiveness and
21
American Educational Research
Association 125
Association of Metropolitan Authorities
(AMA) 8
attendance at school 9, 158
attitudes of pupils, school
effectiveness and 9–10, 108, 110
Audit Commission 121
Australia 136
autonomy see school autonomy

background of schools, historical,
school effectiveness and 106, 111,
113
behaviour of pupils, school
effectiveness and 10
Birmingham LEA, Quality
Development Initiative 66–7
British Educational Research
Association 99

Cambridge Institute of Education 65
Canada
school autonomy in 136
school improvement in 58–60, 95
Cardiff Programme of Institutional
Change 160
cellular automata 77–8

centralized policy change, school
improvement and 40–1
change, school as focus of 56, 58
chaos theory 124–33
modelling of 124–6
choice of school, parental 108, 113
class see socio-economic status
closure of ineffective schools 181–2
Coalition of Essential Schools 46
cognitive outcomes 6
communication networks 153
community values, schools and 146–7
complexity
chaos and 124, 130, 133
illustrations of 79–82
responses to 82–4
school effectiveness and 78–88
science of 75–8
Consortium for Longitudinal Studies
24
contextual effects, school effectiveness
and 17–18
Coopers & Lybrand 141–2
corporal punishment 126
culture of schools 34–7, 43, 57, 98,
106, 107, 153–5, 156, 176
curriculum, content of 107

data
artificial generation of 126–33
collection of 103–4
problems with 121–4
on school effectiveness 56, 103–4,
121–4, 126–33
Department of Education and Science
(DES) 141, 143, 182
development planning 108, 109, 117
dyslexia 107

Project (ISIP) 52, 57, 137
Investors in People 66

language skills, school effectiveness
    and 6–8, 15, 18–19, 20
languages, foreign 107
Latin teaching 107
League of Professional Schools 46
league tables 102, 108, 111, 117–18
learning difficulties 107, 114, 117
Lewisham School Improvement
    Project 60–3
local education authorities (LEAs)
    ineffective schools and 151
    school autonomy and 142, 146
    school closure and 181
    school improvement and 58
        Birmingham Quality Development
            Initiative 66–7
        Hammersmith & Fulham Schools
            Make a Difference (SMAD)
            project 63–5
        Lewisham School Improvement
            Project 60–3
    social justice goals and 102
local management of schools (LMS)
    83, 111
    school improvement and 136, 140–7
London Institute of Education 60, 62,
    64
Louisiana School Effectiveness Study
    13, 53, 56

maintenance structures 38–9
Maldebrot set 132
management arrangements 37–8
marketing of schools 108, 109–10, 115
mathematics, school effectiveness and
    6–8, 15, 19, 20
models
    of chaos theory 124–6
    of school effectiveness 54–5, 122
    of school improvement 41–6, 54–5
monitoring
    of school effectiveness 74–88
    of school improvement 62, 138

National Commission on Education 178
Netherlands, school effectiveness,
    research in 7, 11, 12–13, 14, 15, 20,
    21
new right concepts 136
New Zealand, school autonomy in 136,
    146

Office for Standards in Education
    (OFSTED) 33, 46, 64, 142, 143,
    150, 159–60, 165, 167, 169, 173–6
Organization for Economic
    Cooperation and Development
    (OECD) 146–7

parents
    choice of school and 108, 113
    school effectiveness and 107, 110,
        113, 115
    school improvement and 138, 156
Phoenix High School 181–2
physical punishment 126
Plowden Committee 53, 182
policy implementation, effectiveness of
    40–1
principals see head teachers
prior attainment, school effectiveness
    and 18–20, 23
progress, school effectiveness and 23,
    105
Project Head Start 24
punishment, physical 126
pupils/students
    age of 21
    attendance at school 9, 158
    attitudes to school of 9–10, 108, 110
    behaviour of 10
    ethnic background of 20–1
    gender of 20
    involvement in running schools 108,
        113–14
    part-time work by 121
    physical punishment of 126
    school improvement and 36, 138,
        160, 165, 166–7
    self-concept of 10
    socio-economic status (SES) of